GOOD CAPITALISM, BAD CAPITALISM, AND THE ECONOMICS OF GROWTH AND PROSPERITY

GOOD CAPITALISM, BAD CAPITALISM, AND THE ECONOMICS OF GROWTH AND PROSPERITY

William J. Baumol
Robert E. Litan
Carl J. Schramm

Yale University Press
New Haven & London

Set in Postscript Galliard Oldstyle by The Composing Room
of Michigan, Inc. Printed in the United States of America.

The Library of Congress has cataloged the hardcover edition
as follows:
Baumol, William J.
Good capitalism, bad capitalism, and the economics of growth and
prosperity / William J. Baumol, Robert E. Litan, Carl J. Schramm.
p. cm.
Includes bibliographical references and index.
ISBN 978-0-300-10941-2 (cloth : alk. paper)
1. Capitalism.   2. Entrepreneurship.   I. Litan, Robert E., 1950–
II. Schramm, Carl J.   III. Title.
HB501.B372 2007
330.12′2—dc22   2006036191

ISBN 978-0-300-15832-8 (pbk.)

A catalogue record for this book is available from the British
Library.

10 9 8 7 6 5 4 3 2 1

CONTENTS

PREFACE

Many books take off from one core idea. This book is built on two.

The first notion is that capitalism is not a monolithic form of economic organization but rather that it takes many forms, which differ substantially in terms of their implications for economic growth and elimination of poverty. The implicit assumption underlying the idea of a homogenous capitalism, the notion that all capitalist economies are fundamentally the same, reflects something of the mentality common during the cold war when two superpowers, representing two great ideologies, were struggling for the hearts and minds of peoples of the world. On the one side were countries like the United States, whose economies rested on the foundation of the private ownership of property, and on the other were communist or socialist societies, whose economies essentially did not. This distinction seemed to divide the two economic systems, and not much thought was given to the possibility that there is much more to capitalism.

The fall of the Berlin Wall in 1989 seemed to demonstrate that capitalism (and a democratic form of government) had won and communism had lost. A number of American scholars celebrated this fact, one even suggesting that we had reached the "end of history." The terrorist attacks of September 11, 2001, shattered that illusion, at least as to forms of government. But even before that tragic day, a number of economic developments began calling into question the notion that there was only one form of capitalism in operation.

The most important of these developments was the remarkable resurgence of productivity growth and innovation in the United States in the 1990s, made possible largely by new, innovative companies, and not by the established giants that had previously dominated the U.S. economic landscape. Something new was afoot, and to one of us, it was sufficiently important to merit a special label: "entrepreneurial capitalism," a type of capitalism where entrepreneurs, who continue to provide radical ideas that meet the test of the marketplace, play a central role in the system. This apparently new form of capitalism differed from its counterparts in other countries, especially in Japan and continental Europe, where radical entrepreneurship was noticeably absent and where a combination of large enterprises, often "championed" by their governments, and small retail or "mom and pop" shops dominated the economy.

Drawing on this simple insight, we realized that capitalism in other countries took other forms. In some the state seemed to be directing traffic, hence our term "state-guided capitalism," a form of economic organization that seemed for many—and may still seem—to be the key to jump-starting growth in less developed countries. In other countries, the state may also have played a role, but the leaders of government and the narrow elites who backed them (or feared them) did not seem to care as much about growth as they did about keeping the spoils of the economy to themselves. The economies were capitalist in the sense that private property was allowed; it's just that it was highly concentrated in the hands of a few. These economies seemed to be best characterized as "oligarchic."

At its core, this book is about these four different types of capitalism—entrepreneurial, big-firm, state-directed, and oligarchic—and how they affect growth. We believe these distinctions are important not only for their descriptive value but also for their normative implications. Hence the reference in the book's title to "good" and "bad" forms of capitalism. Clearly, we view some forms of capitalism as worthy of promoting, others as systems to be rejected and eliminated. Our policy suggestions toward the end of the book are aimed at both of these goals.

A second insight or proposition is key to the arguments laid out in the pages that follow. Readers can well be excused if, from the brief recitation of the different types of capitalism, they jump to the conclusion that only the first form of capitalism—the "entrepreneurial capitalism" that has powered the U.S. economy toward a higher growth rate since the 1990s and which seems to be taking hold in other parts of the world, such as Ireland, Israel, the United Kingdom, India, and China, to name just a few— is the only form of "good capitalism." But as one of us (Baumol) elaborated over a decade ago, it takes a mix of innovative firms *and* established larger enterprises to make an economy really tick. A small set of entrepreneurs may come up with the "next big things," but few if any of them would be brought to market unless the new products, services, or methods of production were refined to the point where they could be sold in the marketplace at prices such that large numbers of people or firms could buy them. It is that key insight that led us to the conclusion that the *best* form of "good capitalism" is a blend of "entrepreneurial" and "big-firm" capitalism, although the precise mix will vary from country to country, depending on a combination of cultural and historical characteristics that we hope others will help clarify in the years ahead.

The foregoing insights would not have generated a book without much help from other sources. Here we identify first and foremost the Kauffman Foundation, the world's leading foundation in increasing understanding of and encouraging entrepreneurship. All three of us have benefited enormously from the privilege of being actively involved in the management of this foundation (two of us are officers, the third is a special advisor) and having the opportunity to discuss many of the ideas in this book with our colleagues, not just those at the foundation itself (with whom we have had countless productive conversations), but with its many grantees in the academic community. Because we have the good fortune to be able to direct some of the foundation's resources to further economic research about the nature, causes, consequences, and policies related to entrepreneurship in particular, we have over the past three years gained a worldview that would not have been possible had each of us been on our own. We have been inspired by the research of the scholars the foundation has supported, as well as many others in the profession who have labored in related fields. This book could not have been written without their contributions. Baumol's work, in particular, was also greatly facilitated by the

Berkley Center for Entrepreneurial Studies at New York University, of which he is the academic director, one of the academic organizations generously supported by the Kauffman Foundation.

This book also could not have been written without the exemplary assistance we received on a number of fronts from others to whom we owe our thanks and our gratitude. A team of researchers second to none—E. J. Reedy, Marisa Porzig, Dane Stangler, and Mark Dollard—helped us at various points along the way by finding essential information and offering key insights. Special thanks must also go to two other individuals: Alyse Freilich, who not only contributed to the research effort but also did an outstanding job in drafting the appendix to this book, which explains the many data difficulties that complicate the task of studying entrepreneurship; and Lesa Mitchell, another officer at the foundation, whose pioneering work devoted to understanding and helping to change (for the better) the commercialization of university-based innovation eventually will receive the universal recognition that it deserves.

We are also grateful for the production and editorial assistance of Glory Olson at the foundation and Sue Ann Batey Blackman (a longtime colleague of Baumol's), and to Eliza Childs of Yale University Press. To our editors at the Press, Michael O'Malley and Steve Colca, we owe a large debt; they urged us to write this book on the strength of only the barest outline (which, in retrospect, bore only slight resemblance to the finished product). We take no credit for what we think is a great cover to the book; that honor belongs to Melody Dellinger. Finally, we are grateful for the comments and input we received on portions of this book as it gradually evolved from Zoltan Acs, Edmund Phelps, Robert Strom, and Michael Song.

We hope our readers will share the intellectual excitement that we have enjoyed in working together and in developing the thoughts presented in the following pages. As other coauthors know, it is rare when two authors of a book can finish and still remain friends. This book reflects a unique partnership of three individuals, each of whom brought different fields of expertise to the task and all of whom became much closer friends as the joint venture progressed. We are grateful to one another for being able to pursue this project together.

GOOD CAPITALISM, BAD CAPITALISM, AND THE ECONOMICS OF GROWTH AND PROSPERITY

1

ENTREPRENEURSHIP AND GROWTH:
A MISSING PIECE OF THE PUZZLE

The most astonishing thing about the extraordinary outpouring of growth and innovation that the United States and other economies have achieved over the past two centuries is that it does not astonish us. Throughout most of human history, life expectancy was about half what it now is, or even less. We could not record voices or speech, so no one knows how Shakespeare sounded or how "to be or not to be" was pronounced. The streets of the greatest cities were dark every night. No one traveled on land faster than a horse could gallop. The battle of New Orleans took place after the peace treaty had been signed in Europe because General Andrew Jackson had no way of knowing this. In Europe, famines were expected about once a decade and the streets would be littered with corpses, and in American homes, every winter the ink in inkwells froze.

Today we can create paintings on our laptop computers, put the artwork on a Web page, and quickly receive comments about it from all over the globe. There are two toy-like vehicles driving over the terrain of Mars, analyzing its surface materials and sending back crystal clear motion pictures in color. But after the initial awe and enthusiasm, this ongoing interplanetary research merits only brief notices on the inside pages of our newspapers. For the average citizen, the most plausible explanation of how these things work is that they are acts of magic, yet we have come to take such technological innovations for granted.

Economic growth has been equally astounding. It is estimated that the purchasing power of an average American a century ago was one-tenth what it is today. A moment's thought will make you realize what a significant change has occurred in an individual's economic circumstances over the past few generations. Suppose you were accustomed to receiving the income of an average American today, and suddenly nine-tenths of it were confiscated. We cannot imagine what our mode of living would then be like. Similar calculations can be made for other countries that have grown remarkably fast in recent years: India, China, much of Southeast Asia during the past two decades and, of course, both Western Europe and Japan since the end of World War II.

The fact is that never before in human history has there been anything like the economic progress that citizens of these countries have been privileged to witness and enjoy. The current most critical long-term economic issue for the world is how this performance can be sustained in the wealthiest countries and how it can be transplanted to societies where much of the population lives in abject poverty. To find an answer to these questions, it is necessary to investigate what is different about the economies that have already achieved this spectacular success.

In the past couple of decades, after a long spell of inattention, there has been a resurgence of interest in this topic among economists claiming to have some of the answers. (We will express our skepticism about some of their work in a later chapter.) Of course, we certainly do not pretend to have the "silver bullet" answer to what causes differences in economic growth rates among countries and over time, but we do believe we can contribute to the inquiry by focusing on the overall structure of economies (capitalist economies in particular) that could explain some portion, perhaps a good portion, of the variation. In particular, we will pay special attention to the set of rules and institutions that provide the incentives for entrepreneurs to work unceasingly for the creation, utilization, and dissemination of new products and productive techniques. Indeed, we will argue that these incentives prevent the entrepreneurs in key sectors of different economies from resting on their laurels, forcing them to start planning their next innovative campaign even before the current one has reached its conclusion.

By "entrepreneurs" whom do we mean? The term is commonly used to refer to anyone who starts a business. This definition counts the numbers of self-employed persons and new business starts, regardless of what the business does. Throughout this book, we will use the term in a narrower and, we believe, more significant manner: as any entity, new or existing, that provides a *new* product or service or that develops and uses *new* methods to produce or deliver existing goods and services at lower cost. As management guru Peter Drucker has pointed out, "not every new small business is entrepreneurial or represents entrepreneurship" (Drucker, 1965, 21). He (and we) prefer the definition that Drucker attributed to the nineteenth-century French economist Jean-Baptiste Say, noting that the term: "was intended as a manifesto and a declaration of dissent: the entrepreneur upsets and disorganizes." Joseph Schumpeter (the great twentieth-century economist who celebrated the role of the entrepreneur) coined the famous term "creative destruction" to describe the entrepreneurial process. As Drucker paraphrases Schumpeter's analysis: "[the] dynamic disequilibrium brought on by the innovating entrepreneur, rather than equilibrium and optimization, is the 'norm' of a healthy economy and the central reality for economic theory and economic practice" (Drucker, 27). Or, Drucker puts it more bluntly: "Entrepreneurs innovate. Innovation is the specific instrument of entrepreneurship" (Drucker, 30).

By focusing narrowly on what might be called "innovative" entrepreneurs, we admittedly give short shrift to the many more "replicative" entrepreneurs—those producing or selling a good or service already available through other sources—who are found throughout capitalist economies. Eighteenth-century English writer Richard Cantillon had replicative entrepreneurs in mind (although he probably didn't know it at the time) when he referred to "wholesalers in Wool and Corn, Bakers, Butchers, Manufacturers and Merchants of all kinds who buy country product to work them up and resell them gradually as the Inhabitants require them" (Cantillon, 1931, 51). To be sure, replicative entrepreneurship is important in most economies because it represents a route out of poverty, a means by which people with little capital, education, or experience can earn a living. But if economic growth is the object of interest, then it is the innovative entrepreneur who matters; hence our focus on that form of entrepreneurship throughout much of this book. Put differently, entrepreneurship—as we use the term—is not to be confused with "small business" or even many new businesses.

We recognize, of course, that no economy can be fully successful with entrepreneurs alone. Many such firms will be too small to realize economies of scale. And there is a long distance between what may be the germ of a radical, but useful, idea generated by an entrepreneur and a commercially useful product that is sufficiently affordable and reliable to induce many consumers to buy it. For this reason, the most successful economies are those that have a mix of innovative entrepreneurs and larger, more established firms (often two or more generations removed from their entrepreneurial founding) that refine and mass-produce the innovations that entrepreneurs (and, on occasion, the large firms themselves) bring to market. When we speak of "entrepreneurial economies" at various points in the book, we are referring to this blend of the two types of firms.

What Drives Economic Growth?

To some readers perhaps unfamiliar with much economic writing what we have presented so far may seem obvious. After all, growing economies seem to thrive on new things—new cars, new products, new services. But look through any basic economics textbook and you'll find precious little discussion, let alone analysis, of the entrepreneurs who think up and commercialize many of these new things. In more advanced textbooks and articles, one will find extensive, usually highly mathematical discussions of what determines economic growth. But here, too, entrepreneurship, and the accompanying necessary role of larger firms, is rarely mentioned.[1] Nobel Laureate Ronald Coase put it well when he observed: "The entities whose decisions economists are engaged in analyzing have not been made the subject of study and in consequence lack any substance. The consumer is not a human being but a consistent set of preferences. *The firm, to an economist, as Slater has said, 'is effectively defined as a cost curve and a demand curve, and the theory is simply the logic of optimal pricing and input combination'* (Slater, 1980, ix). Exchange takes place without any specification of its institutional setting. We have consumers without humanity, firms without organization, and even exchange without markets" (Coase, 1988, 3).

Instead, economists generally focus on two main sources of growth: (1) the addition of more inputs (capital and labor), and (2) innovation, technological change, or, in technical economic terms, "total factor productivity" (the increase in productivity of *both* capital and labor, considered together). For simplicity, one could call these two different strategies growth by "brute force" and "smart growth." Robert Solow of MIT won his Nobel Prize in economics for showing in the late 1950s that in the United States and a few other industrialized countries, innovation or "smart growth" was more important than brute force (more inputs) in generating additions to output over time (Solow, 1956, 1957). A number of scholars have since confirmed this basic insight and extended it to many countries around the world (see Denison, 1962, 1967; and Easterly and Levine, 2001).

But what is innovation, beyond something new? As we (and others) use the term, it is the *marriage* of new knowledge, embodied in an invention, with the successful introduction of that invention into the marketplace. Even the best inventions are useless unless they have been designed, marketed, and modified in ways that make them commercially viable. This requires someone who realizes the commercial opportunity presented by the innovation (or even a seemingly small element of the breakthrough), which sometimes is not the purpose the inventor had in mind, and then takes all the steps necessary to turn that opportunity into something many consumers will want to buy. These tasks are inherently entrepreneurial, an insight we will return to repeatedly throughout this book.

So what determines innovation? In Solow's model, innovation is like manna from heaven, something that policy makers largely cannot control. Although they may modestly influence it by way of government-funded research or incentives for research and development, the pace of innovation is essentially taken as a given. A growing number of economists have been uncomfortable with that assumption, and over the past two decades they have put much effort into a better explanation of innovation's role in economic growth. These researchers, using increasingly sophisticated statistical methods, have posited a range of other variables that influence innovation, some of which governments can control (like openness to goods and investment from abroad, spending on research and development, and training of more scientists and engineers), and others of which governments cannot control (like geographic location). We discuss these efforts in chapter 3.

We do not take the position that these factors are unimportant, because many or most of them are. Instead, we suggest that it is more useful to pare down (economize, if you will) the list of suggestions that societies should implement by thinking of economies as potential "growth machines," which need fuel to operate but which also must have some essential primary parts or components that work in harmony if they are to promote entrepreneurship, innovation (and its dissemination), and growth most effectively. The "fuel" for an economy is the right set of macroeconomic policies: essentially, prudent fiscal and monetary policies to keep inflation low and relatively stable and to prevent economic downturns (or even worse, financial crises) from derailing progress toward growth in the long run. We realize that maintaining macroeconomic stability is far from easy. Indeed, it is the focus of much, if not most, of the attention political leaders give to economic policy. But by definition, economic growth is a long-run phenomenon, and so the much greater challenge is to design and implement policies that foster growth in the long run.

We believe that policy makers are most usefully served by having a relatively simple framework for achieving this objective. Not a ten-point list, such as the so-called Washington Consensus list of reforms, or even longer lists of policy prescriptions, which we discuss in chapter 3. The danger in long lists is that they are too easily ignored by busy policy makers, who generally operate under the intense pressure of competing interest groups and have the energy and political capital to concentrate on only a few major endeavors at a time. The other extreme, the search for a single silver bullet answer to the growth problem, is equally dangerous. Economic systems are complicated, and no single policy prescription, even if followed to the letter, is likely to be sufficient to ensure rapid, sustainable growth over the long run.

We attempt to strike a balance between these extremes in concentrating on four factors or conditions that we believe are most important in contributing to long-run growth for all capitalist economies, but especially for those at the "technological frontier," where future progress *requires* continued innovation more than it does mere replication. We flesh these out in greater detail in chapter 4 but give a brief preview here so readers can keep them in mind before proceeding further. The factors should be understood as forming the bare blueprint of a well-oiled growth machine—the "big picture" that busy policy makers can keep in mind when considering more detailed initiatives or programs.

We also limit our attention to growth-enhancing conditions for capitalist economies, or those that at least to some degree allow private ownership of property and reward individuals and firms for serving consumer needs. Although we discuss in some detail in chapter 5 different models of capitalism—and elevate one of them, "entrepreneurial capitalism," above all the rest—the various models differ sharply from the central planning that governed much of the world (the Soviet Union, Eastern Europe, and China) from the end of World War II until the fall of the Berlin Wall in 1989. History has shown that central planning cannot deliver high and rapidly improving standards of living and we therefore will not consider it (even though central planning lives on in a few dark corners of the world, notably Cuba and North Korea).

Our four elements of a well-oiled economic growth machine, the *successful entrepreneurial economy,* are the following:

1. First, and perhaps quite obviously, in the successful entrepreneurial economy, it must be relatively easy to form a business, without expensive and time-consuming bureaucratic red tape. As a corollary, abandoning a failed business (that is, declaring bankruptcy) must also not be too difficult because, otherwise, some would-be entrepreneurs may be deterred from starting in the first place. A reasonably well-functioning financial system must also exist, one that channels the funds of savers to the users of funds, entrepreneurs in particular. And the importance of flexible labor markets cannot be overstated: if entrepreneurs cannot attract new labor, they cannot grow, nor will they want to grow if labor rules are overly restrictive (especially if rules limit the ability of firms to fire nonperforming workers or shed workers they no longer need).
2. Second, institutions must reward socially useful entrepreneurial activity once started; otherwise individuals cannot be expected to take the risks of losing their money and their time in ill-fated ventures. Here, the rule of law—property and contract rights in particular—is especially important.
3. Third, government institutions must discourage activity that aims to divide up the economic pie rather than increase its size. Such socially

unproductive (though, in a sense, entrepreneurial) activities include criminal behavior (selling of illegal drugs, for example) as well lawful "rent-seeking" behavior (i.e., political lobbying or the filing of frivolous lawsuits designed to transfer wealth from one pocket to another).

4. Finally, in the successful entrepreneurial economy, government institutions must ensure that the winning entrepreneurs and the larger established companies (which were launched at some earlier time by entrepreneurs) continue to have incentives to innovate and grow, or else economies will sink into stagnation. The ostensible importance of effective antitrust laws here comes to mind, but we place greater emphasis on openness to trade (which works automatically and without the long lead times inherent in legal antitrust enforcement).

We suspect that there will be a great temptation among some readers to ask: What about this, or what about that? Why shouldn't some other things be on the list? For example, one obvious challenge is from those who believe, as does David Landes of Harvard, that growth is primarily about culture: that some societies have hard-working, enterprising people, and other countries do not. And that those countries with hard-working, enterprising cultures (the United States, much of Europe, Japan, much of Asia, and most recently, India) grow rapidly, while those countries without that culture (much of Africa and Latin America) grow much less rapidly or not at all (Landes, 1999).

We recognize that culture plays a role, but it is—and, indeed, cannot be—the sole factor explaining economic success. If it were, then why have so many Indians, Russians, and some other expatriates been so successful economically outside their home countries, while many others left behind struggle to support themselves and their families? It is not just "self-selection"—that is, expatriates are successful elsewhere because they are the most enterprising to begin with (as demonstrated by their willingness to risk it all by leaving their home countries). The countries they left behind have struggled because their institutions have impeded progress (even in India, the home of the "information technology outsourcing" revolution, where plenty of rules still drag down other parts of that economy).

Or what about the role of geography and the notion that in some countries near the equator the heat makes it impossible for individuals to work hard and exposes them to disease, or that countries that are landlocked have excessive transportation costs and cannot easily trade with the rest of the world? Jeffrey Sachs has placed great emphasis on these factors as determining, or inhibiting, growth (Sachs, 2005). As with culture, there may something to this line of argument. But then there are the counterexamples. If being at the equator is the economic kiss of death, how then does one explain the spectacular economic success of Singapore or the somewhat less stellar but still impressive performance of Thailand? If being landlocked condemns a country to backwardness, how does one explain the remarkable economic record of Switzerland, which is so landlocked by mountains on all sides that it has used its unique geography in the past as a symbol of its neutrality?

And what about education or, as economists antiseptically label it, "human capital"? As we will discuss in later chapters, virtually every theoretical model and empirical test of economic growth assigns a major role to the presence of an educated workforce. We do not dispute the importance of some degree of education for growth but do not single it out as having a unique role for creating an entrepreneurial society or economy, for a simple reason: context matters. Before the Berlin Wall fell (and even since), the countries belonging to the former Soviet Union and many of the Eastern European countries boasted some of the most successful primary, secondary, and even higher-level educational systems in the world. But these systems were embedded in a political and economic atmosphere—socialism or communism—that was the very antithesis of entrepreneurship (admittedly, there was innovation, particularly in military technology and space exploration in the U.S.S.R., but these were the exceptions that prove the rule).

To be sure, an educated workforce can provide a huge boost to entrepreneurship when some or all of the other factors just listed are also present, within a capitalist setting. Highly educated individuals are more likely to come up with cutting-edge entrepreneurial businesses, especially in an increasingly high-tech world. In addition, countries where basic education is widespread can be vital for supplying the human capital that entrepreneurs can draw on to grow their ventures.

Finally, what about democracy? Is it not essential for growth, or as others have claimed, is some degree of autocracy first necessary to enable countries to reach a certain level of development, after which democracy becomes more or less inevitable? These are hotly contested questions, and although the verdicts are still out, our view of the evidence, such as it is, is that democracy certainly can contribute to growth, especially in entrepreneurial economies, but is not essential for this to occur. The growth "miracles" of Southeast Asia, and more recently China, attest to the latter proposition. At the same time, the evidence does not support the view that autocracies are essential for growth; in fact, even among less developed countries, democracies grow faster than countries ruled by autocrats.

The list of "what abouts" certainly goes on, and we will not dwell on all possible permutations in this opening chapter. Suffice it to say that when we examine the various theories and empirical studies of growth in greater detail in chapter 3, we find them wanting, indeed, even crying out for something else. That "something else," we submit, consists of the four basic elements of the successful growth machine we have identified and will later elaborate.

Plan for the Rest of the Book

We flesh out the above propositions and others in subsequent chapters. In chapter 2 we will address the threshold question: why should countries, or their populations, care about economic growth in the first place? This is a seemingly obvious and innocuous question, but as we suggest in the chapter, a number of critiques of growth have been mounted in recent years. We rebut them, and more, in chapter 2.

In chapter 3 we will tackle the key question: what determines economic growth? We don't provide all the answers—after all, that is what the rest of the book is about, and yet neither we nor anyone else has reason to be sure of the answer. But in chapter 3, we outline what, up to now, economists interested in the growth process have theorized and tested. As we have already suggested, we believe the answer to the growth puzzle so far has hardly been fully answered.

In chapter 4, we begin to fill in what remains of the puzzle by advancing some very different views about what capitalism looks like. Since the Berlin Wall fell and communism pretty much has disappeared (except in a few countries), it is understandable that many assume that, at least with respect to economic systems, capitalism has won the ideological "war." More important, subsumed in this view is the assumption that capitalism is monolithic—that it is defined by the private ownership of property and businesses, and little else. In chapter 4 we advance and describe in some detail four different conceptions of capitalism: state-guided, oligarchic, big-firm, and entrepreneurial. These archetypes are starkly drawn and few are prevalent in a pure form in any one country. Nonetheless, societies tend to have economic systems that at any one time are predominantly one of these forms or another. As a gross overgeneralization, developing countries tend to be state-guided or oligarchic. Developed economies tend to be characterized either exclusively by big-firm capitalism or a mix of big-firm and entrepreneurial capitalism. A key point in chapter 4 and subsequent chapters is that, at some point, if and when economies approach the technological frontier and the living standards of rich countries, the only way to ensure that they will remain there is to adopt some blend of big-firm and entrepreneurial capitalism. Furthermore, other countries that have not achieved this level of economic success could benefit from having entrepreneurial features during their transitions toward faster growth.

In chapter 5, we outline what we submit are four key ingredients for building and maintaining the mixed form of capitalism we believe is ideal. Three of those preconditions are important for promoting productive entrepreneurship; the fourth is aimed at ensuring that the winners of the entrepreneurial race keep innovating. We also address the role of the "what about" subjects just mentioned—culture, geography, finance, education, and democracy, among others—and examine whether and to what extent each is unique to either big-firm or entrepreneurial capitalism or, ideally, to a blend of the two.

What steps should developing countries, currently far from the technological frontier, take to move toward the right blend of capitalism, the one we advocate? That is the question we explore in chapter 6. It is not easy to answer because it requires the right mix of economics and politics. The answer is further complicated by the fact that the developing world encompasses many countries at different stages of development, each with its unique culture and historical circumstances.

In chapter 7, we examine two parts of the world—Japan and Western Europe—that are the exemplars of big-firm capitalism and where, only two decades ago, it looked as though per capita incomes would exceed those of the United States. Indeed, Americans were nearly panicked at the thought, although what seemed to concern the United States even more were the large trade deficits that it then had with these two parts of the world. In fact, those deficits, just like the current trade deficits, primarily reflect fundamental macroeconomic imbalances in the United States economy and have essentially nothing to do with relative living standards in different countries, or with the more important question taken up in this book: how close are the economies to the technological frontier (with per capita income being one way to measure that closeness).

In any event, as Japan and Western Europe approached the U.S. living standard, something happened. Their economies stalled (Japan's much more than Europe's), while productivity growth in the United States took off, jumping from an annual rate of 1.5 percent between 1973 and 1975 to 2.5 percent between 1995 and 2000, and then really kicking into high gear over the next four years, speeding at 3.5 percent. The most recent productivity growth acceleration in the United States is especially remarkable, given the 2001 recession and the productivity drag that many thought would be imposed by frictions in trade following the terrorist attacks of September 11, 2001, and the dramatic increase thereafter in private and public security spending.

The debate over why the U.S. economy sped up will undoubtedly continue, but surely one reason Europe and Japan fell by the wayside was the absence of a healthy dose of entrepreneurship in both these parts of the world. Since 2000, Western European leaders have announced that they want to introduce measures to promote entrepreneurship to address this shortcoming. Whether they are likely to succeed is one of the main topics we address in chapter 7.

Finally, even economies that already have a strong entrepreneurial sector, such as that in the United States, face the challenge of remaining that way. After all, societies change. Great Britain, after leading the world, fell back into big-firm and state-guided capitalism for much of the twentieth century, only to awaken from its slumber in the last two decades or so. The United States fell into a stage approaching big-firm capitalism after World War II, a state of affairs that was celebrated by such thinkers as John Kenneth Galbraith and even by the father of entrepreneurship economics himself, Joseph Schumpeter. But the celebration turned out to be prema- ture. America's postwar record of strong productivity growth came to a screeching halt with the first oil shock of 1973–74, and, as we have sug- gested, productivity growth languished for roughly two decades there- after, only to bounce back more strongly than ever since the mid-1990s.

A central challenge for the United State is to keep its productivity mira- cle going. We believe that maintaining the right blend of big-firm and en- trepreneurial capitalism is a key requirement for meeting that challenge. Yet as Mancur Olson (one of the great economists of the twentieth century who, in our opinion, still has not gotten his proper due) warned several decades ago, interest groups can ossify economies (Olson, 1982). Short of war, disruptive technological change can prevent that from happening. But such disruptions are likely to occur only in a climate where risk-taking is encouraged. In chapter 8, we identify a number of trends that worry us, trends that may discourage risk-taking if they are not reversed. It would be a tragedy, to say the least, if the leading entrepreneurial society—the United States—were to forfeit that role, not because of challenges from abroad (the current worry), but from causes made at home.

Concluding Thoughts

We want to be careful about our claims. We are not propounding a silver bullet theory of growth, one that relies on only one factor, such as entrepreneurship, to explain different levels of growth. As we will demon- strate, three of the four types of capitalism we identify have produced and will continue to produce growth. But we are contending that economies that want to advance the frontier—in any sector or many of them—must eventually embrace some mix of entrepreneurial and big-firm capitalism.

Our arguments draw from logic, history, even economic theory (al- though they are not mathematically modeled). We explicitly acknowledge that our claims have not yet been tested by the traditional empirical tech- niques used by economists, although some recent work by others is begin- ning to build a case that entrepreneurship matters—and possibly a lot— for economic growth (Audretsch et al., 2006; Acs and Armington, 2006). The standard statistical technique is to employ some form of multiple re- gression analysis, which allows investigators to sort through the causes of some phenomenon to identify which are significant, and by how much, and which are not.

But policy makers cannot and should not wait for still more formal mathematics and even more statistical work to tell them what to do. We believe that there is enough information already available that can help guide busy policy makers and the citizens who watch them and are affected by what they do. We hope that you, the reader, will agree that this is indeed so.

2

WHY ECONOMIC GROWTH MATTERS

We are interested in entrepreneurship because we hope to explain and ultimately contribute to facilitating economic growth, which is traditionally measured by the increase in a country's output of goods and services (what economists call gross domestic product or GDP). When each of the present authors was trained as an economist, the importance of economic growth was assumed to be self-evident. One of us studied the subject immediately after the Great Depression, when the entire thrust of teaching in the field understandably was how to stimulate growth.[1] After World War II and until the late 1960s and early 1970s, when the other two authors studied the subject, it was still widely assumed that the priority given to economic growth was not controversial and that it was even on a par with the ideals of motherhood and apple pie. Faster growth in the output of goods and services in an economy meant higher incomes for everyone (even though some people would, inevitably, earn more than others). Higher incomes would make it possible for more people to purchase, use, and enjoy more things (and services) in life. So how could anyone question the value of faster growth? In recent years, some observers have done just that, and now (and surprisingly, at least to economists) economic growth needs some defending.

Most people—those who are unemployed and want jobs, or who fear that they may lose their jobs, or who are poor and want the higher wages that faster growth will bring—have no doubts about the benefits of economic growth. But for reasons we hope will be clear shortly, there continues to be a need to persuade many who question the virtue of growth, and it is their criticisms that we will address here.

Before considering their specific critiques, it is useful to consider the big picture. At bottom, economic growth is essential not because humans are greedy or excessively materialistic, but because they want to better their lives. This is a natural aspiration and only with more economic output can more people live a more enjoyable and satisfying existence. Of course, economic growth is not the only goal in life. As economists will be the first to point out, there are always trade-offs: More work leaves less time for play and for family. More output often is accompanied by an increase in unwelcome side effects, such as pollution. But at the end of the day, the richer societies are, the more resources they will have to address the side effects of growth as well as the various maladies that shorten lives or make them less satisfying. Later in this chapter, we will provide some additional reasons why continued growth is especially important for both developing and developed countries in this century and beyond.

Are There Limits to Growth?

One line of skepticism about growth arises from individuals and groups who worry that as the world's population increases and economic growth continues, societies will use up scarce resources and, at the same time, degrade the environment. In the early 1970s, a group called the "Club of Rome" expressed such worries, fearing that eventually (and rather soon) the world would run out of energy and some commodities, so that growth *couldn't* continue at anything like the existing pace. Today, there are those who believe, for similar reasons, that growth *shouldn't* continue.

The doomsayers who projected that economic growth would come to a standstill were wrong. Since 1975, total world economic output has increased more than sevenfold.[2] On a per capita basis, world output is more than five times higher than it was thirty years ago. Growth in output, and therefore income, per person throughout the world advanced at a far more rapid pace (nearly ninefold) in the twentieth century than in any other century during the previous one thousand years (to the extent these things can be measured).[3] Per capita output continues to increase because firms around the world continue to make more use of machines and information technology that enable workers to be more productive and because technology itself continues to advance, making it possible for consumers to use new products and services. There is good reason to hope that this process can and will continue, though there are some lurking dangers, including foolish actions by governments.

But should growth continue? What about the supplies of energy that will be depleted in the process or the pollution that will be generated as ever more things are produced and used? Curiously, economists who tend to be quite rational in their lives urge the worriers to have faith—faith that continued technological progress powered by market incentives will ease these concerns. As it turns out, however, economists' faith has roots in historical fact. In the early 1800s, Thomas R. Malthus famously predicted that the world's population would eventually starve or, at the least, live at a minimal level of subsistence because food production could not keep pace with the growth of population. Technological advances since that time have proved him wrong. Through better farming techniques, the invention of new farming equipment, and continuing advances in agricultural science (especially the recent "green revolution" led by genetic engineering), food production has increased much more rapidly than population, so much so that in "real terms" (after adjusting for inflation), the price of food is much lower today than it was two hundred years ago, or for that matter, even fifty years ago. Farmers, who once accounted for more than 50 percent of the population at the dawn of the twentieth century in the United States, now comprise less than 2 percent of population—and are able to grow far more food at the same time.

The same process of technological advance that undermined Malthus's dire predictions may be able to quiet the concerns of the modern-day Malthusians who worry about disappearing energy, although more active involvement by governments may be necessary to address concerns about global warming. As some sources of energy are depleted—fossil fuels, in particular—their prices will rise, setting in motion several developments that will keep economies from stagnating. For one thing, consumers will cut back on their demand for fossil fuels directly (taking fewer trips, carpooling, or even moving closer to work) or indirectly by buying things (cars, houses, and appliances) that are more energy-efficient. This occurred after the first postwar "energy crisis" of 1973. Energy use as a percentage of GDP in the United States has been cut in half largely as a result of higher prices, and it will continue to drop if fossil fuel prices (adjusted for inflation) rise in the future. Equally important, if prices of fossil fuels increase, the backers of substitute forms of energy (nuclear power, fusion, geothermal, biomass, solar, and possibly other sources) will have stronger incentives to perfect their technologies so that they can be readily used instead.[4]

As for global warming, there is a consensus among scientists that the problem is real and growing. Indeed, some scientists attribute the intense hurricane activity that devastated the Gulf states and parts of Florida during the 2005 season to warmer waters due to global warming. At the same time, there is an emerging consensus among economists and policy makers around the world that the best way to curb the carbon emissions that are contributing to global warming is to employ a mixture of rules and market-like incentives, perhaps the most promising being the establishment of ceilings on pollution by allocating suitably restricted limits on unavoidable emissions by producers and allowing these rights to be traded in markets. Thus pollution can be capped and growth can nevertheless continue. The "cap and trade" approach, applied globally, was the linchpin of the Kyoto agreement reached in the late 1990s but not yet implemented (due in large part to opposition by the United States). Although political and practical problems may inhibit the adoption of cap and trade on a global scale, it may be feasible on both grounds to implement the idea on a national basis.[5]

Those who doubt whether economic growth can continue if resources are devoted to reducing pollution need only look to the U.S. experience— where both the air and water are far cleaner today than thirty years ago, even with a substantially higher production of goods.[6] If the same political energy that has so far fueled the "no growth" or "limits to growth" movements were channeled instead to persuading governments around the world to accept less socially damaging approaches, including a tradable emissions permit system, there is good reason to believe global warming concerns would be much attenuated.

Growth and Globalization

A second line of attack on growth, though not directly labeled as such, stems from the antiglobalization movement. Some of those who object to the increasing economic integration among nations around the world—and who have mounted protests in various places around the globe to make their point—have done so out of the belief that even if this process of "globalization" enhances overall growth, it also contributes to rising economic inequality and even to poverty. Some critics of globalization have followed this reasoning to its logical conclusion, advocating higher barriers to trade, capital flows, and immigration as a way of reversing economic integration and thus ostensibly reducing inequality and poverty in the process, regardless of what it does to growth.

A look at the bare facts validates the concerns about inequality—at least among countries. Figure 1 displays the per capita real incomes (adjusted for price level differences and exchange rates between countries) of three groups of countries as of the year 2000: four "rich" economies (including

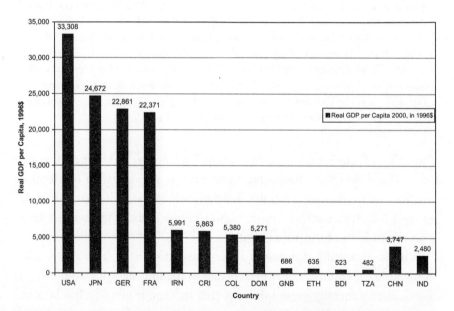

Figure 1. Real GDP per Capita for Advanced, Middle-, and Low-Income Countries, 2000, in Adjusted 1996 Constant Dollars. *Abbreviations:* USA=United States, JPN=Japan, GER=Germany, FRA=France, IRN=Iran, CRI=Costa Rica, COL=Colombia, DOM=Dominican Republic, GNB=Guinea-Bissau, ETH=Ethiopia, BDI=Burundi, TZA=Tanzania, CHN=China, IND=India. *Source:* Alan Heston, Robert Summers, and Bettina Aten, Penn World Table Version 6.1, Center for International Comparisons at the University of Pennsylvania (CICUP), October 2002. Available at http: //pwt.econ.upenn.edu/php_site/pwt61_form.php.

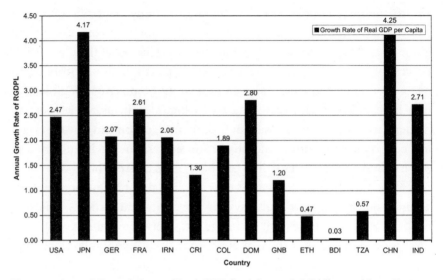

Figure 2. Annual Growth Rate of Real GDP for Advanced, Middle-, and Low-Income Countries, 1960–2000, in Adjusted 1996 Dollars. *Abbreviations:* USA=United States, JPN=Japan, GER=Germany, FRA=France, IRN=Iran, CRI=Costa Rica, COL=Colombia, DOM=Dominican Republic, GNB=Guinea-Bissau, ETH=Ethiopia, BDI= Burundi, TZA=Tanzania, CHN=China, IND=India. *Source:* Alan Heston, Robert Summers, and Bettina Aten, Penn World Table Version 6.1, Center for International Comparisons at the University of Pennsylvania (CICUP), October 2002. Available at http://pwt.econ.upenn.edu/php_site/pwt61_form.php.

the United States), four "middle-income" countries, and four poor countries. The differences among the three groups are vast, with residents of the rich countries earning roughly five times what those living in the middle-income countries earn, and more than twenty-five times the average earnings of residents of the poor countries.

What is especially disturbing about these disparities in per capita incomes among countries, however, is that in the four decades from 1960 to 2000, they generally *grew,* implying that income inequality has become worse. This can be discerned from figure 2, which displays the growth rates in per capita incomes over this period. Although not all the differences in national growth rates are as clear as those shown in figure 2, a distinct pattern does emerge: on average, rich countries grew faster than those in the middle and even faster than those at the bottom. In other words, levels of income or output per capita are diverging rather than converging. Note that at this point, we are simply presenting facts, making no statements about whether and to what extent increased globalization has contributed to this trend or, as Martin Wolf has persuasively argued, has in fact ameliorated it (Wolf, 2004).

In subsequent chapters, we will discuss the continuing controversy over whether income disparities among countries inevitably must converge toward rich country levels of per capita income. But it is important at this point to distinguish differences in the average welfare of citizens among *countries* from differences in incomes of *all individuals* around the world, wherever they may reside. In particular, if one takes account of India and China, where roughly 40 percent of the world's population reside, income inequality among individuals appears to have narrowed over time due to the rapid income growth in heavily populated parts of those two countries (Bhalla, 2002).

Moreover, of particular relevance to the debate about globalization, both India and China have achieved rapid growth while opening themselves up to the rest of the world: trading more extensively and accepting more investment from rich countries. Openness to trade and investment, as we will discuss in later chapters, can be critical to facilitating entrepreneurship and, hence, growth. For now, it is essential to note only that growth and poverty reduction go hand in hand (Dollar and Kraay, 2002). Indeed, it is difficult to think of examples of countries where poverty has declined without economic growth. A rising tide truly does usually lift even the boats at the bottom. From 1978 to 2000, in particular, while the world population grew by 1.6 billion people, the number of people with incomes below $1 per day—the lowest threshold of poverty—declined by more than 300 million (Barro and Sala-i-Martin, 2004, 9).

But even if globalization did worsen inequality (as it may within certain countries, especially because it often disproportionately benefits the most-educated individuals who have skills or products to sell in a global marketplace), steps to slow down or reverse economic integration clearly would reduce growth and very likely lead to lower incomes and average standards of living around the world.[7] A simple thought experiment should demonstrate why. Imagine if residents in each of the fifty states of the United States were limited to doing business only with other residents of their states. Is there any serious question that total output, and therefore incomes, in such a "disunited" America would be lower than it is now, with Americans freely able to buy and sell goods and services, send money to and receive money from, and move to any part of the "united" states, rather than being limited to conducting business only with individuals and firms in a single state? Expanding the size of the market in which individuals and firms can do business enhances prosperity, enabling individuals and firms to specialize in what they do best, insights contributed more than two hundred years ago by Adam Smith and David Ricardo. This is just as true for the United States, as it is for other countries throughout the world.[8]

Growth and Happiness

A third critique of continued growth arises out of the oft-stated aphorism that "money cannot buy happiness." Of course there is plenty of truth to this. Religious leaders constantly remind us, for example, that spiritual health is more important than wealth. At a more mundane level, although the average American household clearly is better off financially today than before, many individuals may be no happier as a result. One obvious reason: With both parents working in many families, the constant struggle to do a good job at work and to spend "quality" (if not "quantity") time with their children makes many Americans feel as though they were on a treadmill. Cornell University economist Robert Frank adds another reason why many Americans may feel no happier, even though they have higher incomes. While most "consumption goods"—houses, cars, and clothes—may make individuals temporarily feel better, that effect is not likely to be permanent. After the "newness" of these items wears off, individuals tend to take them for granted. Moreover, when people look around and find that others have the same or better consumer goods as they do, they may eventually be less happy than they were before (Frank, 2004). Clearly it seems that *relative* wealth or income may be more important to a sense of well-being than absolute wealth or income (Graham and Pettinato, 2002).[9]

Still, economic growth may matter more than people may realize. What individuals report to interviewers in a survey will not necessarily capture the progress that people may take for granted but nonetheless objectively makes them better off. For example, consider the fact that over the past several decades, average life expectancies around the world, even in most developing countries, have been rising.[10] This remarkable result has been made possible by more plentiful supplies of food and better health care, both of which are the products of economic growth. Or consider the significant gains that rich countries, such as the United States, have made over the past several decades in controlling pollution and enhancing the safety of a variety of products (especially dangerous ones, like automobiles). None of these developments would have been possible without growth in incomes that lead people to demand and afford cleaner and safer environments.

Respondents to surveys may not fully be aware of all of these facts when asked for immediate answers. Indeed, as journalist Gregg Easterbrook has noted, one of the "paradoxes of prosperity" is that many individuals in rich countries don't realize how good things really are (Easterbrook, 2003). Instead of assessing the benefits of growth by asking individuals to compare the way things are to the way they were, we believe it is more revealing if the question were asked prospectively—that is, if they would be happier if they had more income in the future, even if everyone else in their neighborhood, city, or country also enjoyed the same increase (whether in absolute or percentage terms). We suspect that not many individuals would question growth if put this way. We are especially confident that the roughly two billion people living on the equivalent of less than $2 a day throughout the developing world would have little trouble answering that they would feel better off.

GDP: Is That All There Is?

A fourth line argument, related to the one about growth and happiness, is that the growth of output as it is conventionally defined does not accurately represent the growth of human welfare. By definition, GDP counts only goods and services that are traded in the market or, if supplied by the government, have prices attached to them. GDP does not measure a whole series of activities that are not traded in the market but that nonetheless contribute to or detract from our overall sense of well-being, including: household activity, human health, selected activities of nonprofit organizations (especially those relying on volunteer labor), and environmental conditions. By focusing exclusively only on what can be found in the market, citizens and policy makers come to have too narrow a view of what really counts in life. A 2006 report by the Organization for Economic Cooperation and Development adds that measures of gross output do not take account of its distribution among an economy's residents (or the degree of income equality or inequality) nor do they count the value of leisure time. Thus, depending on the value society attaches to income equality and leisure, for example, "adjusted" income per capita in some countries in Europe actually may be higher than in the United States (OECD, 2006).

We agree that GDP has its limits, as economists have long recognized. More than three decades ago, two prominent American economists—William Nordhaus and James Tobin of Yale University (the latter a winner of the Nobel Prize)—provided an alternative set of accounts that included various forms of nonmarket activity to arrive at a more comprehensive measure they called "Measured Economic Welfare" (Nordhaus and Tobin, 1972). More recently, a National Academy of Sciences panel has recommended that the federal statistical agencies develop a set of "satellite accounts" to measure these various nonmarket activities, as a way of supplementing the information conveyed by current measures of GDP (Abraham and Mackie, 2005).

None of this should detract from the fact that growth of market GDP is still something to be valued for two reasons. First, the goods and services that make up GDP are valuable to people in and of themselves since they enable people to enjoy a higher standard of living. Second, incomes and output most likely are positively correlated with a number of the nonmarket activities or outcomes that are not currently included in GDP. For example, as we have noted, as economies grow richer, their people can afford more health care and are able to invest in improving the environment (and, indeed, are likely to demand more of these nonmarket goods).

As for income equality or inequality, the value one places on this is inherently subjective, and thus measures of GDP "adjusted" for differences in the distribution of income should not be given undue weight. Nonetheless, extremes in either direction are undesirable. A society where all have the same incomes, for example, would provide no incentives for growth.

Conversely, societies where incomes are highly unequal are prone to political instability and backlashes that are also inimical to growth. No one knows where the happy medium lies, and like beauty, where that point is lies in the eyes of the beholder. The key is not so much how incomes are *currently* distributed but rather the ease or difficulty that individuals have of climbing to higher economic stations and thus to earning higher incomes. In short, it is *opportunity* that matters most—both for growth and for social and political stability.

There has been some debate in recent years, however, about the distribution of the gains from added productivity in the United States, in particular, whether workers as a whole have received their historic share (about two-thirds of the increase in output) or have suffered an erosion in that share. The debate arises from the apparent discrepancy between the faster rate of growth in productivity and that in real wages. But wage income alone does not account for benefits, specifically health insurance, that are included in the compensation of most American workers. Taking this into account, total compensation has been rising at roughly the same rate as productivity (Dew-Becker and Gordon, 2005). Of course, even this fact does not account for the long-run trend toward greater income inequality (pretax) in the United States among workers in different parts of the income distribution. This trend is widely known and accounts for the rising returns to education over time, reflecting increased employer demand for (relative to the supply of) skilled workers (Lazear, 2006).

Is Growth a Zero-Sum Game?

A key premise of this book is that economic growth is good not just for rich countries like the United States, but for all countries, since it is only through growth that people's living standards, whatever they may now be, can improve. But this premise does not seem to be as widely shared as we would like. In recent years, we have heard mounting objections among some political and opinion leaders in the United States who fear economic growth in other countries, especially in less developed countries—China and India, in particular.

To be sure, these fears typically are not expressed as directly as that. Instead, they are often couched as objections to the low labor costs in poorer countries that enable them to provide goods and services more cheaply than can the rich countries like the United States. The suggested remedy to this situation, through one means or another, is for rich countries not to buy as much from poorer countries. To some ears, this may sound like "fairness," but those in the developing world see it as telling them they shouldn't be able to grow as fast as they can or as they would like. Is it true that economic growth somehow is a zero-sum game, meaning that every additional dollar that accrues to a poor country must come out of our own (Thurow, 1980)? If so, doesn't assisting other countries to grow arm our future economic enemies who will take away our jobs or reduce our wages? The answers to these questions are "no" and "no."[11]

Again, the fifty-state example should make the point. New Yorkers benefit when incomes in other states go up because richer citizens elsewhere provide a broader market for goods and services generated in New York. The same is true for each of the other states. The same logic applied after World War II when the United States launched the Marshall Plan to rebuild Europe and supplied extensive aid to Japan to get its economy back on its feet. As per capita incomes in these countries grew, more people could afford the products and services the American economy was able to produce and deliver. That America nonetheless ran trade deficits through much of the postwar era does not contradict this point; it only demonstrates that as Americans' incomes grew, their wants for foreign goods grew at a faster pace than U.S. exports. These new products, services, and production methods find their way to other parts of the world and thus can contribute to rising living standards there. In short, as economists would put it, there are "beneficial externalities" associated with entrepreneurship that crosses national boundaries.

In some minds, perhaps many, the rapid rise of China and India poses a different sort of problem. It is one thing for countries at lesser stages of economic development to advance on the strength of their lower labor costs, making essentially the same things as were once manufactured in rich countries. But there is growing evidence that in some spheres—information technology, biotechnology, and in certain types of electronic equipment—China, India, and their richer neighbors in Southeast Asia have moved beyond mere manufacture or service delivery into research and development, the highest value part of the so-called value chain. Indeed, as we will discuss in chapter 8, some major U.S. corporations have expressed growing interest in supporting university research in these countries rather than in the United States—and not solely for reasons of cost, but because gaining access to and using the results of the research may be easier in these other locales. Should rich countries like the United States be worried about "losing" some of their R&D base to other countries?

In one sense, yes, and in another sense, no. On one hand, as R&D moves abroad, other countries stand to gain some of the profit that would have accrued to United States–based companies and their investors (although some of these may be foreign in any event). Furthermore, R&D success is likely to lead to other successes down the road. Scientists may move to locations where other cutting-edge researchers are located. Moreover, armed with the insights of their initial discoveries, innovators are likely to have a head start on the next wave of related innovations. The net effect of all this is that the countries that are host to the R&D breakthroughs grow more rapidly than they otherwise would, while countries that do not host such breakthroughs will grow somewhat more slowly.

On the other hand, as we will highlight in later chapters, innovation is an inherently "leaky" process. Even with well-enforced intellectual property rights, the vast majority of the profits from innovations accrue to society as a whole rather than the inventor or the initial entrepreneur. That is because innovations lead to new and cheaper products and services, which benefit all who purchase them, improving their standard of living. Thus, even if the "next big thing" should be invented in China or India, Americans and others in the world end up benefiting. That is how the world worked when Americans seemingly were inventing all the "next big things." It will be the way the world works in the future, even if some of those breakthroughs emerge in foreign locations.

There is yet another reason why it is in the economic interest of poor countries to grow more rapidly in the years ahead. As we will discuss shortly, and again in the last chapter, the United States and other rich economies will experience a wave of retiring baby boomers over the next several decades. Those retirees who have been lucky or fortunate enough to have saved for their retirement certainly are counting on the value of their financial assets (as well as their residences and other real estate) not to fall and ideally to continue rising at a rate faster than the growth of their economies. This is unlikely to occur, however, unless investors from emerging markets have the wherewithal to buy the securities that the retirees certainly will be selling, since it is unlikely that the younger generations within the richer countries will have the incomes, and thus savings, to purchase these assets. But investors from abroad will not have the resources themselves unless their economies continue growing. For this reason, investors in all rich but aging economies have a strong economic interest in the continued growth of economies in the rest of the world.

We confine our argument about the benefits of global growth to economics, and not politics. But it could well be that certain countries might use their new-found wealth to enhance their offensive military capabilities and thus increase the chances of conflict. For example, as China's economy continues to grow, its people and its government may not give up on the dream to reunite the mainland with Taiwan. Under the wrong circumstances—in particular, if Taiwan acted too independently—China could move militarily to accomplish that objective. A richer China would be better positioned to finance such a military campaign. The same could be said for a richer India, Pakistan, or any other country in the world where grievances with neighbors are all too common.

Fortunately, economic growth also is accompanied by a countervailing force, which may moderate, though not necessarily eliminate, any impulses toward military action. As we will discuss in chapter 5, there is compelling evidence that as economies grow richer, their propensity to embrace democratic values and institutions is greater. In turn, as societies embrace democracy while also becoming wealthier, they have in the past been less likely to turn to military action to advance their interests. If true, then entrepreneurial capitalism, by advancing growth, may help to diffuse tendencies toward armed conflict in different parts of the world.[12]

Growth and the Demographics of Aging

There is an old saying that there are only two certain things in life: death and taxes. But one of these certainties—death—is getting pushed back, with advances in medical science and nutrition, both made possible by economic growth. As economies grow richer, however, other demographic trends are set in motion. Families have fewer children because they have less need for them as breadwinners. Fewer children and longer life spans mean only one thing: over time, the average age of individuals in society increases. The aging of populations in advanced countries, some with fertility rates below replacement rates, has been known for some time. But what many people may not realize is that the average age in developing countries is rising as well. Indeed, as both the International Monetary Fund and the United Nations have reported, the entire world is aging, and the effects will be even more noticeable in the developing world than in countries that are already rich. Whereas nearly 60 percent of the world's elderly (those over sixty-five) live in developing countries today, that share is projected to increase to 80 percent by 2050 (IMF, 2004; United Nations, 2004).

So what does economic growth have to do with all this, other than helping to make it possible? The short answer is that while growth certainly helped contribute to the aging of the world, it is going to be desperately needed to help pay for the medical care and income support promised to the elderly. To be sure, this is a problem now confined primarily to rich countries, whose governments already have made these promises and have acted on them to a degree. But many developing countries have established similar, though less generous, systems of their own and, indeed, are being encouraged to do so by the World Bank.

The financing problem just for richer countries is enormous. Consider the United States, where the challenge is the least acute among developed economies. As shown in figure 3, in 2004, benefit payments under the United States Social Security and Medicare programs totaled roughly 5 percent of GDP, accounting for about a quarter of all federal spending (which, in turn, is about 20 percent of GDP) and roughly 30 percent of federal tax revenue. In 2010, the earliest baby boomers will begin retiring, a trend that will pick up speed as the years pass. As it does, the promised income and medical benefits will soar.

Thus, the Congressional Budget Office (CBO), the United States government's neutral and official government scorekeeper, has projected spending on these two programs, together with Medicaid (another entitlement program that supports health care for low-income individuals and families) to rise to 13 percent of GDP by 2025 and to 19 percent of GDP by 2050 (CBO, 2003). Compare these figures to the roughly 17 percent of

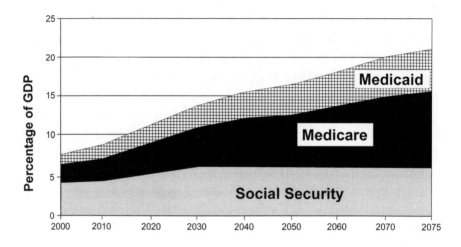

Figure 3. Social Security, Medicare, and Medicaid Expenses as a Percentage of GDP. *Source:* Testimony by Douglas Holtz-Eakin, director of the Congressional Budget Office, on the economic costs of long-term federal obligation, July 24, 2003. Available at http://www.cbo.gov/showdoc.cfm?index=4439&sequence=0.

GDP the federal government collected in taxes in 2004—the lowest share since 1960—or even the roughly 20 percent of GDP tax share that has prevailed in the United States for the past quarter century, and without major policy reforms, a fiscal disaster seems inevitable.

In our view, therefore, some combination of tax increases and budget cuts (especially in entitlements programs) eventually will be required to address this problem.[13] However politically painful these steps may be, they pale in comparison to the economic pain that the country would suffer if, at some point, investors fear they will *not* be taken and then refuse to buy the mounting federal debt required to finance our government except at much high interest rates, which could throw the U.S. economy (and other economies) into deep recession.

In any event, the magnitude of the required fiscal correction, and thus the political pain that decision makers must be prepared to absorb, will depend to a significant degree on how fast the economy grows. The Congressional Budget Office projections assume that output per worker will rise in the future at roughly 2 percent annually, which is a bit above the disappointing 1.5 percent rate of increase during the dark years of the 1973 – 93 period but considerably below the roughly 3 percent growth in annual

labor productivity that the United States has achieved since then. Economists aren't very good at predicting the future rate of productivity growth
since, at bottom, this requires projection of the future rate of innovation,
which essentially is impossible to do with any accuracy. That is why organizations like the CBO, and most economists, when confronted with the
need to make long-run projections adopt a technique called "reversion to
the mean." This principle, which many stock market analysts employ, suggests that if the growth of any variable strays too far away from its historical average, it eventually will bounce back toward that average, though it
may overshoot it. In the case of productivity growth, the long-run average
for the United States since the mid-1900s is about 2 percent, so reversion
to the mean implies that our future productivity growth, over the long
run, will plausibly be somewhere in that neighborhood. Hence the CBO's
long-run projection.

But it doesn't have to be that way. What if the economy changes in some
fundamental way so that past history is not a good guide to the future? For
example, productivity advanced at 2.5 percent annually from the end of
World War II until 1973, when the first "oil shock" occurred. There followed the dismal 1.5 percent growth rate experience for the subsequent
two decades before something kicked in, sending U.S. productivity
growth soaring beyond even the fast pace of the first quarter-century after
the war.

The point of this brief recitation of productivity facts is that economies
are not stagnant. Things change, and when they do, history may well not
be a guide to the future. Here is where growth comes in. What if the
United States were to find a way to continue or even exceed the remarkable post-1993 productivity growth rate of 3 percent rather than settle
down to the 2.1 percent projected by CBO? Over the next forty-five years,
that nearly one-percentage-point annual difference would mean that by
2050 per capita output would be roughly 60 percent higher than the CBO
has projected. With the GDP denominator that much larger, the ratio of
Social Security and Medicare spending to GDP would be substantially
lower. The decline in the spending ratio would be mitigated to some extent by the fact that, under current law, Social Security payments rise as real
wages rise, and wages would increase roughly one percentage point faster
if productivity grew that much more rapidly. But faster productivity growth

certainly would make Medicare spending more affordable, since wages and salaries of health care workers, which would also rise with higher productivity, account for only a portion of overall medical costs. Similar effects would follow if Europe and Japan somehow found a way to increase their rather anemic rates of productivity growth in the future.

In short, growth matters to aging societies because it makes it easier to afford government promises of support made to the elderly, among others. Aging, in turn, has two very different effects on the growth process. On the positive side, aging labor forces—up to a point—mean that the typical worker has more experience. More experienced workers, in turn, are more productive, so that as societies age, they should display faster productivity growth, other things being held constant.[14] But in aging societies, not everything can be held constant. As societies grow older, they are likely to have a lower proportion of young adults without families or children to support, and thus the cohort of individuals that are more likely to take the risks that lead to the formation and growth of high-impact enterprises will be smaller. After some point, aging societies are likely to be less entrepreneurial, in the sense of the term that we are using it in this book: developing and growing enterprises that have high-growth potential. True, many senior citizens or near retirees in the United States are jumping off the corporate ladder to start their own consulting operations or specialty stores, the traditional retirement pursuit of the elderly in Japanese societies. But, other things being equal, it is difficult for older individuals to have acquired the knowledge needed to come up with and commercialize the kinds of breakthrough technologies and services that drive economic growth. That is one of the reasons why, we will argue in chapter 7, countries like Japan and those in Western Europe face an even steeper uphill economic climb than the United States in financing the income and medical needs of their retiring populations in the future.

Economic Growth and Domestic Civility

Finally, economic growth is like a social lubricant that eases tensions while giving hope to populations. Societies with stagnant or, even worse, declining per capita incomes by definition cannot convince younger people that their economic fortunes will improve as they grow older. And without hope there is little or no entrepreneurial spirit to strive to change the existing order or to improve one's own standard of living, let alone the living standards of neighborhoods, cities, or entire countries. In short, the lack of growth itself can become an obstacle, holding back economic progress, or even worse.

As Harvard University economist Ben Friedman has persuasively argued, slow growth, especially when coupled with widening inequality, can provide the environment that breeds distrust and often hate (Friedman, 2005). It is not an accident, he points out, that some of the worst periods of intolerance toward African Americans and immigrants in post–Civil War United States history (the late 1800s, the 1930s, 1970s, and early 1980s) occurred during periods of slow or negative growth. The worst-case example of this was, of course, the rise of Nazism in Germany following World War I, when that country was mired in both hyperinflation and stagnant growth (and eventually depression). In more recent times—for example, in the last decades of slow growth and high unemployment—Continental Europe has again flirted with anti-Semitism, while hosting a strong strain of anti-immigrant sentiment.

The reverse is much more likely to be true for economies that are growing. These have the good fortune to take advantage of a virtuous cycle, since the young can count on a better life, assuming they work hard to achieve it. Visitors to India or China or Ireland or Israel, for example, report a vibrancy and sense of excitement that one doesn't hear about in Western Europe, at the rich end, or much of Latin America or Africa, at the lower end of the world income distribution. Growth opens up opportunities, which in turn unleash not only hope but also the work ethic that helps turn opportunities into reality. Much of this same energy and optimism can be found in pockets of the United States—in high-technology clusters and in parts of some American cities. The challenge will be to maintain this combination of energy and hope in coming decades, when the United States also begins to deal with the many challenges of its retiring baby-boom generation.

Conclusion

The criticisms of growth have some validity but are fundamentally misplaced. Economic growth is and continues to be important, indeed, morally necessary if individuals and society care about improving the living standards of peoples around the world. Michael Mandel, the chief economist for *Business Week,* has written about technology-driven growth in particular in a way that summarizes much of what we have tried to convey in this chapter:

> Such technology-driven growth is essential, I believe, if we are not to drown in our own problems. . . . Without breakthroughs in medical science, it won't be possible to supply the health care to a generation of aging Americans without bankrupting the young. Without breakthroughs in energy production and distribution, it won't be possible to bring Third World economies up to industrialized living standards without badly damaging the environment and stripping the world of natural resources. Without rapid economic growth powered by new technologies, it won't be possible to reduce poverty or ensure the next generation a better life than we have. (Mandel, 2004, xi–xii)

Just citing the hope for improvements in future technology begs the question: who comes up with it and, just as important, how does it get introduced into economies? As for the first question, economists generally agree that technological development is at least loosely tied to investment in the process of discovering new technologies, or research and development (R&D). But the more interesting question that so far has not been well studied, in our view, relates to the conditions under which new technology is introduced and used in economies. The answer to this puzzle turns very much on how an economic system is organized. We will address that critical question in chapter 4, after pausing in chapter 3 to survey what economists have concluded so far about what generates economic growth and why those efforts still leave room for further improvement through analysis and research.

3

WHAT DRIVES ECONOMIC GROWTH?

Modern economics as a separate academic discipline began with Adam Smith's *The Wealth of Nations,* whose central preoccupation was the question: what made economies rich? One of Smith's most important insights was that specialization, and therefore trade, within and across a country's borders was critical to growth. Individuals, he posited, would be far better off if each person specialized in what he or she did best and simply bought the things that other people could make more cheaply. In Smith's view, even if you were a jack-of-all-trades, it would be to your advantage to concentrate on the one or two things you did best because there always would be someone who could do the other things better. Thus, rather than grow your own food, build your own house, or make your own clothes, it would be better to specialize in one activity, or to work for someone else who did, and then buy the rest of what you needed from others. Smith was optimistic about future economic prospects as long as individuals and firms could freely trade with one another across as wide a geographic area as possible (as long as transportation costs did not offset the advantage of trading from afar).

Only a few decades later, Thomas Malthus did his best to turn that optimism around. Malthus is widely known, of course, for his infamous prediction that population would grow faster than the food supply, thereby leading to mass starvation and death. With this one forecast, Malthus did much to cement the reputation of economics as "the dismal science."

As the few statistics cited in the beginning of chapter 1 demonstrate,

Malthus was wrong. And, as we discussed in chapter 2, Malthus failed to take into account the continued advances in the technology of food production that have made it possible to feed more and more people with the same amount of (or even less) land and far fewer people engaged in the production of food. Nonetheless, one could excuse the roughly two billion people in the world who today earn less than $2 per dollars a day for believing that Malthus was right to be so pessimistic. For this reason alone, one would think that economists would have been consistently interested in why some countries grow faster than others, as well as why individual countries grow faster or slower in different time periods. But after Malthus, interest in the topic of economic growth declined among economists and did not pick up again until the era of the Great Depression, when economies around the world not only were *not* growing but were actually contracting at historically unprecedented rates.

The renowned British economist John Maynard Keynes supplied the solution to the problem at that time. Keynes argued that the classical remedy—waiting for high and rising rates of unemployment to drive wages down to a level where it would be profitable for business firms to begin hiring workers again—would not work, or that it would take so long as to be practically useless. For one thing, there was a downward rigidity to wages; workers who still had jobs resisted efforts by employers to lower wages simply to create new jobs. Equally if not more serious, firms would have little or no interest in hiring any more workers—even at lower wages—without confidence that whatever goods and services they produced or delivered actually would be bought by consumers or other firms. In short, Keynes's diagnosis of the Depression was that it was caused by insufficient demand for goods and services and could not be cured any time soon by waiting for wages and prices to fall.

A major economic field of study—macroeconomics—was born out of this basic insight. Associated with it was a set of straightforward economic prescriptions. If the private sector was generating too little demand, then government needed to come to the rescue, either by cutting taxes or increasing spending, or both. In other words, when the economy is weak, government deficits can help jump-start growth—but again, from the demand side of the economy. Conversely, if private sector demand growth was too strong, so strong that it was pushing up against the limited capacity of the economy to produce goods and services and thereby causing prices and wages to rise, then one appropriate policy response would be tighter fiscal policy, higher taxes and/or cuts in government spending. This latter problem of inflation would not become evident in U.S. experience until many years after World War II, but it was anticipated in Keynes's thinking and, indeed, was the corollary of one of his prescriptions for getting an economy out of a recession or a depression (which is, in essence, a severe and prolonged recession).

Keynes's emphasis on government responsibility for managing the economy—keeping it propped up when private sector demand was weak and dampening it when private sector demand was too strong—has survived him. Although some economists have since questioned the ability or wisdom of governmental attempts to smooth out economic fluctuations, the fact remains that in virtually all capitalist economies, macroeconomic policy management remains a central job of government. Understandably, therefore, to the average investor (and, indeed, the average citizen) economic growth is largely or only a demand-side phenomenon, driven by the growth in private sector and government demand for goods and services.

But although demand is certainly important, particularly in the short run, it cannot explain growth in the *long run*. Like any machine, the economy at any given point in time has a certain maximum capacity. Over the long run, economic growth is about the growth in that capacity, or what economists often call "potential output," that is, the amount of goods and services the economy could produce if all its resources, people, and machines were fully utilized. In the 1980s, this focus on potential output was popularized under the rubric of "supply-side" economics and addressed the role that tax cuts play—or were alleged to play—in stimulating growth in economic capacity by encouraging individuals to work harder and to save more.

We will not wade into the controversy that continues to this day about how important taxes are in this process. The important point for our purposes is that supply-side economics was not new. A number of economists had theorized in previous decades about what determines growth of potential output. In this chapter, we want to review briefly what insights they had, then turn to recent empirical studies of growth, and finally conclude with some thoughts about what we believe has been missing from these efforts to understand the process of economic growth.

Explaining Economic Growth: The Theory

In one sense, understanding how economies grow is like understanding how to make a cake: one must simply find a recipe. Recipes for making a cake include some basic ingredients (sugar, flour, leavening, and so on), some labor (measured in minutes or hours), and some equipment (a mixer and an oven). For economies, there are as many recipes as products and services, but typically all of them require essentially the same three ingredients: raw materials, labor, and machines (also called physical capital).

Actually, there is a fourth ingredient for both cakes and economies: technological change. Just as the mixers and ovens today are more efficient and cook more evenly than those of yesteryear, technological advances in whole economies lead to new products and services that are more desirable than those already on the market, as well as to more efficient ways of generating and delivering all products and services, whether existing or new.

In chapter 1, we boiled down the recipes for economic growth into two broad categories, which we labeled "growth by brute force" and "smart growth." By brute force, we meant the addition of more inputs—more labor and more capital that will lead to more output, although more capital alone will substantially raise output per worker. Yet one of the basic tenets of economics is that there are diminishing returns associated with the addition of any one factor of production. For example, with a given labor force, adding more and more machines will produce more output, but at a steadily declining rate. So although raising the share of output an economy devotes to both saving and investment can lead to higher growth for a while by providing more plant and machinery, it cannot do so in the long run. Put another way, in the long run, more investment can raise the level of total output but not its growth rate. This is one of many insights of one of the founding fathers of modern growth theory, MIT professor Robert

Solow (1956), and of another growth model published at the same time by Trevor Swan (1956).

Our second category—smart growth, that is, technological advance—can rescue an economy from diminishing returns. Steadily equipping any given labor force with better machines or equipment, such as personal computers instead of typewriters, can raise both the level and growth rate of output. Indeed, a central contribution of Solow's early work on growth theory (for which he was eventually awarded the Nobel Prize) is that technological advance (or increases in total factor productivity [TFP]) is the most important source of growth. Solow reached this finding for the United States using U.S. economic data through the 1950s and estimating an equation linking output to measures of capital and labor (Solow, 1957).[1] Since the estimated equation explained only about 12.5 percent of the variation in output, Solow attributed the leftover, residual variance to technological change. Subsequent work by the late Edward Denison, for the Committee for Economic Development and later for the Brookings Institution, reached similar conclusions through a somewhat different procedure—growth accounting,—which apportions out growth to a number of possible causes (Denison, 1962 and 1974). Other economists have since come to a similar conclusion, that technological change is a key driver of growth (Easterly and Levine, 2001).

The theoretical growth models constructed by Solow, Swan, and others since are shorthand ways of expressing in mathematical terms the relation between certain input variables—labor, capital, and technological advance—and the growth in the output of goods and services. Although abstract, such models can provide useful insights. For example, in one mathematical form, the models imply that responsiveness of output to changes in labor or capital (what economists call elasticity) is equal to the respective shares of labor and capital in overall output. Roughly speaking, therefore, since workers' incomes typically account for roughly two-thirds of output in most capitalist economies, a one-percentage-point increase in the labor force (from some combination of population growth, immigration, and increases in the participation rate of individuals wanting to work) would, in this model, lead to a 0.67 percent increase in output.[2]

But even the best mathematical models have their limits, and the postwar growth models were no exception. In the basic Solow-Swan model, for example, technological change is considered to be exogenous—something that happens with some combination of serendipity and policies aimed at promoting it (for example, government spending on basic research or legal protection of intellectual property rights). As we discuss below, the statistical studies of economic growth that have been performed over roughly the last two decades are largely aimed at attempting to unravel the mystery of technological change, or what many economists call the Solow residual. Why does the pace of innovation speed up in some periods and in some societies, and why does it slow down at other times and in other places? To be able to answer these basic questions is, at bottom, to be able to explain what can speed up or retard economic growth itself.

A growing number of economists have wrestled with these questions over the past several decades. Most have followed in the model-building and testing tradition pioneered by Solow; we will discuss their efforts in the next section. A few others, however, have taken an entirely different and nonmathematical path, one that stresses the importance of institutions, that is, the rule of law and informal norms that ensure that productive economic behavior will be rewarded. The leader of this institutionalist school of growth is another Nobel Prize winner, Douglass North, although others have contributed to the field.[3]

Economists who stress the importance of institutions typically point to the enforcement of rights to property (both physical and intellectual), contracts, and limited liability for investors in companies as being among the most important of these rules. Institutions take much time to develop, however, and generally cannot be copied or transplanted wholesale from some societies where they seem to work well into other societies that seem to be sorely in need of them. Instead, the institutions work most effectively, if at all, if they are home-grown. This can be frustrating to policy makers, whose time horizons are typically measured in years to the next election, not in decades—which may explain why the somewhat autocratic leaders bent on achieving economic reform (notably those in Korea and Singapore) have been so successful. The long time lags inherent in the development of institutions also frustrate the ability of economists to test their importance empirically, for lack of available data. But just because the contribution of these institutions cannot easily be validated by standard statistical tests does not mean they are unimportant. On the contrary, economists and policy makers who ignore the importance of institutions in economic growth run the risk of committing the proverbial lamppost fallacy: looking for one's lost money under a lamppost because that is where there is light, not necessarily because that is where the money was lost.

As readers will see in subsequent chapters, our own thinking on the subject of economic growth has been strongly influenced by the institutionalist school of economic growth. This also explains our mode of argument, which is heavily historical, logical, and even anecdotal rather than statistical. We acknowledge the limitations of our work, which can be fairly described as informed guesswork. Some of our prospective critics (if there are any!) may emphasize the guesswork aspect of our work, but we hope most readers will recognize that our analysis is informed by a substantial body of facts.

Explaining Economic Growth: The Empirical Evidence

For roughly two hundred years, from the time of Adam Smith up through the contributions of Solow and Denison, the topic of economic growth was largely the stuff of abstract theorizing. All this has changed over roughly the past two decades for a simple reason: the historical data that economists need to run standard statistical tests have been generated and made available by several economists who pioneered this unglamorous, but very important, aspect of the field. Accordingly, growth theory has been elaborated and subjected to a wide number of statistical tests by various economists in recent years, the essence of which we will review now.

Still, even with the best of data—and we will argue shortly that the data here have their limits—economists, like other social scientists, face obstacles that their counterparts in the physical sciences (physics, chemistry, and biology, for example) do not. Physical scientists generally are able to test their theories or hypotheses by running experiments, in which they can test one population that has been subjected to some intervention (such as a drug or a procedure) against a control group to see if that intervention makes the difference that theory suggests. These experiments often generate results very quickly, in a matter of days or months. In the case of highly sophisticated particle accelerators, physicists get results in literally a flash of a second (although it may take a bit longer to analyze the results of smashing atoms at the speed of light). Astrophysicists can also look backward—over many millions of years—by looking into space through increasingly powerful telescopes or probes launched into space to take advantage of the speed of light to find out what certain objects looked like or how they behaved many millions of years ago.

Economists do not have these luxuries for several reasons. For one thing, economists cannot run controlled experiments, with results observable only after a substantial delay, with entire economies, although in some rare cases, social scientists can conduct more modest experiments on selected populations (giving different groups various economic incentives or rewards for certain types of behavior, or providing groups of students different curricula or other educational interventions, for example).[4] But no government will allow its country to serve as a control group or a guinea pig for a study on what encourages or inhibits economic growth, especially given the long time lags involved in collecting and analyzing sufficient data for economists to draw definitive conclusions. If some policy has at least a reasonable chance of raising growth, governments and the people they serve will or should want to implement it right away, not wait to find out many years later whether it might work (although interest groups in societies that might be hurt by growth-oriented policies, which inevitably create disruption, may be successful in resisting their adoption).

Accordingly, economists are almost always looking backward in an effort to develop policies for the future. They do this by applying statistical techniques to bodies of historical data to sort out one or more variables whose patterns might explain growth. If economists can do that with some grounds for confidence in the results, then they can offer prescriptions to government leaders with at least some hope that what has worked in the past has a reasonable chance of working in the future.

For example, in the case of economic growth, economists seek to find out which ones of some set of "independent variables"—such as capital, labor, and various other factors they believe might contribute to technological change—drive economic growth (which is the "dependent variable," typically measured by per capita GDP or some variable designed to measure innovation or technological change directly). Once economists know, or believe they know, what factors have been most important in stimulating innovation in the past (ideally, factors over which governments have direct control, like spending on research and development, tax rates on income or sales, or openness to foreign trade and investment, for example), then they have some basis for proffering advice to political leaders that has some grounding in facts, not simply theory or, worse, political or personal bias.

Yet even in this endeavor, economic analysis has its limits. One problem is that in prescribing policies that have worked in the past, economists—and the politicians who listen to them—implicitly are assuming that the economies to which they are applying these policies will continue to behave or operate in the future in fundamentally the same way as in the past, or at least in similar fashion. This is equivalent to saying that the individuals and firms who make up these economies will act in the future much as they have in the past. While this is a plausible assumption, reality may intrude in some way or another, and this possibility at the very least raises questions about that assumption. This is especially true where some event—like a war, a major depression, or a sharp change in political or economic systems (the sudden transition from socialism to some form of capitalism in the former Soviet Union and Eastern Europe, for example)—has marked a sharp break between two historical periods. In such cases, people, firms, and even governments may behave very differently after the break than before.

A second limitation is that the statistical techniques that economists typically use (such as multivariate regression analysis) have their own shortcomings. For one thing, the results they generate are only as useful as the data to which they were applied, a limitation about which we have more to say in the following section. For another, statistical techniques often do not generate consistent or even clear answers, which is a limitation that we believe plagues the statistical work on growth in particular. There is always the problem of omitted variables or influences that really matter but which have not been included in the statistical tests, sometimes unintentionally or, more often, because the data to measure those influences do not exist or are highly imperfect.

And then there is the nagging problem of how to interpret the statistical results. Strictly speaking, regression analysis—which seeks to find the mathematical formula that best "fits" the behavior of some independent variables to the behavior of another dependent variable—usually generates at most what economists or statisticians call correlation. One variable is correlated with another if it moves in roughly the same direction as the other. For example, rainfall patterns are generally correlated with agricultural yields. Or the frequency of sunspots may be correlated with the ups and downs in the stock market. But correlation is not causation. The fact that two variables are highly correlated does not necessarily mean that one causes the other. The hypothetical sunspot example should be proof of that.

This distinction between correlation and causation is critical in social science, and in economics in particular, since political leaders who adopt a policy that economists recommend will generally assume that if they take that step they will get the positive results they desire—that adoption of a policy will cause some desirable outcome, like faster economic growth, to occur. But the regression results on which the policy recommendations rest may not justify such causal inferences. Or even if they do, when the policy is adopted, other forces—within or outside the economy (such as the weather)—may interfere with the experiment. Economists, politicians, and pundits will then debate for years thereafter about what truly caused what. The continuing debate in the United States over the impact of government budget deficits is one example of how controversies can seemingly go unresolved for years.

With these many caveats in mind, we now briefly describe the various statistical tests economists have deployed to unlock the puzzle of growth. As we have already suggested, these tests rest on the availability of statistical data on levels of output and other variables in different countries that might contribute to economic growth. Why different countries? Because the reliability or "confidence" of statistical tests improves as the quantity of data analyzed increases, especially if one wants to test the presence and magnitude and influence of many variables at the same time. As statisticians like to say, the more data they have relative to the number of variables tested, the more "degrees of freedom" they have. When statistical tests are limited to one country, the statistician only has data for that country for a given number of variables of interest over as long a period as they have been collected. In the United States, this is probably since 1950, and because the measures we are interested in are released annually, the data base can cover about fifty-five years or data points, at maximum. For other countries, the time series—the available set of statistics—may be even shorter. But when time series data for different countries are pooled together, the number of observations is greatly magnified and so is the power of the statistical tests, at least in principle.

These fine points of statistical testing were not an issue in the first generation of post-Solow statistical tests of growth, which used the data series on output, output per worker (or work-hour), and output per capita that were compiled by Angus Maddison (1982), who is one of the leading figures in the highly specialized field of cross-country data collection, and Matthews, Feinstein, and Odling-Smee (1982). The tests asked a seemingly simple question: have standards of living, as measured by productivity (output per hour of work) or output per capita in different countries, converged over time? In other words, do advances in leading countries spill over to a set of follower countries, through exports of goods, capital, and ideas from the advanced guard to the followers? And does this spillover and imitation process happen in such a way that the follower countries catch up to the leaders by growing more rapidly for a time (perhaps by investing and saving greater fractions of their output while adopting the leaders' technology)?

Several early studies of different groups of countries confirmed that this had indeed happened. Matthews and colleagues found it to be the case over the 1870–1973 period for seven countries that were industrialized by the early 1970s (Matthews et al., 1982). One of the authors of the present volume reached a similar finding, using Maddison's data, for a larger sixteen-country group over a slightly longer period, 1870–1979 (Baumol, 1986), but found that convergence had not occurred among the much larger set of countries for which the requisite data were provided by Summers and Heston (1991). That is, for the converging countries one could explain the growth rate of their productivity over a little longer than a century almost entirely by knowing only one thing: their initial level of productivity in 1870. If a country started out far behind the productivity leader (which, in 1870, was Australia), it grew much more rapidly than if its productivity level was already at or close to the frontier. This simple proposition, that the further behind the leader a country was in 1870, the faster it grew later, explained the very rapid growth of Japan, Sweden, France, and Germany over this long period, and the relatively slower growth of the United Kingdom and the leader itself, Australia.

Yet even the author of one of these studies cautioned that too much should not be read into this apparent finding of convergence, noting that the 1870 productivity levels were measured with considerable error and that Maddison constructed them using a method of backward extrapolation that would have biased the finding toward convergence (Baumol, 1986, 1076). Baumol could have added that the 100+ years covered by the data series included two world wars, and that after World War II, in particular, one of the countries in the data set (the United States) provided ample financial and technical assistance to both Europe and Japan that should have enabled them to catch up to U.S. productivity levels after the war.

Thus, a more interesting question is whether, since World War II, convergence has occurred among a larger group of countries, including many that were once or still are less developed. Baumol (1986) used a data set of per capita incomes (which provide a rough approximation to productivity data) compiled by University of Pennsylvania professors Robert Summers and Alan Heston for that larger group of countries (these statistics have since become the data set of choice of a large body of researchers).[5] Unlike a similar set of statistics assembled by the World Bank at that time, the Summers and Heston data for output in different countries are adjusted for differences in the relative purchasing power of currencies, not just for differences in exchange rates between countries. This distinction is very important because the prices of the same commodities or services may be very different in different countries. Measures of output that do not take purchasing power differences into account do not capture the true disparities in standards of living among countries.

When Baumol analyzed the Summers-Heston data for seventy-two countries over the 1950–80 period, he found a very different set of results from those he had reported for the narrower set of industrialized countries over a previous longer period: for the entire group of countries, convergence had essentially disappeared. Indeed, there was even a mild positive relationship between a country's initial level of productivity and its subsequent growth: that is, the countries that were richer to begin with tended to grow a bit faster than other countries. Baumol did find, however, various country clusters where convergence seemed to take place within (but apparently not across) those groups, between 1950 and 1980, among the (then) centrally planned economies (the Soviet Union, China, and Eastern Europe) and again among the industrialized countries. This convergence clustering did not appear to take place within developing economies as a whole, although we know from subsequent experience that at least one group of developing countries, notably those in Southeast Asia, has displayed rapid convergence among themselves and relative to the world's leading countries.

Baumol's finding of a lack of overall convergence in the postwar era through 1980 has continued to hold up. Figure 4 displays the growth rates in per capita income over the 1980–2000 period, together with initial per capita incomes for 106 countries in a more recent version of the Summers-Heston data set (with coauthor Bettina Aten). The figure clearly fails to support the convergence conjecture (the tendency for initially poorer countries to grow more rapidly than countries with initially higher incomes, as catch up would require). Indeed, if anything, simple visual in-

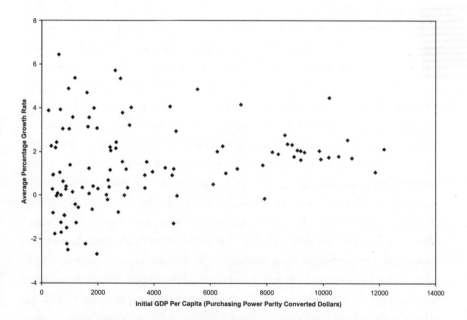

Figure 4. Cross-Country Initial GDP per Capita vs. Average Growth Rates, 1980–2000. *Source:* Alan Heston, Robert Summers, and Bettina Aten, Penn World Table Version 6.1, Center for International Comparisons at the University of Pennsylvania (CICUP), October 2002 (106 observations: countries having complete data set). Available at http://pwt.econ.upenn.edu/php_site/pwt61_form.php.

spection of figure 4 suggests that initially richer countries may have grown faster than initially poor countries, a result consistent with figure 1 in chapter 2.

If countries are not converging in their standards of living, then what explains the continuing economic differences across countries? Attempts to answer this simple, but vital, question have spawned a separate industry within the economics profession. These research efforts would not be possible, of course, without the Summers-Heston-Aten data, which contain information only on the variables to be explained—the levels and growth rates of output (per capita or per worker or per work hour). A variety of data sources have since arisen for variables that might "do the explaining," such as measures of physical and human capital (labor force and education levels), institutional variables (law and corruption, for example), international trade, financial indicators, government and private investment in research and development, and measures of climate and geography provided by such organizations as the World Bank, the United Nations, and individual researchers.

The search for answers to the growth puzzle—and, specifically, the causes of the variation in the Solow residual (the rate of technological advance)—has engaged some of the most distinguished figures in economics, including two Nobel Prize winners (Stanford University's Kenneth Arrow and Robert Lucas of the University of Chicago), as well as many leading lights in the profession (such as Robert Barro, Greg Mankiw, Andrei Shleifer, and Edward Glaeser of Harvard University; Jeffrey Sachs and Xavier Sala-i-Martin of Columbia University; Stanford University's Paul Romer; Barry Bosworth and Susan Collins from the Brookings Institution; Yale University's William Nordhaus; Ross Levine from the University of Minnesota; Steven Durlauf from the University of Wisconsin; Elhanan Helpman of Harvard and Tel Aviv Universities; and William Easterly of New York University, among others). It is difficult (if not impossible) to summarize all of this work in a short space, but certain broad generalizations are possible. (Readers who want a more thorough guide to this research, and indeed to the evolution of the discipline of economics in general, are strongly encouraged to read Helpman, 2004, and Warsh, 2006.)

First, many of the economists who have conducted these studies now believe that if the right model of growth can be identified, it will show that there is a fundamental dynamic toward conditional convergence. That is, if one controls for the right variables, it remains true that countries with low initial levels of productivity will have faster growth in productivity and economic output than richer countries. Of course, this conditional convergence process may occur slowly—or rapidly—depending on one's patience or expectations. Some of the cross-country statistical tests suggest that on average throughout the world, the gap between the richest and poorest countries closes at the rate of about 2 percent annually.[6] At this rate, it takes about a generation (thirty-six years) for a lagging economy to close half the gap between its per capita income and that of the leading economies. Those looking for miraculous turnarounds in a short span of time will be disappointed by this figure. But for others, the prospect for closing this much of any income gap in just a generation may seem remarkable.

Second, despite the substantial statistical investigations of growth that have been undertaken over the past two decades, economists who believe that the statistical work has helped to unlock the growth puzzle (as we will note shortly, this includes most, but not all, economists who pursued this line of work) still fall broadly into two groups. In one camp are those whose views adhere closely to the assumption built into the initial Solow-Swan growth model: that technological progress is primarily determined by forces—such as climate (which affects the rates of disease), geographic location (which determines costs of transportation and thus propensity to trade), and institutions (which are man-made but may take decades, if not centuries, to change)—that are outside the economic system and over which policy makers have little or no immediate control (see Bosworth and Collins, 2003, and Frankel, 2003). To this list some add culture, which is difficult to incorporate in formal statistical tests, but which some economic historians argue is the dominant driving force behind growth, a subject we will explore further in chapter 5.

In a second camp are economists who contend that the statistical studies lend support for the view that active policy intervention, in the short to intermediate run, can accelerate the growth of either or both labor productivity (output per worker or hour of work) or technological advance (measured by additions to output that arise even if labor and capital investment are held constant). Growth-enhancing policies can include governmental decisions to open up an economy to more trade and foreign investment, to support more research and development (through direct spending or tax incentives), to increase human capital by broadening the availability of primary and secondary education, and to conduct sound macroeconomic policies (avoiding consistent and large budget deficits or inflationary monetary policies). At its core, economists who fall into this second camp are more optimistic about the ability of governments to encourage more rapid improvements in living standards than what might otherwise occur naturally.

In the technical language that economists often use, economists in this second camp are suggesting that technological advance is endogenous, that is, it is determined by forces within the economic system itself rather than such exogenous factors outside the system as climate and geography. Much of the intellectual impetus for this way of looking at growth was provided in the 1980s through the work of Paul Romer, then at the University of Chicago and currently at Stanford (Romer, 1986).[7] Romer (and others who followed in his wake, including Robert Lucas and William Nordhaus) built on the earlier insights of Kenneth Arrow (1962) and Eytan Sheshinski (1967), who believed that the ideas that underpin technological advance are the unintended by-products of investment in new equipment that spilled over and thus benefited the rest of the economy. In this way, more investment would lead to more technological advance, suggesting that the latter somehow depended on the former.

One unspoken policy implication of this view that investment generates beneficial spillovers is that governments do indeed have a potentially important role to play in encouraging growth. To the extent that governments can stimulate investment, through tax incentives in particular, and also to the extent that they can encourage more domestic saving, which should enlarge the pool of funds available for financing investment (thus bringing down its cost), government can enhance the long-run prospects for growth. This implication sharply departs from the investment pessimism of the Solow-Swan growth model, which implies that additional investment eventually stops adding to growth because of diminishing returns. But if investment can actually enhance technological advance, this pessimism may be misplaced.

In his modeling, Romer went one step further, observing that technological advances often were not simply by-products, but were the objects of economic activity itself—the products of deliberate investments of time and money by individuals and firms seeking to improve on what already exists and ultimately to commercialize any successful results. In this sense, business firms' investment in knowledge creation is analogous to their investment in new equipment that promises to make employees more productive. But unlike investment in a new machine, which has more or less predictable productivity-enhancing consequences, investment in knowledge discovery (and, if successful, its subsequent commercialization) is fraught with uncertainty. It is not surprising, therefore, that the statistical work that has gone into trying to explain the sources of technological advance has come up with varied answers, and some controversy over certain variables (such as openness to foreign trade) still continues.

One other policy implication stands out from Romer's work, however: that technological advance is not likely to occur, at least in economies at the frontier where imitation is not an option, unless those who undertake it are assured of some reward. Hence the importance of imperfect competition, or something other than the perfectly competitive ideal where so many firms are making an identical product that they compete away any excess profits. If some extraordinary profits are not available to the individuals or firms who leap into the unknown, taking the risks to develop and commercialize something new, then technological advance would not occur. That is why economists typically defend the importance of an effective system of intellectual property rights that confers monopoly status on innovators for some limited period of time, or why market structures should not be perfectly competitive in dynamic industries, at least in the short to intermediate run. Continuing technological advance, however, competes away any short-run profits so that over the long run they disappear.[8] We draw on these key insights in our discussion of what is essential to entrepreneurial capitalism in subsequent chapters.

Third, there seems to be some rough consensus among economists in both camps that institutions—such as well-enforced property rights and the absence of corruption—are important to growth. But debate still continues over whether Anglo-Saxon or so-called civil code legal systems are more effective in advancing growth.[9] The key challenge with respect to institutions is how best to create them. Must countries wait decades, or even centuries, for institutions to evolve naturally? An open question is whether the right institutions can be manufactured or transplanted in short periods of time.

Fourth, included implicitly if not explicitly in the view that institutions matter is the rough consensus that one of those institutions is the development of human capital, which is the steady improvement in the skills of the labor force. In their empirical work, economists have typically measured human capital by years of education, although they admittedly recognize this to be an imperfect proxy for skills. A number of statistically based studies of growth find a strong link between human capital measured in this fashion and economic growth.[10] That link can arise through two channels. A more educated workforce has a larger effective labor supply, since an hour of work by a more skilled individual is equivalent to more than hour of work supplied by an individual with lesser skill. In addition, as a society's workforce becomes more educated, the greater is the likelihood that some of its members will contribute to technological advance in some way, by inventing or commercializing inventions or somehow assisting others who do. Here the possibility of reverse causation constitutes a key problem: may things not work the other way, with growth providing the resources needed to expand education so that growth stimulates education rather than the other way round? The answer is far from certain.

Finally, the debate is perhaps most contentious over the role of foreign aid: whether it enhances, has no effect on, or even may detract from growth. We will discuss this subject at length in chapter 6.

Limits of Statistical Analyses of Growth

Laymen and political leaders can be forgiven for wondering how very smart economists can analyze seemingly the same bodies of data and come up with very different conclusions about the impact of such governmental policies as foreign aid (among others). Do these statistical tests affirm nothing more than the old saw that there are three kinds of untruths: lies, damn lies, and statistics?[11]

One answer is that the economists who have argued over the role of aid have *not* used the same bodies of data, nor the same models to analyze or test them. Another reason for the differences is that analysts have conducted statistical tests over different time periods, examining different sets of countries. Indeed, the mini-industry of economists running "cross-country regressions" has grown as new economists come into the field, finding or constructing new data series to add to those already available.

To broadly generalize, a wide range of results has been obtained from the statistical tests that have been reported in the leading studies. Essentially, one can pretty much find whatever result or results one is looking for, depending on what variables, countries, and time periods one wants to include in the regressions. This state of affairs is hardly comforting to policy makers and others outside the profession. But it is the reality, and, to some extent, it should be expected. After all, a number of the data series constructed to represent some of the more qualitative variables thought to influence growth—such as the "rule of law," corruption, and openness to trade, among others—are indexes compiled either by the researchers themselves or some organization or body interested in the subject (such as Transparency International, a nongovernmental organization that measures corruption). As a result, these data series have an element of subjectivity that is not present in the more objective variables, such as investment expenditure and hours worked (although even these standard variables have their own measurement problems, especially for developing countries, where resources for economic data collection are less plentiful than in richer countries).

It is not surprising, then, that some of the economists who have carried out these statistical tests have questioned their usefulness and reliability. Ross Levine and David Renelt were early skeptics (see Levine and Renelt, 1992). More recently, Easterly has suggested that no standard variables, even including such theoretical stalwarts as investment in equipment, are consistently and reliably linked to economic growth (Easterly, 2001). But Easterly and Levine are in the minority of economists in this area. Most other economists who have studied growth believe, to one degree or another, that at the very least the statistical tests help identify which variables contribute to growth, although admitting that much uncertainty remains about the relative and absolute magnitudes of each contribution. It is difficult to believe, for example, that investment in physical and human capital has made *no* difference toward increasing output. Similarly, we know at the very highest level of abstraction that incentives matter for growth, as Easterly recognizes. It cannot be an accident that countries that have allowed individuals and firms to own their own property and to reap the rewards of their efforts have enjoyed much more prosperity than centrally planned economies where individuals and firms did not enjoy these rights. The challenge for economists, policy makers, and citizens around the world is to see if more definitive statements can be made about the factors that are most important for growth. We take up that challenge in chapters 4 through 8 of this book.

Growth and the "Washington Consensus"

In 1989, well before most of the empirical tests of the determinants of economic growth were conducted, John Williamson (an economist who has worked at both the World Bank and the Institute for International Economics) attempted to resolve the growth puzzle by way of another technique. He asked a number of economists and policy experts in Washington, D.C. (including people working for think tanks, the United States government, and the international financial institutions and whom he thought were expert in economic growth), what policies they thought would contribute most to growth in Latin America in particular (Williamson, 1994). The top ten answers are displayed in table 1 and have since come to be known as the "Washington Consensus" set of policy prescriptions.

In the 1990s, the Washington Consensus became more than just a list compiled by one economist. It evolved, largely by accident, into a recipe for growth and financial stability that the world's major international financial institutions, especially the International Monetary Fund, imposed in the 1990s on a number of developing countries that required bridge financing to enable them to weather financial crises (such as suddenly falling exchange rates, shortages of domestic currency reserves, and shaky financial systems). Presumably, officials thought these conditions were necessary for both growth and stability for at least two reasons.

First, many of the policies that made up the Washington Consensus—fiscal discipline, open markets, competitive exchange rates, and privatization, among others—already were largely in place in developed economies. If the policies were good for the rich, then by implication they must be good for the poor. Further, presumably some participants in Williamson's survey listed policies they thought foreign investors were most interested in seeing before committing their funds to developing countries.

Table 1 The Washington Consensus Policy Prescriptions for Growth in Developing Countries

---

- Fiscal discipline
- Redistribution of government funds on the basis of need rather than politics
- Broadening of tax bases and reduction of marginal tax rates
- Liberalization of financial markets (absence of entry and price controls for institutions, national treatment for foreign firms, and absence of capital controls)
- Competitive exchange rates
- Replacement of trade quotas with tariffs
- Removal of barriers to product market competition
- Privatization of state-owned enterprises
- Abolition of barriers to foreign direct investment
- Strong and effectively enforced property rights

Source: Williamson, 2004.

The Washington Consensus list has since become a topic of much discussion and controversy among economists and policy makers in developed and developing countries alike. While some notable scholars and policy makers generally have supported the policy prescriptions on the list (see Fischer, 2003), others have argued that, in the fifteen or so years since the list was compiled, experience has not borne out the validity of its prescriptions (Rodrik, 2003). As Williamson himself has noted, the regions of the world that have done the most to stabilize, liberalize, and integrate their economies with the rest of the world economy were Latin America and the transition economies of Eastern Europe and the former states of the Soviet Union (Williamson, 2004). Yet the growth record of Latin America since the early 1990s has at best been relatively poor, and the growth of the transition economies has been uneven.

At the other extreme, the fastest growing economy of the past twenty years has been China, which admittedly has moved in the pro-market direction suggested by the Consensus list, but only in a gradual fashion. Nonetheless, in criticizing the list, Harvard University's Dani Rodrik has asked a provocative question: if the best economic minds of the late 1970s had been surveyed about what policies China should have adopted to stimulate economic growth, they almost certainly would have given some variation of the "Big Bang"—that is, the simultaneous adoption of all of the reforms on the Washington Consensus list. Yet, as we will discuss in more detail in chapter 6, China pursued a very different course with much success, retaining its state-owned enterprises but gradually encouraging them to shrink while at the same time privatizing the Chinese economy "at the margins" by gradually allowing individuals to own their own plots of land for growing crops and allowing villages to own and operate new firms. In chapter 7, we will suggest a similar incremental strategy for promoting entrepreneurship in Europe.

One unfair, though highly publicized, criticism of the Washington Consensus is that Argentina, which was supposed to be a shining example of the success of the Consensus policy prescriptions, suffered one of the worst financial crises of any country in the world in 2001. But this criticism is misplaced. Again, as Williamson (2004) and others have noted, Argentina may have followed some of the prescriptions on the list—notably, privatization, openness to foreign direct investment (until recently, Argentina had the largest share of foreign banks of any Latin American country) and property rights protection—but ignored two other critical items on the list, fiscal discipline and a competitive currency.

Nonetheless, the Argentine and Chinese experiences, among others, highlight one of the central problems of the Washington Consensus list. The list provides no guidance to countries about the *relative* importance of the different prescriptions on the list or about their timing or sequence. In fairness, that was never the point of Williamson's exercise and he himself has since expressed some surprise (and regret) about the extent to which the list has become the centerpiece of debate in economic policy circles around the world. Furthermore, although it was not Williamson's intention, the IMF and others confused the purpose of the list. Over time, the policy prescriptions came to be viewed as more essential because of their contribution to financial stability (and some of them, such as fiscal discipline and competitive exchange rates, surely are) than for sustained economic growth.

Accordingly, any consensus about the right set of policy prescriptions for growth in particular has broken down. Indeed, analysts since have moved in two opposite directions. Williamson, together with Peruvian economist Pedro-Pablo Kuczynski (2003), has proposed a sharp narrowing of the list to just four key factors:

1. Policies aimed at avoiding financial crises, especially by avoiding fixed exchange rates, which clearly can derail a country from its long-run growth path for a very long time;

2. Liberalization of domestic markets, not just product markets (by lowering trade protection measures such as tariffs) but also labor markets, which impede the growth of rising industries and firms and inhibit the necessary shrinkage of uncompetitive industries and firms;

3. Strengthening of domestic institutions that foster growth, an insight that the two economists assert was one of the most important changes in the thinking of development economists in the 1990s; and

4. Recognition that the distribution of economic rewards is a subject that cannot be ignored when a country is trying to promote growth, if only because highly inequitable distributions of income can give rise to political pressures that inhibit or defeat growth (in this regard, the two analysts put greater weight on assuring widespread educational opportunities than on redistributive tax policies).

Rodrik, a noted critic of the original Washington Consensus, proposes moving in a very different direction: augmenting Williamson's initial list with another ten factors that he believes are central to growth. Table 2 lists Rodrik's ten *additional* policy prescriptions.

We agree that many, if not all, of the additional items on Rodrik's list are desirable, not just for growth but also for financial stability and the equitable distribution of income. But the problem with lists of this type is that they give readers, let alone policy makers, no sense of proportion. The question is, given the limited attention spans of leaders and their citizens, as well as the many competing pressures and objectives, which items on the original or additional lists should policy makers implement first? The lists do not provide answers to this vital question.

Indeed, as we suggested in chapter 1, laundry lists of desirable policy prescriptions can be very problematic, especially if they do not provide some sense of priorities. Faced with a daunting lineup of ten or twenty "musts," policy makers can easily suffer from information or obligation overload. Feeling that they must make progress toward carrying out most, if not all, of the prescriptions, political leaders and their advisers can too easily be tempted to throw up their hands and say "it's not possible"

Table 2 Additions to the Washington Consensus List of Growth Policy
Prescriptions Proposed by Professor Rodrik

- Legal/political reform
- Effective regulatory institutions
- Effective anticorruption laws and enforcement
- Labor market flexibility
- Adherence to WTO trade agreements
- Implementation and enforcement of effective financial codes and standards
- "Prudent" opening of capital accounts
- Exchange rate regimes compatible with financial stability
- Effective social safety nets
- Effective programs for reducing poverty

Source: Rodrik, 2003.

and ignore the lists altogether. Like students who are given a mass of as-
sorted facts to memorize but have no structure or context in which to
place them, the consumers of these policy lists may simply look at them,
perhaps memorize the items for a short while, but then quickly forget
them when confronted with the everyday challenges of having to run governments and meet the unceasing and often conflicting demands of their
citizens.

In short, while there may at one time have been a consensus at least
among Washington-based policy makers and economists about policies
that are most conducive to growth, that consensus no longer exists. This is
evident among the policy analysts (such as Williamson and Rodrik, among
others) who write about growth, as well as in the different, and sometimes
inconsistent, results of the growing body of statistical studies that attempt
to explain the great difference of patterns of growth among countries.

The Four Faces of Capitalism: A New Way to Look at Growth

The time is ripe, in our view, for some fresh thinking on the subject of growth. In particular, may there be a different way of thinking
about this vital subject that policy makers in various countries can actually
use to accelerate the pace of improvement in living standards of their populations? We believe the answer is yes, and that is what we undertake to
supply in the rest of this book.

We begin with the fundamental proposition that economies are complicated systems that cannot be reduced to one or two central driving forces, and cannot be turned around by applying one or even a few of the policy prescriptions various development economists or institutions have recommended over the years. To return to the analogy in chapter 1 of the economy as a well-oiled growth machine, the economic machine has a number of parts that are interconnected and that work together. Likewise, if economies are to grow at their maximum possible rate, they must have in place at least some elements of four basic characteristics that we outlined in chapter 1 and will elaborate further in chapter 5.

We say "at least some elements" because the specific policies that are appropriate will vary for different countries at different times. Context, culture, and history all matter. There is no single detailed blueprint that can or should be imposed on every country. The fact that various countries have achieved rapid growth rates with somewhat different institutional structures is testament to that fact. Yet before we address these four key characteristics of the well-oiled growth machine, we believe it is useful to examine growth through a different lens. Specifically, in our view, one can learn much about what it takes for economies to generate sustained growth by keeping in mind what we believe are the four broad types of capitalism that have been and currently are in place in different parts of the world.

These archetypes of capitalism admittedly are very rough generalizations. Furthermore, few economies fit neatly into any one category. More commonly, economies possess different elements of these archetypes at any point in time, and the composition of these elements varies over time. Even more to the point, these archetypes are not handed down from some higher authority, though there is some cultural inertia behind any one. History shows, however, that through deliberate actions, sometimes with unintended consequences, economies can move from one archetype to another, and in shorter order than many people may commonly believe.

Having these archetypes in mind serves as a useful reference point for our discussion later about how countries, through their leaders, can in fact choose different paths to growth. Ultimately, however, we will argue that there is one path—actually, the right *blend* of two of these archetypes—that promises the most rapid and sustained path for growth.

4

CAPITALISM: THE DIFFERENT TYPES
AND THEIR IMPACTS ON GROWTH

For many of us, November 9, 1989—the day the Berlin Wall fell—
marked the end of the terrifying cold war struggle between communism
and capitalism. Capitalism had triumphed and communism was reduced
to a mere historical curiosity. Looked at that way, the term "capitalism"
seemed to refer to a simple and uniformly characterized form of economic
organization, something we would recognize if we saw it even if we had no
formal definition for it. But this view of capitalism turns out to be a seriously misleading oversimplification. As we will emphasize in this chapter,
in the countries that we would all consider "capitalistic," the organization
of the economy, the economic role of government, and a variety of other
attributes differ profoundly. Some capitalist economies come close to being socialistic, while others are far more regulated. Moreover, the form
taken by capitalism in a particular country has profound implications for its
growth performance, and that is why, for our purposes here, it simply will
not do to put all forms of capitalism into a single category. Rather, we will
classify the economies of the different capitalist countries in four categories:

1. state-guided capitalism, in which government tries to guide the market,
   most often by supporting particular industries that it expects to become "winners";
2. oligarchic capitalism, in which the bulk of the power and wealth is held
   by a small group of individuals and families;

3. big-firm capitalism, in which the most significant economic activities are carried out by established giant enterprises; and

4. entrepreneurial capitalism, in which a significant role is played by small, innovative firms.[1]

About the only thing these systems have in common is that they recognize the right of private ownership of property; beyond that they are very different. In particular, the economies in one category tend to have growth records very different from those in another, and that is because their mechanisms of growth, innovation, and entrepreneurship vary substantially. We will maintain that one of the most promising ways to promote growth in an economy that is currently characterized by a slow-moving form of capitalism is to adopt reforms that move it toward a type of capitalism with a more powerful growth engine. For the same reason, economies that already are characterized by a fast-growing form of capitalism must vigilantly watch out for developments that might undermine their membership in that group.

No type of capitalism is dominant within and across economies and over time. Economies can be and are different mixes of the various types at different stages in their histories. There are even some "precapitalist" economies that readily fit into one or another of the four archetypes. A precapitalist economy is typically very poor (with annual per capita income of $1,000 or less), with few if any of the institutions one associates with capitalism of any sort, particularly rights of property that are protected by the state. In some precapitalist economies, many of which can be found in parts of Africa, Central America, and western Asia (such as Afghanistan or Pakistan), governments are very weak; precapitalist societies instead consist largely of clans or tribes that set the rules. In some cases, these clans may forbid private property, while in others property rights may be informally recognized. But the governmental institutions associated with capitalism are so primitive in these economies that it doesn't make sense to include them in our classification. It is nonetheless important to consider these precapitalist economies because they are home to tens, if not hundreds, of millions of people living at subsistence levels whose plight deserves the world's attention, not simply for moral reasons but because they cannot be good customers for our products and, more important, at least for those of us who live in other societies, they can be breeding grounds for diseases and for terrorists who threaten the lives of those in more developed societies. Fortunately, however, we believe that the same set of recommendations we offer to developing countries that do fit within one of our categories also apply, with appropriate adaptation, to precapitalist economies.

In describing each of the four archetypes of capitalism, we will be painting a picture that depicts more about their outcomes than the inputs required to attain those results. Frankly, it is easier to envision the outcomes since, in many instances, they are already there to be seen. It is much harder determine what steps will achieve or even contribute to those outcomes. That is the job we will attempt in later chapters.

In the appendix to this book, we address another important topic: how does one *measure* the degree to which economies fit into one or the other of these paradigms? We will outline some suggestions, in principle, but fuller answers must await further research and, most important, time-consuming data collection.

Before describing our four prototype variants of capitalism, we should first specify what we mean by the term. Generally, an economy is said to be capitalistic when most or at least a substantial proportion of its means of production—its farms, its factories, its complex machinery—are in private hands, rather than being owned and operated by the government. No economy is perfectly capitalistic. For example, in the United States, some electricity is produced by municipal governments and also by the federal government. In a communist regime, some pieces of small-scale productive equipment, such as sewing machines, are owned by private individuals. In our descriptions of the four capitalisms, we will encounter cases that might be described as "state socialism." But the societies in question often also possess substantial capitalistic attributes, and it is those features that will be our primary concern.

State-Guided Capitalism

As the label suggests, state-guided capitalism exists where governments, not private investors, decide which industries and even which individual firms should grow. Government economic policy is then geared to carry out those decisions, using various policy instruments to help out the chosen "winners." The overall economic system nonetheless remains capitalist because, with the exceptions to be discussed shortly, the state recognizes and enforces the rights of property and contract, markets guide the prices of the goods and services produced and the wages of workers employed, and at least some small-scale activities remain in private hands.

Why do governments try to direct economic traffic? In part, it may be because political leaders want to take advantage of their power to extract wealth and other benefits from the winner industries and firms. This form of state-guided capitalism is little different from oligarchic capitalism, which we discuss in the next section. The main objective of leaders of oligarchic economies is patronage, not economic growth. In contrast, under state-guided capitalism governments typically take the position that centrally planned direction of or influence on the allocation of resources in the economy is the best way to maximize economic growth.

Governments have a number of means at their disposal to guide growth. Perhaps the most important is explicit or implicit ownership of banks, which are the principal conduits in virtually all countries for transferring the resources of those who save to those who invest the savings. Only in the United States, at least so far, is this task of transmission of financial resources from savers to producers carried out primarily in organized capital markets, such as stock and bond markets, rather than by banks. It is true that the last few years have produced a wave of privatizations of publicly owned enterprises around the world—driven as much by the need of governments to acquire revenues from the sale of these assets to help deal with their deficits as to improve the efficiency and lower the price of the services offered by these formerly government-owned enterprises. Nevertheless, in developing economies, as well as in some developed ones (such as Germany), the government still owns a significant share of the banking system (see Hanson, 2004). In India, state ownership accounts for fully 75 percent of all bank assets (see Patel, 2004). And not surprisingly, given its command-and-control heritage, four state-owned banks in China dominate the financial system in that country, although under China's agreement upon joining the World Trade Organization, it is scheduled to privatize those banks completely in 2007.

Even without direct ownership, governments can still direct or strongly "persuade" banks to do their bidding. South Korea is a good example of the former, and Japanese "administrative guidance" an example of the latter. Governments can and do guide capitalism in other ways as well, for example, by favoring certain companies or sectors with tax breaks, exclusive licenses (legalized monopolies), or government contracts. Favored companies thus can become "national champions," whose success is assured by government policy. Governments can also support industries through protective measures, such as tariffs, insulating domestic companies from foreign competition. In addition, governments can guide the activities of foreign investors or partners, allowing them only in certain sectors and under certain conditions (commonly, that the foreign partner share and eventually transfer its technology and know-how to the local partner). China's joint ventures with American manufacturers and Japanese arrangements with U.S. aerospace companies are examples of this type of guidance.

State-guided capitalism can overlap to some degree with big-firm capitalism, but the two systems are fundamentally different. They overlap when, for example, national champion firms are favored by the state. These firms typically have large numbers of employees, who are managed in a highly structured way. Innovation, to the extent that it exists, is organized, separately budgeted for, and closely managed. It is rare in a state-guided system to have more than a few national champions, if only because the size of the domestic market may not allow more than a certain number. Meanwhile, other large firms may prosper, perhaps by conducting substantial business with government or by tapping into domestic and/or foreign markets that generate growth of the enterprise. Economies can then come to be dominated by big firms, but not necessarily directed toward that outcome by government policy.

It also may be tempting to equate state-driven capitalism with central planning, but the two systems also are very different. In centrally planned economies, the state not only picks winners, it also *owns the means of production, sets all prices and wages, often cares little about what consumers may want, and thus provides essentially no incentive for innovation that benefits the individual.* On the contrary, the bureaucrats who ran the large "firms" in the former Soviet bloc countries, which were the apotheosis of central planning, were paid according to the amounts their plants produced, regardless of quality or whether consumers actually wanted the output. Central planning, by its nature, is not conducive to the adoption of break-through technology, the Soviet space program that launched Sputnik in 1958 being perhaps the only exception. But this effort was the kind of thing state socialism does best: a massive command-and-control activity for a specific, even limited purpose. It generated little in the way of pervasive long-run economic benefits.

Indeed, in the old Soviet bloc—where progress was mapped out in five-year plans and where entrepreneurship was, to use computer terminology, not supported by the operating system—the high-tech industries that have propelled growth in the industrialized capitalism world, especially in the United States, never even got off the ground. The Soviet system was capable of producing superbly trained scientists but literally incapable of capitalizing on their work. Like the ending in the movie *The Wizard of Oz*, when the curtain is pulled back to reveal an ordinary human being at the controls, the crumbling of the Berlin Wall revealed to the whole world the miserable economic failure of the Soviet-bloc economies, surprising even many experts in the West (including the United States Central Intelligence Agency), who had believed that the Soviet Union, in particular, was a rather powerful economy that had to be reckoned with.

It is important to note that, without adopting "state guidance" in the sense in which we use the term here, government nonetheless can play an important role in providing public goods and services whose benefits are shared widely throughout the population without necessarily seeking to decree *which particular sectors or industries should prosper.* For example, governments routinely provide basic infrastructure—roads, water and sanitation systems, education, police and judicial systems—and fund basic scientific research. In undertaking these activities, governments are simply providing a platform on which all economic actors can carry out their activities. Providing "public goods," or those whose benefits no single individual or firm can fully appropriate, is the basic job of governments (along with national defense). Doing so does not mean that governments are thereby "guiding" the economy. Providing public goods is normal in every form of capitalist economy, and not only in those that are guided by the state.

What are some prominent examples of state-guided capitalism? One immediately thinks of most of the countries in Southeast Asia, where governments have used one or more of the instruments of guidance already outlined to favor certain sectors, primarily for exports. For several decades, many countries in Latin America followed policies of "import substitution," which were designed to promote the growth of sectors, and often of individual firms that had been selected for such support, by sheltering them from imports. There also have been elements of state planning or direction in France, Germany, and the United States, indicating that no single and pure form of capitalism is likely to dominate any economy to the exclusion of elements of the others, the mix of the different systems being what is most important for the economy's growth. To be more specific, though it primarily limits itself to providing the kind of public goods that governments should supply, the federal government in the United States also engages in a limited form of state guidance by subsidizing its agricultural sector directly and through tariffs or quotas and cash subsidies (like Europe and Japan); its energy sector through tax breaks; and its housing industry through tax breaks and a subsidized secondary mortgage market (dominated by two large government-sponsored enterprises, "Fannie Mae" and "Freddie Mac").

The Advantages of State-Guided Capitalism

As the remarkable growth of the state-guided economies of Asia attests, this form of capitalism can be highly successful and last over long periods (although, in the case of the Southeast Asian economies, economic growth was interrupted by one major postwar financial crisis in 1997–98). The sources of this success are not difficult to comprehend. Economies that lag well behind those at the technological frontier need only find some way to gain access to cutting-edge foreign technology, or something reasonably close to it, and then combine it with lower-cost labor to turn out products (and, increasingly, services, for example, "call centers") that will sell well in international markets. Foreign technology can be imported through foreign direct investment. Knowledge can be gained by sending nationals abroad for university study (most commonly, to the United States). A bolder strategy is to encourage, or at least not limit, the ability of domestic residents to emigrate to technology-leading countries like the United States and hope that they succeed and later either return to their home countries or facilitate from abroad the start-up and growth of new home-grown enterprises. India is the leading practitioner of this "reverse brain drain" strategy, which may have looked like a gamble several decades ago but seems to have paid off handsomely now that successful Indian entrepreneurs in the United States have either returned home or invested in Indian enterprises (Saxenian, 1999).

However it has been accomplished, countries that have adopted a strategy of "export-led growth," facilitated largely by state guidance, have been successful only because their exports have had someplace to go, largely to the United States and more recently, in the case of the Asian exporters, to other countries in Asia, where incomes are rising and governments have the foreign exchange, earned through exports, to pay for imported goods. State-guided, export-led growth would not have been successful if markets around the world had not been opened by successive multilateral liberalizations of tariffs and other at-the-border restrictions, first under the auspices of the General Agreement on Tariffs and Trade (GATT) and later through its successor, the World Trade Organization (WTO).

Pitfalls of State-Guided Capitalism

There are drawbacks, even dangers, to state-guided capitalism. Indeed, given our proclivity to favor the other forms of capitalism, it may not surprise readers to learn that we see many more drawbacks than advantages, especially once these successfully state-guided capitalist economies approach the per capita income levels of richer, less state-guided economies.

BELIEVING THAT STATE GUIDANCE WILL WORK FOREVER Governments that guide their economies with some success can learn the wrong lessons from the past. For countries whose economies have grown rapidly under the guiding hand of the state—one thinks of many Asian economies in particular—it can be tempting to conclude that indefinite continuation of the same approach will yield growth benefits. But the world changes. After picking the low-hanging fruit, the difficulties of harvesting grow much greater. So it is, and has been, for a number of countries where state guidance has worked for a period.

EXCESSIVE INVESTMENT A good example of what can go wrong is what happened to South Korea in the late 1990s. Long accustomed to directing its banks to provide loans to the larger South Korean conglomerates ("chaebols"), South Korea's government induced too many banks to invest excessively in the expansion of the semiconductor, steel, and chemicals industries. When the financial crisis that began in Southeast Asia during the summer of 1997 spread to South Korea, the country's banks and, more important, the companies that had borrowed to expand were so overextended that the South Korean economy came close to collapse. It was rescued only when the United States government led an international effort to prop up the country's financial institutions by extending the maturities of their deposits (Blustein, 2001). Only later would the South Korean government force a number of the chaebols to restructure and induce its banks to apply commercial, rather than government-directed, criteria to the country's lending.

South Korea is not alone. China has had a huge banking problem, resulting from decades of central planning during which the state banks essentially were government instrumentalities for financing state-owned enterprises (SOEs). As China has moved away from central planning toward its own unique version of capitalism, many of the SOEs have been unable to repay the state banks, leaving the Chinese government to pick up the enormous tab for the losses, a process we describe in chapter 6. In chapter 7, we discuss a similar banking mess that has plagued the Japanese economy ever since that country's stock market and real estate bubbles burst at the end of the 1980s. Although Japan had not adopted central planning, its form of "administrative guidance" to its banks eventually led to overinvestment by corporate borrowers, who could not repay the debt they had taken on. The government's halting and delayed response to this problem contributed to the stagnation of the Japanese economy throughout the 1990s and well into the current decade.

PICKING THE WRONG WINNERS AND LOSERS Excess investment is not the only drawback of state-guided capitalism. As such countries approach the technological frontier, they no longer can just pick a sector or an industry, figuring, "We'll find out how the firms in that industry work and 'one up' them." Instead, once at the frontier, a country comes to the proverbial fork in the road. Which direction to choose? That is the question that firms in advanced economies face every day. They are not sure which new products and services consumers will want. They also don't know the outcome of their R&D efforts, however planned they may be.

In rapidly innovating economies, individual firms—often working in parallel at the same time—race to be the "first mover" and to take advantage of that market position. Sources of finance back their efforts, effectively placing their bets on which horses they believe most likely to win the race. A Darwinian process of market selection eventually produces a winner or winners, who may not be the most technologically sophisticated of the horses to enter the race, but who have the most effective production, marketing, and distribution plans and appeal widely to many consumers. Examples in the United States include the Model T made by Ford (certainly not the most sophisticated automobile of its day), the Windows personal computer operating system developed by Microsoft (not as secure as its latest competitor, the "open-source" Linux), or even the personal computer itself, where Dell has made its way to the top of the pack by selling the equivalent of the Ford of computers, not the Cadillac (made by Sun and others).

Governments in state-guided economies are not comfortable with the seemingly chaotic, unplanned, rough-and-tumble process that is the hallmark of capitalism unconstrained by bureaucracy. Instead, having seen firsthand their initial success at picking sectors for their export prospects (with sales in the domestic economy to follow), these governments are apt to believe that the same process of guidance can continue to produce the winners of the future. But once economies are at the frontier where success is not so easy to generate—because there are no clear leaders to copy or follow—mistakes are easy to make. That is how Malaysia ended up building one of the world's largest high-technology parks in the 1990s, a multibillion-dollar venture that still does not seem to have paid off. And it is what has led Singapore to launch a major effort aimed at making the country one of the world's leaders in biotechnology, offering large salaries and perquisites to leading researchers from all over the world if they would spend significant time in Singapore. That gamble may yet work, but Singapore is not alone in believing that it can become the next Silicon Valley of biotech. South Korea has made major strides in the biotechnology field, in part because its government does not have the strict laws against cloning that are found in the United States. Meanwhile, in the United States, numerous states and localities are staking out their claims to be the center of the biotech revolution. Some will be successful in this biotech race, but not everyone.

SUSCEPTIBILITY TO CORRUPTION In economies where a business firm's success depends on whether it receives favors from government, there is always a danger of corruption. Firms will find subtle or not-so-subtle ways to earn those favors. China, where corruption is a well-known feature of the system, is a good example. As we will suggest shortly, although China has grown rapidly, it could grow faster were it free of corruption.

DIFFICULTY "PULLING THE PLUG" AND REDIRECTING GOVERNMENT RESOURCES A final danger of state-guided capitalism is that once a state has committed its resources and prestige to particular ventures or sectors, it can be hard to "pull the plug" if it becomes clear that major restructuring is called for or that competitors in other countries are surpassing them. Either governments don't want to lose face, or more commonly, politically powerful interests impede the ability of well-intentioned governments to abandon their interventions. The best examples of this problem are the agricultural subsidies extended by virtually all rich-country governments, despite the falling and now relatively small share of employment engaged in agriculture (in the United States, it is under 3 percent). Furthermore, despite the liberalized trading rules negotiated under GATT and then the World Trade Organization, rich countries still attempt to protect certain manufacturing industries from import competition, whether through "temporary" protection authorized by the so-called escape clause in the WTO agreement or via the more permanent variety: antidumping duties and countervailing duties to offset foreign subsidies (despite overwhelming condemnation of antidumping remedies in particular by economists). Indeed, it is ironic that political pressures often force governments to support failing industries rather than those industries with promise for the future, largely because the dying industries and their employees can be counted upon to cry most loudly for government assistance.

In sum, states can often successfully guide their economies when they have well-defined targets to aim for. But as economies catch up to the technological frontier, the low-hanging fruit will have been picked. At this point, or perhaps well before it, the drawbacks of state-guided capitalism become more evident: excessive investment, an inability to come up with radical innovation, susceptibility to corruption, and the reluctance to channel resources from low-yielding activities toward potentially more rewarding ventures become the norm.

Oligarchic Capitalism

As already suggested, the form of capitalism we call "oligarchic" is easily confused with state-guided capitalism because under the former the state also is apt to be heavily involved in directing the economy. Capitalism is defined as "oligarchic" when, even though the economic system is nominally capitalist and property rights protect those who own substantial property, government policies are designed predominantly or exclusively to promote the interests of a very narrow (usually very wealthy) portion of the population or, what may be worse, the interests of the ruling autocrat and his (or her) friends and family (in this instance, the system is better characterized as a "kleptocracy"). This form of capitalism is, unfortunately, all too common in too many parts of the world, encompassing perhaps one billion or more of the world's population. It is prevalent in much of Latin America, in many states of the former Soviet Union, in most of the Arabic Middle East, and in much of Africa.

In these societies, economic growth is not a central objective of the government, whose main goal is instead to maintain and enhance the economic position of the oligarchic few (including government leaders themselves) who own most of the country's resources. This fact distinguishes oligarchic capitalism from other autocratic, or less-than-democratic societies, where growth clearly is a central objective but where capitalism is repressively "guided" by the state. Of course, even in oligarchic economies, governments and the ruling elites to whom they respond may be and probably are interested to some degree in promoting growth, but only as a peripheral objective or a "constraint": to achieve enough growth to keep "the natives" from rebelling and overthrowing those in power as well as giving the ruling elites a larger accumulation of national wealth from which to expand their larceny. It is these circumstances, along with the repressive powers that such governments exercise, which lead us reluctantly to conclude in chapter 6 that revolution may be the most effective (and perhaps the only) way to undo oligarchic capitalism and move toward a system where economywide growth becomes a primary goal of government.

Inequality and Sluggish Growth

Oligarchic capitalistic economies generally have several features in common. First, and perhaps most obviously, their incomes are distributed extremely unequally (and their wealth tends to be distributed even more unevenly). We can use the so-called Gini coefficient, a standard measure of inequality, to illustrate this.[2] Table 3 reports the Gini coefficients in 1998, 1999, or 2000 for Latin America, a region we believe to be broadly characterized by oligarchic capitalism. The higher the Gini—on a scale from 0 to 100—the more unequally income (or wealth) is distributed. For contrast, table 4 shows the Ginis for countries belonging to the Organization for Economic Cooperation and Development (OECD), which includes the world's rich countries (along with a few exceptions, such as Mexico and Turkey). The differences are striking. The Ginis are much higher in Latin America, roughly near 50 to 60, suggesting a high degree of income inequality. In contrast, the Gini's in the OECD fall in the 25–40 range (with the United States at the top of the range).

Table 3 Gini Coefficient for Selected Latin American Countries

Country	Gini coefficient	Year
Bolivia	44.7	1999
Chile	57.1	2000
Colombia	57.6	1999
Costa Rica	46.5	2000
Dominican Republic	47.4	1998
Ecuador	43.7	1998
El Salvador	53.2	2000
Guatemala	59.9	2000
Honduras	55.0	1999
Mexico	54.6	2000
Panama	56.4	2000
Peru	49.8	2000
Uruguay	44.6	2000
Venezuela	49.1	1998

Source: World Bank. *2004 World Development Indicators* (Washington, D.C.: International Bank for Reconstruction and Development/ World Bank, 2004).
Note: Gini coefficients for other Latin American countries were unavailable from this source.

Table 4 Gini Coefficient for OECD Countries

Country	Gini coefficient	Year
Australia	35.2	1994
Austria	30.0	1997
Belgium	25.0	1996
Canada	33.1	1998
Czech Republic	25.4	1996
Denmark	24.7	1997
Finland	26.9	2000
France	32.7	1995
Germany	28.3	2000
Greece	35.4	1998
Hungary	26.9	2002
Ireland	35.9	1996
Italy	36.0	2000
Japan	24.9	1993
Korea	31.6	1998
Mexico	54.6	2000
Netherlands	30.9	1999
New Zealand	36.2	1997
Norway	25.8	2000
Poland	34.1	2002
Portugal	38.5	1997
Slovak Republic	25.8	1996
Spain	32.5	1991
Sweden	25.0	2000
Switzerland	33.1	1992
Turkey	40.0	2001
United Kingdom	36.0	1999
United States	40.8	2000

Sources: For Gini coefficients, World Bank, *2004 World Development Indicators* (Washington, D.C.: International Bank for Reconstruction and Development/World Bank, 2004); for OECD members, OECD web site at http://www.oecd.org/documentprint/0,2744, en_2649_201185_1889402_1_1_1_1,00.html.
Note: Data not available for Iceland and Luxembourg.

To be sure, a number of Latin American countries seemingly attempted to enhance growth in the 1980s and beyond, shedding the import-substitution strategy pushed by Argentine economist Raoul Prebisch in the 1950s and adopted throughout much of Latin America for two decades thereafter. The rationale offered for this policy was that it would protect local "infant industries" from foreign competition so that they could, in time, grow up and withstand competition from any source. But powerful and wealthy local families typically owned those infant industries, underscoring the consistency of such import protection with the oligarchic capitalism we describe here. The abandonment of this approach by some countries in Latin America and the hesitant steps toward opening their economies to foreign competition would seem to indicate some weakening of the oligarchic-capitalist model and faster growth as a result.

So far, the results are not consistent with this view, however. Table 5 compares the growth rates of major Latin American economies over two time periods, 1960–80, and 1980–2000. The first period roughly coincides with a time when the import-substitution economic policy was dominant throughout Latin America; the latter period loosely covers the "market reform" era. Yet, as table 5 shows, with the exception of Chile (where the Gini coefficient was among the lowest in Latin America), economic growth in the period 1980–2000 was not materially different, and in many cases it was actually *lower* than in the period 1960–80.[3]

In 2006, the World Bank devoted its entire *World Development Report,* an annual document that is scrutinized closely by policy makers and development experts around the world, to the relation between equity and economic development. Although it has been commonly assumed that there is a tradeoff between the two in developed economies (Okun, 1976), the Bank makes a compelling case that at least for developing countries as a whole, income and wealth inequality can impede economic growth through two ways. Those with power and wealth can and do tend to distort the cost of capital across social groups, thus leading to wasteful and inefficient allocation of resources while impeding opportunities for those who are penalized. Narrow, powerful elites also tend to put in place and maintain institutions and rules that benefit only themselves, at the expense of wider publics. Both of these tendencies are apparent, and indeed accurately describe economies where oligarchic capitalism dominates.

Informality

Latin American economies, among other developing-country economies, have been plagued by a second feature associated with many if not most oligarchic economies: a high share of "informal activity." Econ-

Table 5 Average Growth in GDP per Capita and Gini Coefficient for
Latin American Countries

Country	Import substitution era, 1960–80	Free market era, 1980–2000	Gini coefficient
Argentina	1.94	0.42	52.2[a]
Bolivia	1.40	−0.53	44.7[b]
Brazil	5.12	0.66	59.3[a]
Chile	1.87	3.20	57.1[c]
Colombia	2.72	1.13	57.6[b]
Costa Rica	2.28	0.48	46.5[c]
Dominican Republic	2.89	3.07	47.4[d]
Ecuador	3.91	−0.94	43.7[d]
El Salvador	1.23	0.38	53.2[c]
Guatemala	2.80	−0.16	59.9[c]
Honduras	1.56	−0.48	55[b]
Mexico	3.35	0.75	54.6[c]
Nicaragua	0.54	−2.53	43.1[a]
Panama	4.32	0.73	56.4[c]
Paraguay	3.18	0.28	57.8[a]
Peru	2.17	−0.07	49.8[c]
Uruguay	1.62	1.08	44.6[c]
Venezuela	0.18	−1.01	49.1[d]

Sources: For GDP, Alan Heston, Robert Summers, and Bettina Aten, Penn World Table Version 6.1, Center for International Comparisons at the University of Pennsylvania (CICUP), October 2002, available at http://pwt.econ.upenn.edu/php_site/pwt61_form.php; for Gini coefficient, World Bank, *2004 World Development Indicators* (Washington, D.C.: International Bank for Reconstruction and Development/World Bank, 2004);
[a] Gini coefficient in 2001.
[b] Gini coefficient in 1999.
[c] Gini coefficient in 2000.
[d] Gini coefficient in 1998.

omists have been aware of the informality phenomenon for some time (see Tanzi, 2000), and it was popularized in two best-selling books by Peruvian economist Hernando De Soto (see De Soto, 1989, 2000).

Informality, in the sense in which De Soto uses the term, exists when individuals and firms carry out economic activities that are inherently constructive—such as building homes, selling goods and services, and so on—but in ways that are technically illegal because they lack the requisite official approvals, licenses, or, in the case of land, titles. This definition of informality distinguishes it from criminality, which is also an extralegal activity but which society condemns because it undercuts the fabric of society (through such activities as theft, assaults, kidnapping, murder, and in many countries, the use and sale of certain drugs and the money laundering that typically accompanies it).

Informal activity is constructive and contributes to growth, but as we argue in the next chapter, economies where it is widespread could grow faster if informal businesses were allowed to surface from the underground and do business in the open, with access to formal credit and networks that facilitate more rapid expansion. The key point for our present purpose is that we do not believe it to be an accident that in oligarchic capitalism informality tends to be widespread and persistent. The ruling families in such societies do not consider the extension of formal rights throughout the population to be in their narrow economic interests. They don't want the competition that new, formal entrants into the economy can provide. Governments backed by oligarchic elites seem to go out of their way to make it difficult for informal firms and individuals to operate formally.

The problem of informality is now recognized far beyond Latin America, where De Soto first studied it in the 1980s; it is also prevalent in Africa, Asia, India, and China. Indeed, even Russian President Vladimir Putin has acknowledged the difficulties of establishing new businesses in Russia, a country that, somewhat to its dismay, has facilitated the influence of oligarchs. Thus, Putin has lamented: "The government and the regional authorities (in Russia) have failed to create conditions for small-and-medium-sized businesses to flourish. *Everyone who opens a new business and registers a company should be given a medal for personal (bravery)*" (as quoted in Arvelund, 2005).[4]

Corruption

Oligarchic economies typically are plagued by corruption, even more than in state-guided capitalism, though corruption certainly is not unknown in any economic system. Governments that make it difficult for citizens to obtain licenses or approvals—the preconditions that lead to informality—also create opportunities for lesser officials to take bribes. Indeed, firms that pay bribes typically face more intrusion from government officials than law-abiding enterprises (see Kauffman and Wei, 1999). Furthermore, although the few firms and families that dominate oligarchic countries can be "powers behind the throne," ultimate power still rests with government officials who have the means to make life easy or hard for the oligarchs. As a result, firms and families in this position may be subject to demands for side-payments by the leaders in charge.

Corruption should stunt growth in a number of ways. For one thing, it diverts entrepreneurial energy away from productive activities like the development and adoption of innovations and toward socially wasteful endeavors. The "opportunity cost" of losing the productive services of these potential innovators is perhaps the greatest cost of corruption. In addition, by increasing the cost of doing business, corruption discourages investment, both at home and from abroad. One largely anecdotal but persuasive account of the problem blames corruption for much of the economic misery suffered in Africa and other poor countries in the world (see Baker, 2005; Naim, 2005b). There is some more formal statistical evidence confirming that corruption is costly, finding it to discourage foreign investment in particular.[5] For example, Shang-Jin Wei of the Brookings Institution and the International Monetary Fund has estimated that corruption can impose as much as a 50 percent tax rate on foreign investment, which understandably discourages foreign inflows of capital (see Wei, 2000).[6] One might suppose that China, where despite widespread corruption the country has been highly successful in attracting foreign investment, is an exception to this pattern. Yet Wei finds that China would attract even more investment from abroad, and thus grow even more rapidly, if it were able to reduce corruption (Wei, 2001).[7]

The Dangers of Abundant Natural Resources

Finally, there are some oligarchic countries where abundance of a natural resource—oil, in particular—helps cement that form of capitalism and makes it difficult to dislodge. New York Times columnist Thomas Friedman has advanced an even broader hypothesis, which he calls "the first law of petropolitics," that asserts that in oil-rich economies, "the price of oil and the pace of freedom always move in opposite directions" (Friedman, 2006, 31). The notion is that when oil prices rise in oil-rich economies, the ruling oligarchies have the wherewithal to "buy off" opponents to their regimes and also the resources to ignore what other countries may think of them. For our purposes, the most relevant aspect of Friedman's hypothesis is that in high oil price regimes, there is less incentive or need to foster entrepreneurship as well.

Saudi Arabia, where one family (the House of Al Saud) has been in power for generations and also owns the state oil monopoly (Aramco), is perhaps the prototypical example of these propositions. Enriched by oil revenues, the family is able not only to control the oil business but to use the revenues to acquire or establish many other businesses. The Saud family also has used oil revenues earned by the government to support other businesses, such as petrochemicals, thus displaying features of state-guided capitalism as well. The situation in other parts of the Middle East is similar, but the families that rule the oil-rich countries of Oman, Bahrain, Dubai, the United Arab Emirates, and Kuwait seem to have been more successful in their efforts to encourage broader-based growth of their economies. Our impression is that one reason for this is that despite the apparent ease of opening a business in Saudi Arabia (as judged by the World Bank's annual *Doing Business* rankings, discussed in the next chapter), and state plans to use the vast increase in the country's oil revenues to develop more giant manufacturing complexes and petrochemical facilities, the country is still far more culturally and economically closed than the more successful oil-rich economies, which are more open to foreign goods, ideas, and capital.[8]

For example, although significant hurdles must still be overcome, Dubai is doing its best to become the Middle East's center for banking and securities trading (Spindle and El-Rashidi, 2006). Dubai's leaders recognize that this effort will not succeed without the active on-the-ground presence of major foreign financial institutions, and so far a number of them have responded by opening or expanding their operations in the country. Dubai is also building "Internet City," which, as of mid-2006, has attracted many of the leading high-tech names from the United States (Microsoft, Hewlett-Packard, and Cisco) to establish major Middle Eastern operational facilities there. The leaders of Oman and Bahrain have also opened their economies in a different way, seeking to attract tourists from within and outside the region.[9]

Still, for all the recent progress of the Emirate states, the economic progress of the Middle East (excepting Israel) has been abysmal, despite the oil riches in most of these countries. As one study has reported, "since 1975, per capita GDP growth in the Middle East has been worse than that of any other region in the world" (Askari and Takhavi, 2006, 83).

In sum, economies governed by oligarchic capitalism are not driven by a growth imperative but rather, in a worst case, are homes for corrupt leaders and, even in better cases, manage to preserve income and wealth only for a favored few. Indeed, a high degree of income inequality is one of the defining characteristics of oligarchic capitalism. Other characteristics include an extensive network of informal economic activities and pervasive corruption (which can be magnified when an economy is heavily dependent on a single natural resource).

Big-Firm Capitalism

Ironically, toward the end of his life (in the late 1940s and early 1950s), Harvard economist Joseph Schumpeter—one of the only economists to recognize the central role of entrepreneurs in capitalist economies—was pessimistic about the future of innovation in the United States. Schumpeter feared that entrepreneurial activity was gravitating toward the large, established enterprises, which not only had the resources to finance creative activity but also enjoyed positions in their markets large enough to earn profits sufficient to make the investment in the development of innovations worthwhile. Schumpeter was also concerned that the growing bureaucracies within large U.S. companies, especially in the wake of the mass production required during World War II, were going to stifle innovation in the future (Schumpeter, 1942, 81–86).

Another Harvard economist, John Kenneth Galbraith, who was even better known to the public, also wrote about the growing power of large, established companies during the early part of the postwar era. But unlike Schumpeter, Galbraith was not worried that Corporate America would run out of commercial ideas. On the contrary, he feared that large corporations were becoming so powerful that society would need "countervailing powers"—unions and government—to check corporate excesses, in wasteful advertising, in lavish perks, and in profits (Galbraith, 1967, 388–99).[10]

Both Schumpeter and Galbraith concerned themselves with what we call big-firm capitalism, in other words, economic systems dominated by large companies, where the original founder of the company either has passed from the scene or is no longer in effective control of the company. Ownership of such enterprises is widely dispersed among many shareholders, often including some large institutional investors (insurance companies, pension funds, universities, foundations, and the like). Professional managers are the "agents" of these "principals," giving rise to the well-known "principal-agent" problem, that of ensuring that the managers continually act in the best interests of the owners of the firms they manage.[11]

Here and in chapter 7, we identify big-firm capitalism primarily with Continental Europe, Japan, Korea, and pockets of other economies, including the United States. This isn't to say that the former group of economies is totally dominated by large enterprises, because in fact each of them also hosts many small entrepreneurs. But there are few entrepreneurs in big-firm economies that are innovative in the sense of the term as we use it. Instead, the entrepreneurs in big-firm economies live at the margins and do not provide the economic fuel for the large firms in the way that is done by innovative entrepreneurs in the United States and increasingly in other countries where entrepreneurial capitalism is a central feature of the economy or becoming so. Big-firm economies also tend to be powered more by certain national champion firms that are selected or promoted by governments, out of national pride and stemming from the belief that only such firms can realize the economies of scale to take on powerful global competitors from other countries (typically from the United States).

Disadvantages of Big-Firm, Oligopolistic Capitalism

Often, but not always, big-firm capitalism is *oligopolistic*. That is, it is characterized by large firms operating in markets that, because of their limited size, are capable of supporting only a few competitors who may be able to take advantage of any significant economies of scale provided by the current technology. Or these markets may contain only one or a few firms because of "network effects," where the value of a good or service depends on how many others use it, as is the case for communications networks, stock markets, and various high-technology products, notably computer software. Such markets tend to be highly concentrated, some-times even monopolies, because the firms that succeed in building a sub-stantial body of customers can thereby out-compete would-be entrants.

Oligopolies nonetheless have been frowned on by many economists and policy makers because they depart from the competitive ideal of many small firms, each working hard to outdo the others. In such "atomistic" markets, no one firm controls enough of the market to be able to set its price; rather, prices are determined by the impersonal interactions of many consumers and many firms and are represented graphically by the intersec-tion of the supply and demand curves found in every introductory text on economics. In contrast, oligopolies are distrusted because in industries with few competitors, individual firms may have some control over the prices they set, especially where they are able to differentiate their products and services from others in their market (economists label this "monopo-listic competition"). Firms with pricing power can thus earn "supranor-mal" profits—or profits above those earned by firms in purely competitive markets—via higher-than-competitive prices, which can hurt consumers.

In addition, firms in oligopolies can be lazy, living off their cash flow without innovating, and can leverage their power in one market into other markets, thereby stunting the growth of new technology and handicap-ping the entrepreneurs who could commercialize it. Oligopoly firms some-times "rent-seek" from government, asking for protection by the courts or regulatory agencies from more efficient domestic and foreign competitors. The U.S. automobile and steel industries are prime examples of large firms in oligopolistic markets that lost their competitive zeal and then sought and obtained trade protection to blunt—but not totally thwart—more efficient competitors from abroad. The domestic counterpart of trade pro-tection here is antitrust litigation aimed at benefiting particular big-firm competitors rather than the entire economy, with such litigation mounted by increasingly enterprising plaintiffs' lawyers, state attorneys general, and occasionally federal antitrust authorities (Baumol, 2002).

Advantages of Big-Firm, Oligopolistic Capitalism

Oligopolies do have advantages, however. If the cost structure or network effects in a market support only a few firms, then oligopoly could be the most efficient outcome for consumers, even if prices reflect a markup for higher profits. Indeed, because of their supranormal profits, firms in oligopolies have the cash flow to finance the development of the incremental improvements in technology that are the hallmark of large firms. Two Japanese giants, Honda and Toyota, exemplify the best of big-firm enterprises, firms that not only have continuously improved their automobiles, but have been radical innovators as well (most recently, in the case of hybrid cars that combine two sources of power, gasoline and a rechargeable battery). A few large Korean manufacturers—Hyundai and Samsung—also have displayed innovative zeal in recent years. Western European economies are also host to a number of successful and innovative large firms, which are strong in the automobile, capital goods, and consumer appliance industries, among others.

Indeed, large firms are essential to the functioning of *any* economy if for no other reason than because founders of vibrant, new companies—the entrepreneurs—eventually must pass the reins of power to nonfounding managers. At this point, the firms confront a fork in the road: down one path lies successful expansion and ideally other rounds of innovation, down the other lies stagnation and possible demise of the firm. If the initial firm was a radical innovator, it is unlikely that it will repeat that success in its second and third generations of management, however. Larger, second-generation companies typically have flatter, more lock-step compensation systems that cannot reward individuals or groups within the firm for breakthrough inventions to the same degree that the market rewards lone inventors or entrepreneurs. In addition, breakthrough technologies can quickly make existing products and services obsolete and for that reason may be fiercely resisted within large organizations.

These factors help explain a number of seeming conundrums: why only a small fraction of the R&D budgets of large firms is devoted to radical research (Branscomb, 2004); why research and patents filed by small firms are at least twice as likely to be "high impact" patents as those filed by bigger firms (see CHI, 2003, and Council on Competitiveness, 2004); why large U.S. firms like Proctor & Gamble, Intel, and large pharmaceutical companies, among other large enterprises, increasingly seem to be "outsourcing" much of their R&D to smaller firms, which come up with new products and then sell themselves to those larger companies (some of which may make equity investments in them in the first place);[12] or why Sony of Japan—which originated the transistor radio, the Walkman, and the Trinitron television and was once one of the most successful innovative large firms—seems to have lost its way. As one commentator has put it, Sony has become (at least as of this writing, since its new CEO is doing his best to turn the company around) a classic victim of the "not invented here" syndrome, refusing to imitate or cooperate with other companies (Surowiekci, 2005).

But big firms nonetheless can grow and prosper by constantly refining existing products and services and occasionally developing new ones, typically after considerable market research about what consumers will and won't buy. The innovation process becomes routine and predictable, picking up "three yards at a time" (to use an American football analogy) rather than seeking the breakaway touchdown. Such constant, albeit routine, refinement is necessary in any economy.

Indeed, big firms are also essential to mass-produce some of the innovations that radical entrepreneurs are unable by themselves to manufacture in a cost-effective way. Examples are legion: Ford with the mass production of the automobile, which had seen a long line of inventors before;[13] Boeing, Lockheed, McDonnell-Douglas, and Airbus with the airplane that was invented by the Wright brothers; IBM with the mainframe computer that was developed at the University of Pennsylvania; Dell with the personal computer that had been developed by Apple; Microsoft with the PC operating system that apparently was developed by Gary Kildall; and large pharmaceutical companies, which have the resources to conduct the expensive and time-consuming clinical trials on breakthrough therapies invented in universities and in small companies.

In these and many other cases (including the radical innovations we discuss below), the early innovations were usually in a primitive state, limited in capacity, and often subject to frequent breakdown. It eventually took the bigger firms, with their permanent and well-trained research staffs, to refine them and to turn the innovations into products that consumers wanted and could afford. Understandably, in such environments the research arms of these firms give priority to product improvements that enhance reliability and user-friendliness rather than to imaginative breakthroughs. Nonetheless, these incremental refinements are essential. Without such "routinized" research and development activities of big corporations, economies in developed (and developing) countries would be far less productive, and the reliability, practicality, and user-friendliness of many innovative products would be far more circumscribed.

In rare cases, big firms even can be entrepreneurial. One example is General Electric, which during CEO Jack Welch's tenure was run more as a collection of individual entrepreneurial enterprises than as one large company. Indeed, Welch streamlined GE's central office and decentralized power to the company's individual business units. Another big company well known for encouraging its employees to come up with new ideas, and then backing them as if they were starting new businesses, is 3M Corporation. And in Japan and now in its operations throughout the world, Toyota and Honda have demonstrated that large automobile companies can continue both to make incremental improvements in the already high quality of their vehicles and to innovate with new hybrid cars that are substantially more fuel-efficient than anything else on the market.

There also are cases of established, once-entrepreneurial firms that develop and market innovations when their backs are to the wall, having suffered declining fortunes from their other operations. The transformation of Nokia, the Finnish cellular telephone company, is one of the world's leading examples of this genre. More recently, in the United States, Apple has been resurrected by "iTune" players and online music and video stores, radical technologies that have rescued the company from its perennial status as a niche producer of personal computers.

And then there are large firms that simply buy radical innovation from smaller, more entrepreneurial firms. As one *Economist* survey put it in 2006: "Most of the innovation in pharmaceuticals these days is coming from small new firms. Big Pharma's R&D activity is now concentrated as much on identifying and doing deals with small, innovative firms as it is on trying to discover its own blockbuster drugs" ("New Organization," 2006, 9). Much the same can be said for a number of the larger information technology firms, such as Cisco, Intel, and Microsoft.

The more typical pattern among larger firms, however, is one that is the Achilles' heel of big-firm capitalism itself: the tendency *not to innovate*. The temptation to live for the status quo is especially strong if the large firms that dominate a market are successful in thwarting competition, either through acts on their own or by enlisting governments to shelter them from competition. Either way, the drive for continued improvement may wane. Or big firms may simply become so bureaucratic that they become incapable of recognizing and acting on radical ideas even when they see them. One noted expert on entrepreneurship, Amar Bhide of Columbia Business School, argues that such tendencies may be endemic in large companies (Bhide, 2006).

The sclerosis of larger firms threatens the growth of entire economies not only because of missed opportunities but because it can infect the attitudes of those who work for them. The labor market counterpart of a stagnant product market is when workers see job security, rather than personal growth and contribution to their company's welfare, as their highest priority. It is not an accident that in the leading exemplars of big-firm capitalism—continental Europe and Japan—labor markets are rigid, employment security is taken for granted, and firing is rare. The irony, of course, is that big-firm economies have failed to provide the employment security that workers in them so fervently seek. After outperforming the United States with lower unemployment rates through the 1950s, 1960s, and 1970s, Western European economies over the last decades have suffered structural unemployment rates that substantially exceed those in America. Restrictive labor rules that make it difficult for firms to fire or lay off redundant employees also discourage them from hiring new ones to begin with. More problematic, the fear of being stuck with a labor force that they cannot later modify deters entrepreneurs from getting started in the first place, or if they do manage to begin, from hiring beyond any threshold that triggers the job protection requirements. Yet both Europe and Japan now find themselves aching to create an entrepreneurial culture to help generate the new jobs that their existing big firms cannot. Whether either or both will succeed is the major topic we take up in chapter 7.

In short, big-firm capitalism at its best generates sufficiently large cash flows to finance internally the continuing, incremental improvements in products and services that are staples of any modern economy. At its worst, big-firm capitalism can be sclerotic, reluctant to innovate, and resistant to change.

Entrepreneurial Capitalism

Finally, we come to our fourth category: entrepreneurial capitalism, the capitalist system in which large numbers of the actors within the economy not only have an unceasing drive and incentive to innovate but also undertake and *commercialize* radical or breakthrough innovations. These innovations are bolder than the incremental innovations that characterize big-firm capitalism. Together, these innovations, as improved and refined by the entrepreneurs themselves or by other existing firms, have improved living standards beyond anything our ancestors could have believed. Examples include the automobile and the airplane; the telegraph, which led to the telephone and eventually the Internet; the generation of electricity, which has transformed the way we work and live; and the air conditioner, which has permitted massive migrations of peoples from colder climates to warmer climates, not just in the United States but around the world, and increased worker productivity by no small amount along the way.

This is just a small sample of the radical innovations that have transformed our lives and have spawned entire industries around them. They either become "platforms" on which other products or technologies are built (electricity or personal computer operating systems, for example), or "hubs" that help create and support many "spokes" (automobiles and their supplier industries). The industries spawned by these radical innovations in turn enhance productivity and thereby contribute to economic growth, both nationally and within regions where new firm formation is especially strong (Acs and Plummer, 2005; Acs and Armington, 2004).[14] Or, as David Audretsch and his colleagues at the Max Planck Institute have argued, "entrepreneurship makes an important contribution to economic growth by providing a conduit for the spillover of knowledge that might otherwise have remained uncommercialized" (Audretsch et al. 2006, 5).

New Firms and Breakthrough Innovations

But where do these radical, breakthrough innovations come from? The answer is that transformational technologies, and hence entrepreneurial capitalism, would not exist without *entrepreneurs,* who recognize an *opportunity* to sell some thing or service that hadn't been there before and then act on it. Radical breakthroughs tend to be disproportionately developed and brought to market by a *single individual or new firm,* although frequently, if not generally, the ideas behind the breakthroughs originate in larger firms (or universities) that, because of their bureaucratic structures, do not exploit them (Moore and Davis, 2004, 32). As Jean-

Baptiste Say noted at the beginning of the nineteenth century, without the entrepreneur, "[scientific] knowledge might possibly have lain dormant in the memory of one or two persons, or in the pages of literature" (Say, 1834, 81). Although the finding is now somewhat dated, one thorough statistical study has found that smaller, younger firms produce substantially more innovations per employee than larger, more established firms (Acs and Audretsch, 1990).

With rare exceptions, truly innovative entrepreneurs can only be found in capitalist economies, where the risk of doing something new—and spending time and money to make it happen—can be handsomely rewarded and the rewards safely kept (these are key preconditions for entrepreneurial capitalism, which we will discuss in chapter 5). Given the importance of innovation, the virtue of a free-market, opportunity-maximizing economy is that it taps the talents of the many. Such an economy is open to continual brainstorming and experimentation, which pays off because the people at large—vast numbers of them, having a diverse mix of skills and different kinds of knowledge—are more likely to come up with and implement good ideas than any group of planners or experts. Thus, the very "un-plannedness" of a free-market economy, which might seem to be a great weakness, turns out to be a great strength.

One of us (Baumol) has offered several reasons why radical innovations seem to emanate from entrepreneurs rather than large firms (at the same time being careful to note that most entrepreneurs are replicative rather than radical).[15] For one thing, successful radical innovation, if undertaken by the entrepreneur, promises what might be called "mega-prizes"—hundreds of millions, if not billions, of dollars of wealth. Nothing comparable awaits the radical innovator in a large firm, who might get a special recognition award and a onetime bonus.

Beyond this, paradoxically, studies have found (for the United States at least) that the *typical* entrepreneur earns *less* monetary compensation than her employee counterpart. Why then do so many entrepreneurs willingly engage in what is inherently risky activity? Because the additional psychic rewards—being one's own boss, pride in self-accomplishment, and so forth—make the entrepreneurial endeavor worthwhile even if the entrepreneur does not gain the mega-prize. This, in turn, helps explain why entrepreneurs have a comparative advantage relative to large companies in attempting to discover and commercialize breakthrough innovations. Because a not insignificant portion of the entrepreneur's "income" from her activity is psychic, the entrepreneur is the low-cost provider of radical innovation. Often, therefore, it is more economical for the large firm to wait for entrepreneurs to develop the radical innovations and then buy them out.

Large Firms and the Contagion of Innovation

Why then does this low-wage competitive advantage of the independent innovator-entrepreneur not extend also to less radical innovations, the cumulative incremental improvements that are specialties of large firms? Part of the answer lies in the greater complexity and capital cost of incremental innovation. A Boeing 777 obviously is far more complicated than the primitive airplane developed by the Wright brothers. It has taken Boeing a century to continually refine the original airplane into the complex and rather amazing piece of machinery that is today's modern airplane. Boeing has accomplished this feat by amassing an army of engineers and designers and spending billions of dollars—money the Wright brothers did not have. This, too, is not accidental. By its very nature, the original revolutionary invention known as the airplane, like so many that came before and after it, grew ever more complex as it was repeatedly modified and improved. In this respect, the independent innovator-entrepreneur was at a marked disadvantage in the financing of the incremental improvements that have led to the modern airplane.

None of this is to imply that large firms are incapable of radical innovation or that they never achieve it. The fact is that even in America, entrepreneurs have not had a monopoly on all radical innovation, and large second-generation firms are essential to ensure that radical innovations take root. For example, Bell Laboratories, which was perhaps the most successful research arm of any major corporation (when it was owned by AT&T), was responsible for two of the more important big-firm radical innovations in recent decades: the transistor and then the semiconductor.

These were seminal breakthroughs indeed, but it is also noteworthy that they helped to launch a wave of innovation by newer, entrepreneurial firms. In 1958, when American scientists were scrambling to catch up to the Soviet Union's successful launching of Sputnik, Jack Kilby at Texas Instruments expanded on the Bell Labs work by conceiving an integrated circuit, a silicon chip containing transistors along with other circuit elements. Building upon these two innovations, others brought to market a series of new consumer and business goods, from transistor radios to pocket calculators and, eventually, personal computers—which were developed and commercialized in the 1970s by entrepreneurs at a time when existing firms did not yet see the value of PCs (an industry launched by another entrepreneur, Steve Jobs, the founder of Apple).

Innovation didn't stop there. The PC industry, in turn, gave a huge boost to the fledgling software industry that also had been launched by cadres of independent entrepreneurs. Even the legendary start and growth of Microsoft into one of the world's largest and most profitable companies, as the pioneer of PC operating systems, thereafter provided a market for other computer application software. Advances in computing, in turn, have enabled advances in biotechnology, a new field started by university researchers experimenting with recombinant DNA, which was developed into an industry by entrepreneurs and venture capitalists. Computing and biotech have since played instrumental roles in the emergence of nanotechnology—miniature devices no larger than molecules—that may revolutionize medicine and other fields in ways that cannot yet be imagined.

No one could have planned these events. No one even foresaw them. Yet they led to entirely new industries employing millions and benefiting hundreds of millions (if not billions) more.

Other countries have witnessed these remarkable developments and are learning from them. As we discuss in later chapters, such countries as Ireland, Israel, and the United Kingdom have or are in the process of shedding the guiding role of the state in their economies and putting their bets on entrepreneurs, with growing and even remarkable success. India, a long-time practitioner of state-guided capitalism, has embraced entrepreneurship, more by accident than design, in a small but growing corner of its economy: call-in centers and software design. China, formerly the world's largest centrally planned economy, has developed a new form of semi-state-guided entrepreneurship that has helped make that economy the world's fastest growing of the last decade. We will have more to say about both the Indian and Chinese embrace of entrepreneurship in chapter 6.

The United States and the Brave New World

For now, however, we simply point out that Americans must learn to live with the fact that they no longer have a monopoly on their country's unique blend of entrepreneurial and big-firm capitalism. This is a good thing if it spurs the United States to maintain its commitment to both radical innovation and incremental improvement. It will be unfortunate, however, if the fear of stiffer competition induces American policy makers to adopt a more defensive form of capitalism that, over time, retards the remarkable growth in innovation that has so far characterized the U.S. economy.

The fear we speak of grows out of the necessary and inevitable consequence for any entrepreneurial economy, what Schumpeter called "creative destruction." The creativity and the destruction are often brought about by the entrepreneur and successor firms, who commercialize the new technology that replaced the old: the car instead of the horse, electricity instead of the steam engine, the semiconductor instead of the cathode ray tube, and computer hardware and software that have eliminated (and continue to eliminate) many tasks once formerly carried out by human beings, among many other examples.

Successful entrepreneurial economies *embrace* and generally *encourage* change. They do not erect barriers that prevent money and people from shifting from slow-moving or dying sectors to dynamic industries. They do not wall off their existing producers from more efficient ones in foreign countries. And they seek out better ideas wherever they can find them, even abroad (we will have more to say about the importance of imitation in chapter 5).

Radical innovations and the changes they spawn have a tendency to come in waves, accompanied by much disruption over an extended period of time, with many losers and just a few winners. At one time, for example, several thousand firms or individuals were making and trying to sell automobiles in the late nineteenth and early twentieth centuries; only a handful survived. A similar story can be told about the telephone industry and, more recently, the numerous dot-com companies that quickly came and went in the 1990s. Financial bubbles attend these technological revolutions, with investors placing bets on numerous competitors, pushing up their share prices only to see most prices fall to earth when most of the companies fail. This boom-and-bust nature of financial markets is inherent in any economy that spawns radical or paradigm-shifting innovation (see Perez, 2002).

Economies characterized by entrepreneurial capitalism are also dynamic in another sense: there is a constant churning of firms in the pecking order among all firms, in contrast with greater stability in firm rankings in economies characterized by big-firm capitalism. Consider, for example, the contrasting experiences of the United States and Europe. Of the twenty-five largest firms in the United States in 1998, eight did not exist or were very small in 1960. In Europe, all twenty-five of the companies that were the largest in 1998 were already large in 1960. Moreover, the pace of the change in America seems to have accelerated. Whereas it took twenty years to replace one-third of the Fortune 500 companies in 1960, it took just four years to accomplish this task in 1998 (Commission of the European Communities, 2003).[16]

Because radical change is so disruptive, entrepreneurial economies can benefit from properly constructed safety nets that shield some of the victims of change from its harsh impacts (without at the same time destroying their initiative to get back on their feet). This may seem paradoxical or counterintuitive. The former chief scientist of Israel once told two of the present authors in conversation that she believed one reason Israel was so entrepreneurial was that its people had a high level of discomfort, brought about largely by external threats to their physical security. In societies where individuals may be too comfortable—much of Western Europe, for example—people may be reluctant to take the risks inherent in any entrepreneurial endeavor. Indeed, in 2004, a French government employee wrote a best-selling book called *Bonjour Paresse* (Hello Laziness), which extolled the virtues of not working hard. This "avoidance of work" ethic is now a serious cultural issue across Western Europe, manifesting itself in a noticeable drop in average hours worked per year by employed individuals in major European countries (see chapter 7).

But context makes a big difference. In Europe, where there is job security for those who have a job, it is not surprising to find authors hailing laziness. In societies where this is not so and where people have much to lose if they lose a job, as is true in the United States, change from any source can be highly threatening. And when change hits home, it is easier to put a foreign face on it—blaming trade, outsourcing, or direct investment by American companies abroad—than to recognize that most change is domestically driven by continuing improvements in productivity that allow firms to make do with fewer workers, with or without foreign competition or outsourcing. In such an environment, then, actual and potential losers from change have a strong incentive to try to disrupt very visible sources of change, such as trade, outsourcing, and the like.

Thus, although it may seem counterintuitive, constructive safety nets that catch the fallen without destroying their incentive to get back up can be more important in high-income, entrepreneurial economies than in economies with lower average standards of living. This is because the potential losers from change in high-income countries have more to lose and thus greater incentive to try to stop it or slow it down.

To summarize, entrepreneurial capitalism is the system we believe is most conducive to radical innovation. But no advanced economy can survive only with entrepreneurs (just as individuals cannot survive by eating just one type of food). Big firms remain essential to refine and mass-produce the radical innovations that entrepreneurs have a greater propensity to develop or introduce. One area for future research is the optimal mix of entrepreneurial and large firms. To address this challenge, however, requires better data sets than currently exist. (Readers interested in the important but overlooked topic of what data are required to test the hypotheses advanced in this book should consult the appendix.)

The Challenge Ahead

Now that we have outlined the four types of capitalism, a number of obvious questions beg for answers. In particular, how can governments set out to create or accelerate the growth of entrepreneurship? Assuming they can, how can governments ensure that the successful large firms that result continue to innovate? Or is government essentially helpless, taking a back seat to the informal norms and practices of a society—its "culture"—which may take decades, or even centuries, to change? Chapter 5 takes up these and other related questions that are vital to understanding and promoting economic growth.

5

GROWTH AT THE CUTTING EDGE

Growth failed to respond to any of the (standard macro) formulas because the formulas failed to take heed of the basic principle of economics: people respond to incentives.

—William Easterly, *The Elusive Quest for Growth,* p. 143

Throughout most of recorded history and in almost all societies, accumulation of wealth has been a primary goal of enterprising individuals. In the vernacular familiar to American readers, individuals have pursued one of the two primary roads to acquire wealth: increasing the size of the pie and taking one's fair share from the increase, or simply taking more of the pie, whether or not it grows. Until the time of the Industrial Revolution, the second of these options—redistribution of what was already there—was pursued overwhelmingly. That fact, ultimately, explains why the economic growth achieved by industrial countries in the last two centuries is unparalleled in previous history, ancient or recent.

There are straightforward reasons why redistribution rather than growth has for most of human history been the preferred method of wealth-accumulation. Perhaps the most obvious is that it looks easier simply to acquire riches by taking them away from others who are weaker. Indeed, when unrelenting dangers lurked from every side, violence was understandably deemed a manly, heroic activity. More than that, in such an environment there was little certainty that the fruits of the other avenue to wealth—contribution to production and growth of the economy—would accrue preponderantly or even in any substantial part to the individuals who endeavored to make those contributions.

So manifest are the immediate advantages of wealth-grabbing activities over activities that increase the total wealth of society that it is not easy to explain what led modern free-market economies to move toward the latter. The obvious answer is the appearance of new institutions that reined in the enterprising wealth-grabbing options and limited their benefits, while at the same time offering greater reward and certainty of payoffs to the enterprising individuals who contributed to economic growth. Put that way, it becomes clear that such a revolutionary change in incentive structure must have been a piece of great good luck for societies where the revolutions occurred; indeed, something of a miracle. This chapter will seek to describe those changes in institutions and associated incentives.

The blend of big-firm and entrepreneurial capitalism we extoll here may not be right for all economies at all times. It may be that in their initial stages, economies need or benefit more from the guiding hand of the state, or so some have argued. We will not enter that debate here. We are surer, however, that *once economies approach the technological frontier—that is, once their living standards are among the highest in the world—they can remain at or become the frontier only by shedding state guidance and adopting some blend of entrepreneurial and big-firm capitalism.* The nature of this blend, as well as the characteristics of entrepreneurial capitalism in particular, will differ from country to country, depending on historical circumstances and differences in culture. Simply put, all economies need some degree of entrepreneurship to generate radical innovation, yet they also need effective big firms to refine it and commercialize it on a mass scale.

This chapter is about those economies that are ready for a blend of entrepreneurial and big-firm capitalism but want to know the key ingredients for achieving and maintaining it. We do not mean to be overly prescriptive since there is no single recipe for growth, even in economies at or near the frontier. The precise rules and institutions that may work well in one country, or within a country, may not and probably will not work elsewhere. But whatever their precise form, we believe that the institutions must satisfy four key conditions, which are unique, in our view, to the blend of entrepreneurial and big-firm capitalism we have described. At the same time, we recognize that other factors—not unique to this form of capitalism or even necessary for growth—also can enhance growth. We examine those factors at the conclusion of the chapter.

Four Conditions for Maximizing Growth at the Cutting Edge

An entrepreneurial economy must have entrepreneurs—not just any entrepreneurs, but innovative entrepreneurs. We submit that three preconditions are necessary to generate them. But just as important, entrepreneurial economies must have ways to ensure that the successful entrepreneurs that grow into large firms are kept on their toes. Otherwise, as suggested in chapter 8, big-firm capitalism can become sclerotic. Our fourth condition addresses this particular danger.

Easy to Start and Grow a Business

To encourage the formation of innovative entrepreneurial enterprises, governments should lower the costs of "formality" (business and property registration and ease of hiring and firing workers); have a workable bankruptcy system in place; and facilitate the formation and growth of their formal financial sectors, which channel resources to innovative entrepreneurs. The first condition should hardly be a surprise. If entrepreneurship is about starting and growing a commercial enterprise (we ignore for this purpose so-called social entrepreneurs who might have other objectives in mind), then it must be easy and inexpensive to do so—formally, that is. In other words, licensing requirements should be few (unless the business requires some kind of special expertise, such as a medical care facility), the time and the cost required to fill out the necessary applications should be kept to a minimum, and so should time required for approval. These same elements apply to registration of property and collateral (to secure loans); these steps should be easily managed.

In an age increasingly dominated by the Internet, many or all of these activities can be conducted online, and in parts of developed economies, they already are. For developing countries that lack the infrastructure for high-speed Internet communication from remote locations, the application process can be accelerated at the appropriate registry with relatively low-cost electronic kiosks or similar equipment.

BUSINESS REGISTRATION We underscore the word "formal" in these registration requirements because, as we noted in the last chapter, in many developing economies, entrepreneurship is alive and well but in an *informal way*—that is, without all of the necessary formal approvals. That is because the formal processes are so time-consuming and expensive.

In his first book, *The Other Path,* Hernando De Soto documented how significant this problem was in Peru in the mid-1980s (De Soto, 1989). He and his colleagues at his institute in Lima started a business and tried to obtain the necessary approvals, only to discover that it took nearly three hundred days to obtain them—and that was with payments of bribes to officials along the way. Before and after this book, De Soto and his colleagues were invited to other developing countries and found similar or longer waiting periods (along with corruption).

De Soto argued that because the cost and delay in "being formal" were so substantial, it was rational for individual homeowners and entrepreneurs simply to do business without the approvals, to opt for "informality" instead. Although informality can be rational for individuals who choose it, economies as a whole suffer when vast numbers opt out of formality.

Specifically, informal firms must operate at a small scale to avoid detection by the authorities (especially since they typically do not pay taxes). Because they are not official and any "property" that they may control is not formally registered, informal entrepreneurs cannot obtain formal bank credit, for they have no legally recognized property to pledge as collateral. As a result, they either can expand only as they generate and save income, gain support from friends and family (often meager because they, too, are likely to informal and have little means), or if they can, borrow from informal lenders (known in some countries as the "curb market") who can charge exorbitant interest rates. To underscore the point, De Soto estimated in his second book, *The Mystery of Capital* (2000), that due to the absence of title registration of informally "owned" property (typically buildings), there was at that time throughout the world more than *$9 trillion* in "dead capital," property that could not be used to finance investment and growth. Societies plagued by large informal sectors are like poorly oiled engines, operating at far less than their full potential, with much waste and inefficiency.

De Soto's work has had its skeptics. Some question his statistical methods. Other dispute whether informality is as costly to economies as De

Soto argued. And others object to the silver bullet implication of De Soto's work—namely, that if businesses and property could be registered properly, poor countries suddenly would grow a lot more rapidly.

Even if exaggerated, De Soto's argument strikes home, and indeed it is becoming somewhat the conventional wisdom (always a dangerous position to be in) in international policy circles. The United Nations formed a commission in 2004 on advancing entrepreneurship in the developing world and appointed De Soto to it, no doubt in recognition of the importance of his work.[1] More important, at least for future economic research, the World Bank has begun a major effort to compile the kind of data on time and expense in business registration and property recordation that De Soto claimed he was finding. The Bank included additional variables on its list, notably the costs of hiring and firing employees, given the importance of well-functioning labor markets in all economies.

Tables 6 through 9 provide some illustrative data on the ten best and ten worst performing countries on the costs of business registration, property registration, ease of hiring workers, and ease of firing workers, from the Bank's second report, *Doing Business in 2006* (World Bank, 2006). The costs of hiring and firing workers are included not so much because they affect the ease of business formation (though they may) but because they (presumably) affect their rate of growth once they do are formed.

The data in Tables 6 through 9 reflect reports as of early 2004 and are based on extensive analyses of local laws and regulations, coupled with surveys of more than three thousand local government officials, lawyers, consultants, and other professionals familiar with registrations in various countries. Viewed together, the results presented in the tables are not surprising: most of the best performers are in developed economies and the worst in developing countries, though there are exceptions.[2]

Taken together, the tables demonstrate that it generally is more difficult and expensive to start and grow a business in poor countries than in rich ones. For example, the Bank concludes that on average it takes fifty-nine days and 122 percent of per capita annual income to start a business in the poorest countries, but only twenty-seven days and 8 percent of annual per capita incomes to do so on average in countries belonging to the Organization for Economic Cooperation and Development, or OECD (World Bank 2005, 18).

The results in the tables should be interpreted carefully, however. One

Table 6 Cost of Business Start-up (% of Income per Capita, $US)

Least	%	Most	%
Denmark	0.0	West Bank and Gaza	275
New Zealand	0.2	Cambodia	276
United States	0.5	Rwanda	280
Sweden	0.7	Congo, Rep.	288
United Kingdom	0.7	Chad	360
Canada	0.9	Niger	465
Puerto Rico	1.0	Congo, Dem. Rep.	503
Singapore	1.1	Angola	642
Finland	1.2	Sierra Leone	835
France	1.2	Zimbabwe	1442

Source: World Bank, 2006.

cannot automatically infer that because developed economies tend to have the lowest costs of registration and hiring and firing that those lower costs are the reason (or a reason) for their higher level of economic development. As economists say, the causation could run in the other direction. It could be the case that in developed economies entrepreneurs have sufficient political clout to ensure that their costs of registration are low, and conversely that they lack such clout in developing countries where registration costs are high.

Table 7 Property Registration Cost (% of Property Value)

Least	%	Most	%
Saudi Arabia	0.0	Central African Republic	17.3
Slovakia	0.1	Senegal	18
New Zealand	0.1	Burundi	18.9
Belarus	0.1	Cameroon	19
Switzerland	0.4	Mali	20
Azerbaijan	0.4	Chad	21.3
Russia	0.4	Congo, Rep.	22.1
United States	0.5	Zimbabwe	22.6
Estonia	0.5	Nigeria	27.1
Armenia	0.5	Syria	30.4

Source: World Bank, 2006.

Table 8 Difficulty of Hiring

Least	*Most*
Australia	Iran
Georgia	Burkina Faso
Hong Kong, China	Mozambique
Israel	Central African Republic
Malaysia	Congo, Rep.
Mauritius	Sierra Leone
Namibia	Congo, Dem. Rep.
Russia	Mauritania
Switzerland	Morocco
United States	Niger

Source: World Bank, 2006.

The Bank purports to find that the causation runs in the right way, however, from costs to growth. In particular, it cites statistical work (admittedly subject to all of the qualifications we highlight in chapter 3) that controls for the causation problem and estimates that by moving from the seventy-fifth percentile in the costs of starting a business to the twenty-fifth percentile (lower costs are better), poor countries could increase their annual rate of GDP growth by anywhere from .25 to .50 percent a year (Klapper, Laeven, and Rajan, 2004). Those fractions may not sound like

Table 9 Difficulty of Firing

Least	*Most*
Costa Rica	Angola
Hong Kong, China	Cameroon
Iceland	Egypt
Japan	Lao PDR
Kuwait	Sri Lanka
Oman	Togo
Saudi Arabia	Ukraine
Singapore	India
Thailand	Nepal
Uruguay	Tunisia

Source: World Bank, 2006.

much until one applies them to some base number, like all GDP in developing countries. When that is done, the Bank reports that raising the growth rate by just .25 percent would enhance GDP in the developing world by $14 billion annually, an amount equal to a quarter of all development aid (World Bank, 2005, 24) and roughly the size of the foreign aid budget of the United States.

The costs of business registration (both direct and indirect) are important not just for domestic businesses but for foreign-owned ones as well. Countries can benefit hugely from "start-ups" or acquisitions of existing companies by foreign investors, or "foreign direct investment" (FDI). This is because foreign investors, often major foreign enterprises, typically bring their knowledge, technology, and experience along with their money to the countries they invest in. Yet many countries, both developed and developing, restrict foreign investment, either across the board (for populist reasons) or in particular sectors (in the United States and other countries, in communications and defense industries, for cultural and national security reasons). As discussed in the last chapter, foreign investors also appear to be highly sensitive to levels of corruption, which can act like a tax, and not simply on registration but on the regular conduct of business.

BANKRUPTCY PROTECTION It may seem paradoxical, but another important, but indirect, factor affecting the costs of the entry is the cost of *exit* or failing. In most societies and throughout history, bankruptcy has been a mark of shame, if not a criminal offense requiring the bankrupt to serve time in jail. The United States and some other countries have taken a more enlightened attitude toward debtors who cannot pay their debts when they come due (one of the definitions of bankruptcy): depending on the part of the law they invoke, those who "declare" bankruptcy are excused from some of their debts, provided they agree to repay the balance over some rescheduled time period.[3] Effective bankruptcy protection is critical to promoting entrepreneurship, since without it, many would-be entrepreneurs would be unwilling to take the risks of starting a business, knowing that if they fail they could lose everything, on top of facing the severe social stigma of having declared bankruptcy. Indeed, it is safe to speculate that there is a strong negative correlation between the strength of that stigma and attitudes toward entrepreneurship in any given society: the more society penalizes failure, the less entrepreneurship it will get. (This proposition has its analogue in labor protection: the more difficult it is to fire workers, the less incentive firms have to hire them.) Those social scientists who attribute differences in entrepreneurship rates between countries to differences in cultural attitudes (a subject we will soon explore) thus may be missing an important underlying policy that influences culture, namely, the policy toward bankruptcy.

ACCESS TO FINANCE A third essential factor in starting most businesses is access to capital. J. R. Hicks, one of the great British economists, observed that the liquidity of capital markets in eighteenth-century England helped ignite the innovation associated with the Industrial Revolution by allowing inherently illiquid long-term investments in capital equipment to be financed (Hicks, 1969, 143–45). Early in his distinguished career, Joseph Schumpeter emphasized the importance of banks in funding entrepreneurs and established businesses, spurring technological innovation and hence economic growth (Schumpeter, 1911). In recent years, with more attention paid by economists to the sources of growth, there is a growing consensus that economic growth depends to at least some degree on the maturity and soundness of economies' financial systems (Levine, 2004). After all, the central role of financial systems—financial intermediaries and capital markets—is to channel funds of those with excess funds (savers) to those who are likely to earn the highest returns on those funds (investors). As banks, other financial intermediaries (insurance companies, pension funds), and capital markets (stock and bond markets) grow in size and sophistication, they become more efficient in performing this critical function. The more efficient they are, the more risk that savers are likely to take with their funds, which should foster more investment and entrepreneurship. As Columbia University economists Massimiliano Amarante and Edmund Phelps succinctly put it: "Financiers are the channel through which innovations can be transformed from mere ideas to a source of economic growth" (Amarante and Phelps, 2005).

What makes the financial systems of entrepreneurial economies unique is that they are more likely to finance new, risky firms than are economies characterized by other forms of capitalism. As we suggested in chapter 4, one of the primary instruments governments use to guide their economies is ownership of the nation's banks or at least the ability to influence their loan operations. These practices inevitably favor large, state-favored enterprises to the detriment of new and smaller businesses, even if the latter hold innovative promise. Banks in bureaucratic capitalist societies do not act much differently. As we will discuss in chapter 7, in both Japan and Western Europe, where big-firm capitalism is perhaps practiced at its best, banks have close ties, through ownership or director positions (or both), with the companies that are their borrowers. Indeed, for a long time, and even now, many of Japan's leading companies had "main" banks as shareholders. This sort of lending behavior, coupled with "administrative guidance" as to where to place funds, works to the detriment of any entrepreneurial sector.

In contrast, the U.S. financial system has long been decentralized and much more "democratic." After a brief flirtation with federally owned banks in the early decades of its history, the United States abandoned any notion of state ownership of banks and instead went in the opposite direction by allowing a proliferation of many smaller banks, which for most of the nineteenth and twentieth centuries were not allowed to expand across state lines. United States stock exchanges developed gradually after the nation was formed, soaring in importance after World War II, to the point where today U.S. equities and bond markets are a primary source of new capital for both established and new firms, while serving as a more important home for the holders of financial assets than banks (unlike all other countries, where banks still hold most private financial wealth).

Indeed, America's financial system has evolved in ways that continue to underscore Hicks's maxim about the importance of finance in funding innovation. For a long time, banks were a primary source of funding for new enterprises, but only as lenders. New companies that reached a certain size could issue stock of their own on America's stock markets—as "initial public offerings"—but the stock markets did not provide the so-called early stage funding to help new companies get started. Entrepreneurs had to have either some wealth beforehand or access to funds from family and friends, which is still true for most replicative entrepreneurs and also for innovative companies in their early stages.

What has made America's financial system conducive to innovative entrepreneurship is that it has developed institutions that have financed the *growth* of innovative enterprises. For most readers, the best-known institution of this sort is the venture capital fund, which was first developed after World War II but did not bloom until the mid-1970s, when Congress permitted pension funds and various nonprofit organizations (including universities and foundations) to invest a limited portion (up to 5 percent) of their assets in these funds. Venture funds pool the funds of these institutional investors and wealthy individuals to provide equity financing for companies in their early stages. Although only a tiny fraction of U.S. companies have received venture money, venture funds have played a very significant role in launching many of America's high-technology firms— Intel, Sun, Amazon, Cisco, and Google, to name a few.

Venture funds could not exist without an active stock market, however, for it is through initial public offerings (or IPOs) that the venture capitalists traditionally have found a way to liquefy their original investments and thus compensate their investors for the substantially higher risks involved in innovative start-ups. Other countries have begun to copy the U.S. venture capital model, but they have found it tough going since investors must have an appetite for risk, faith that the legal system will protect their investments, and have active stock markets where the shares of IPOs can be readily traded.

Since the bursting of the Internet stock market bubble (not just in the United States but also in other developed country markets), the venture capital industry and its investors have become more risk averse, even bureaucratic, concentrating on "second" or "third" rounds of funding new companies. A new financial "industry," loosely speaking, appears to be taking on the role of providing start-up equity for innovative entrepreneurs: "angel investors," or wealthy individuals who alone or in groups are providing the equity, along with family and friends, to help launch what America hopes will be the innovative companies of the future.

As the U.S. experience with venture and angel investing spreads to other parts of the world, other countries should experience an increase in the number and growth of innovative firms and thus import one of the features that makes the United States the leading example of entrepreneurial capitalism. Indeed, U.S. venture firms, to the extent they are still involved in funding start-ups, increasingly are looking abroad for entrepreneurial opportunities rather than within the United States. This is not a cause for alarm but rather another illustration of how "technology"—in this case "financial technology"—eventually diffuses across national borders.

Rewards for Productive Entrepreneurial Activity

A cursory reading of history indicates that the pursuit of wealth by at least some individuals has been present in virtually every society (there are exceptions—medieval serfs, monks in monasteries, and the like—but these are the exceptions that only prove the rule). As we noted at the outset of the chapter, there are fundamentally two ways in which wealth may be acquired: by undertaking productive activities that enlarge the size of total output for any society, or by ignoring that objective and seeking instead to gain a larger share of whatever output is generated. In the vernacular, the choices are to expand the pie or to seek larger slices.

Clearly, economic growth requires activities of the first type—those that expand the pie or total output—and we will refer to this as *productive entrepreneurship*. In turn, we have previously identified two types of productive entrepreneurship: innovative and replicative. For entrepreneurial societies, we are interested in the former, for it is only by commercializing new products and services or by adopting new and better ways of making or delivering existing ones that the economic frontier moves out.

It is not sufficient for entrepreneurial economies to make it easy for entrepreneurs to start their businesses. Such individuals and the firms they found must be rewarded for their success. Several institutions are important are in this regard: the rule of law (effectively enforced), intellectual property protection (but not too much), taxes that are not unduly onerous, and rewards and mechanisms to facilitate imitation in certain environments.

THE RULE OF LAW, PROPERTY, AND CONTRACT RIGHTS Innovative entrepreneurship is a risky undertaking, and individuals who bear these risks must be appropriately compensated.[4] That is, entrepreneurs must have rights to the property—money, land, goods, or all three—they gain as a result of successfully pursuing their endeavors. In addition, entrepreneurs (and all firms) must have confidence that the contracts they enter into with other parties will be honored (and if necessary, enforced by an independent judicial system). As Professor Kenneth Dam reminds us, it is not sufficient for statutes or regulations protecting contracts and property to be on the books; both must be effectively *enforced*. China would appear to be an exception to these propositions, which otherwise are well established. Yet Dam argues that even in China legal protections have improved as the economy has grown (Dam, 2006).

AVOIDING ONEROUS TAXATION Property rights serve as a powerful positive incentive for productive entrepreneurship, but of potential equal importance is minimizing *disincentives* that can discourage such activity. One obvious disincentive to productive entrepreneurship, or indeed any activity, is taxation. Clearly, no one likes paying taxes, perhaps least of all entrepreneurs, who tend to credit themselves for their success and deeply resent efforts by government to take away any part of the earnings to which they believe are fully entitled. But the reality, of course, is that taxes are essential in any free society. Some compulsory means must be found to provide for basic public goods—those whose benefits cannot be fully appropriated by any individual or group but instead are widely dispersed through society. Examples include national defense, a police force, an effective legal system, roads, sanitation facilities, and education (whose benefits accrue only in part to those who receive it, society also benefiting from having citizens learn shared values and knowledge and from advances in knowledge that education makes possible).

Entrepreneurs, along with everyone else in a society, benefit from public goods and services, and we presume that those public goods are present as a precondition for growth under any economic system and any of our different types of capitalism in particular. So the optimal level of taxation for any society—whether or not it aims to be entrepreneurial—clearly is not zero. The critical challenge for entrepreneurial societies is to fund public goods at such a level and in a fashion that least punishes entrepreneurial success.

Somewhat surprisingly, little empirical research exists on this question.[5] Common sense suggests that the more highly and directly tied taxes are to entrepreneurial success, the less entrepreneurship one can expect will take place. Thus, other things being equal, if promoting entrepreneurship and growth are the sole objectives of any tax system, taxes on sales or property are to be preferred to taxes on income, which perhaps is the most direct measure of entrepreneurial success. There is an additional reason to tax sales, or value-added: such taxes discourage consumption and reward saving, which is also essential for growth (though not as important, according to empirical studies, as innovation, which is diffused throughout economies by entrepreneurs and well-established larger firms).

We recognize, of course, that few societies eschew income taxes altogether in favor of consumption taxes. More commonly, governments tax both, on grounds of fairness and also by historical accident. Nonetheless, if additional funds are needed—as we suggest, in chapter 8, they will be in all developed economies as their populations age—then policy makers should think seriously about taxing consumption before raising additional income tax rates if they want to avoid unduly penalizing entrepreneurship and hence growth.[6]

PROPER REGULATION (OR DEREGULATION) Regulation (or deregulation) also can be a powerful force affecting entrepreneurial incentives. For example, in the United States until quite recently, regulation of prices charged in long-distance telecommunications, freight and passenger transportation, and some forms of energy sought to prevent monopoly profits by adopting ceilings on profits, defined in terms of rate of return on investment. It is hard imagine a system that more effectively invited inefficiency and waste and minimized the incentives for innovation. The firms were not only exempted from penalties for wasteful outlays, they were *rewarded* for incurring such expenditures since the price ceilings typically took the form of some markup over cost. As the United States undid these forms of "antimonopoly regulation"—eventually out of the recognition that these industries were *not* monopolies—new entrants came in, existing inefficient firms have been forced out or shrunk, and the overall efficiency of these sectors, as measured by increases in productivity, has improved.[7] In addition, deregulation of transportation industries in particular made it possible for such important innovations as "just in time" shipping (adopted from Japan) to exist. Under the previous, highly regulated, transportation system, airlines, trucks, and railroads would not have had the flexibility to accommodate rapidly shifting shipping demands (Barone, 2005, 79).

REWARDING NEW IDEAS Having established the importance of rewards for successful entrepreneurial behavior, an obvious question begs for an answer: where do entrepreneurs get their *ideas?* By definition, replicative entrepreneurs have no difficulty coming up with the ideas for their businesses: they simply copy what some others have done. Their only challenge is to pick one of countless businesses or business models already in the marketplace that they believe are best suited to their talents, experience, and interests.

The more interesting questions are where do innovative entrepreneurs get their ideas, and do incentives matter here too? In answering these questions, it is useful first to dispel the notion that innovation is something that is entirely new. Of course, innovative products and services are new, but they could not exist without many other components or ideas that already exist. As the famous scientist Isaac Newton once said, "If I have seen further than others, it is by standing upon the shoulders of giants." So, too, with innovative entrepreneurs, or any inventor for that matter: technological breakthroughs happen only when related ideas or products, already in the marketplace, are put together in new ways (Hargadon, 2003). Successful innovative entrepreneurs are the ones who *recognize and then realize the commercial opportunities* that such recombinations offer.

Indeed, it is safe to say that virtually every product that has ever been sold has features that were previously developed but are now combined in new ways to yield something different. A few recent examples illustrate the idea: the airplane (piston and then jet engines; the airframe; nuts, bolts and many other parts that go into making a plane; radar and wireless forms of communication); the automobile (engines; gears; steel and aluminum castings; rubber; and now increasingly, semiconductors); and the Internet (computers; networking technologies; communications protocols; fiber optics; network servers; among other components). We are confident that readers can think of countless other examples simply by looking around their office or their home.[8]

So what does government policy have to do with all this? The answer is: plenty. Although inventors will tinker simply because they are good at it or love to do it, as with any other activity, one will get more innovation if it is actively encouraged and rewarded. European monarchs recognized this as early as 1300, providing inventors with temporary exclusive rights, or what today we call "monopoly profits," for their innovations. The concept really took hold in England several centuries later and was formally embodied in the United States Constitution by America's founding fathers (Jaffee and Lerner, 2004). Congress implemented the constitutional guarantee initially by providing seventeen years of monopoly protection, since extended to twenty years, both periods running from the date the Patent Office awards the patent (after determining it to be an advance of the "prior art"). Other nations have since introduced their own forms of patent protection, though it is common outside the United States for the protection to be awarded to the "first to file" the application, and to that date in particular.

Yet even with the temporary monopoly profits awarded to innovators under patents, the lion's share of the gains from innovation still spill over to the rest of society. This is a good thing, as long as patent holders are adequately compensated, since societies benefit most from innovation when it is rapidly diffused. For example, one noted study of one hundred American firms found that "information concerning development decisions is generally in the hands of rivals within 12 to 18 months, on the average, and information containing the detailed nature and operation of a new product or process generally leaks out within about a year" (Mansfield, Schwartz, and Wagner, 1981, 911). William Nordhaus estimates that inventors capture as little as 3 percent of the total social benefits of their inventions (Nordhaus, 2004).

Still, even with spillovers of this magnitude, having a patent remains a prized possession and thus must continue to act as a powerful force for stimulating innovation. Indeed, there is a danger that this force can be too powerful. If patents are too easy to come by—that is, temporary monopolies are awarded for developments that are not truly novel but instead are "obvious" and thus unworthy of legal protection—then society will stimulate too many "temporary" monopolies. Patents that are unjustly awarded will then *discourage* entrepreneurship because they will prevent others with truly novel ideas that are deserving of patent protection in their own right (or at least the ability to be left alone without fear of lawsuits) from entering markets and competing against those whose patents are not deserved. This is an increasingly serious problem in the United States, which we discuss further in chapter 8.[9]

GOVERNMENT-SUPPORTED R&D Government can play another important, but more indirect, role in stimulating ideas that eventually are commercialized by entrepreneurs: subsidizing basic scientific research. Though it rarely finds its way soon into the marketplace, basic scientific understanding provides the building blocks for subsequent applied research that eventually leads to commercial products. The semiconductor, for example, would not have been possible without fundamental knowledge about the atom, molecular structure, and the like. Likewise, the components of the Internet would not have been possible without fundamental understanding of the way in which light and information travel over fiber optic cables. Similar statements can be made for the myriad pharmaceutical wonders that extend or save lives.

Rich countries, like the United States, can afford the resources to devote to basic research at levels and in ways that poorer countries cannot. Indeed, as a share of gross domestic product, the United States has led the world in government-funded civilian (nonmilitary) research and development expenditures for some time. Although other countries may be catching up to the United States, this is not the cause for alarm that many in the United States may think. It is foolish to believe that when entrepreneurs and innovators in other countries develop new things, they will somehow keep the innovations to themselves. To the contrary, they have strong incentives to sell their innovations to purchasers around the world. Who wouldn't want to be "number one in the world" if it were possible?

Of course, there are benefits to being first or a global leader that should not be dismissed, but they should not be overstated either. For one thing, innovators reap profits from the intellectual property that may temporarily protect their inventions, but as we have just noted, the economic spillovers from innovation typically dwarf profits. Historically, the more important benefits from innovation are the localized networks that it can help create. Firms in industries tend to cluster in certain locations. In the United States: high-tech in Silicon Valley, autos in Detroit, furniture in North Carolina, entertainment in Los Angeles, securities and banking firms in New York, insurance companies in Hartford. In the rest of the world: software programming in Bangalore, India; consumer electronics in Taiwan and Japan; fashion in Italy, to name a few. Locations hosting vibrant economic activity and innovation develop largely by serendipity, but once one or two firms in a location in a particular industry (or industries) become successful, they attract labor and entrepreneurs, and other services and suppliers, who build thicker and thicker networks, which in turn help spawn other new firms. Those who fear the rise of scientific advance in India and China, wittingly or unwittingly, base their logic on this virtuous cycle of development: if either or both of those countries (or some other economy) somehow gets "ahead" in an existing or new sector, America's growth rate allegedly will suffer.

Such fears cannot be dismissed, but they are overstated in our view, for at least two reasons. One consideration is that in the age of the Internet, location may not be as advantageous in the future as it has been in the past. Indeed, India owes its current and likely future high-technology success to the "death of distance" created by high-speed satellite-based communications that allow processing and programming to be performed while employees in client countries are sleeping and then zapped back to their sources at the end of the Indian work day, just when clients elsewhere are just waking up. With the Internet, networks increasingly are becoming untethered from geography, and thus so should innovation.

The second mitigating factor is that whether or not India, China, or some other country takes a lead in one or more particular sectors, living standards in America or any country, for that matter, depend as they always have on rising productivity *at home*. America (and all other countries) should take advantage of innovations developed elsewhere and use them then to develop something new or adapt them to the local market—just as other countries have done with our innovations for decades. *Innovation is a positive-sum exercise, not a zero-sum game.*

COMMERCIALIZING UNIVERSITY INVENTIONS There is also an important interaction between government funding of basic research and patent rewards that should not overlooked. Much government support of R&D in the United States, in particular, is provided to university-based researchers. Until 1980, it was not clear what rights those universities, or the researchers themselves, had to obtain patents on discoveries that followed from this research. Under one line of thought, it could be argued that those rights belonged to the government, since it after all had provided the funding.

But this was and is a shortsighted view. The ultimate aim of government research is to benefit society, and to do that, discoveries in the lab must find their way into the marketplace, ideally as quickly as possible. In 1980, the United States Congress acknowledged, through passage of the Bayh-Dole Act, that the best way to do this was to assure that universities had the right to patent innovations developed with federal funding (in turn, universities typically share a portion of the licensing royalties they receive on these patents with the professors who come up with the innovations). Bayh-Dole marked an important watershed in innovation policy in the United States and is credited by some with encouraging more rapid diffusion of university-based discoveries. Yet, as we discuss in chapter 8, the law is not working as well it could. This is especially important given the increasing sophistication of modern technology and the likelihood that high-growth businesses of the future will be technology based.

REWARDING IMITATION Not all ideas from innovative businesses need to be new *but instead just new to particular environments and locations*. Countries in the early stages of economic development cannot realistically be expected to grow by originating ideas for new products when it is easier and less expensive for them to adapt technologies and products already in use in other settings for use at home. Indeed, according to 1999 data published by the United Nations (the most recent year for which such data were available), just two countries—the United States and Japan—received more than 50 percent of the world's patents (United Nations, 2003). If the rest of world is to avoid falling hopelessly behind, other countries must find ways of availing themselves of as much of this intellectual property as they can.

There are several ways to do this: by importing products that embody cutting-edge foreign technology, by attracting foreign investment from abroad, by sending residents abroad for training and hope they come back, or by just stealing the technology. We do not dwell on last option other than to note that piracy of intellectual property is a well-known problem (especially, it seems, in China) and one that continues to be at the top of the trade agendas of the rich countries that try to stop it.

Much of Asia has followed the first option—importing technology embodied primarily in capital equipment and using it with local, low-cost labor to manufacture goods for export to third markets. Of course, export-led growth has worked primarily because the United States has been so willing—at least up until now—to be the world's consumer of last resort. Furthermore, eight successive "rounds" of international trade negotiations have brought tariff rates down to single digits in most other countries, which has allowed poorer countries to catch up through exports.

To be sure, export-led growth is not necessarily an entrepreneurial strategy. Most Asian countries that have succeeded with it have done so with a heavy dose of state guidance. India is an exception. The Indian government is notorious for having attempted to micromanage its economy, except in the fields of software development and call center operations, where the government looked the other way as entrepreneurs used first-world communications technology and highly trained local talent to become world leaders in services exports (Srinivasan, 2005). In effect, these sectors were lucky and benefited from benign neglect. As we suggest in the next chapter, the rest of India could benefit from a similar form of "neglect."

Many developing countries have been more resistant, primarily for reasons of national pride, to adopting the second strategy for importing ideas—welcoming foreign direct investment (FDI). China is a notable exception. Its national and provincial governments compete to land investments by foreign companies, often in joint ventures that entail the transfer of foreign technology. In 2002, China became the world's leading destination of FDI, passing the United States. Ireland is another major FDI success story. Once the poor cousin of Europe, Ireland dropped its corporate tax rate in the 1980s to 12.5 percent and then watched as foreign multinationals poured money into the country, making it a launching pad for sending goods and services to the European Union. By 2004, Ireland's per capita income was only 10 percent below that of the United States. Israel, too, has benefited greatly from foreign direct investment, as well as from an influx of technology "embodied in people" through the emigration of nearly two million Russians, many of them highly educated.

A number of countries have tried and are still using the third strategy—allowing, and indeed encouraging, their nationals to go abroad to be trained in universities of developed economies, returning home with first-world skills. Japan and Korea used this approach with much success, and both have been followed by India and China. India's expatriates are unusual in that many of them have remained abroad, especially in the United States, where they have gone on to found or work in high-technology start-ups. Indeed, between 1980 and 2000, Indian and Chinese immigrants accounted for an astonishing 30 percent of the successful startups in California.[10] As we noted in chapter 4, India's "human capital bet" is now paying off now that many Indians are returning home, either part-time or full-time, to participate in that country's high-tech boom.

American immigration policy has become much more restrictive since the terrorist attacks of September 11, 2001, but this hasn't stopped developing countries from sending their best and brightest abroad. Rather, some of the destinations are different: universities in Australia and Europe have been filling some of the void created by the drop in foreign students accepted by the United States. In chapter 8, we suggest that American immigration policy can safely reverse course and should actively welcome foreign students—assuming they still want to come.

Disincentives for Unproductive Activity

The evil twin of entrepreneurship is *unproductive activity* that detracts and even subtracts from an economy's income and wealth. By unproductive activity, we broadly mean to include both unlawful and lawful efforts to redistribute the economic pie rather than to contribute to the growth of the pie. Examples of the former, of course, are theft or bribery (or other forms of corruption), which have had such a clearly destructive social and economic impact that virtually all societies condemn them with criminal sanctions. Lawful redistribution or "rent-seeking" can be pursued either by lobbying governments for special benefits that help narrow interests rather than society as a whole, or through litigation that shifts resources from one pocket to another without effectively deterring undesirable behavior. One particularly egregious form of such activity entails misuse of the antitrust laws to undermine competition rather than to preserve it, as intended. This happens when a firm, finding that its inferior products or its inefficiency condemn it to failure, takes its competitive battle out of the marketplace and into the courtroom, complaining (falsely or on questionable evidence) that a rival has engaged in "predatory" behavior. In the United States, lobbying and litigation are not only lawful but are protected either by the Constitution or by specific statutes.

Whether or not redistributive activity is lawful, it almost always has the effect of leaving the overall size of the economic pie not just unchanged but actually diminished in size. Where the negative effect is small, as it may be for redistributive tax systems that aren't too onerous, it can be tolerated if society deems the improvement in equity worth the negative effect on overall growth.[11] Indeed, when income and wealth are too unequally distributed, then economies are at risk either of oligarchic elites dominating policy or of populist backlashes, both of which are inimical to growth.

But when the objective of entrepreneurial activity is narrowly redistributive—to the entrepreneur and not for large portions of society—then we can find no defense for it. Indeed, if left unchecked, the quest for this kind of redistribution, at its worst, can so reduce the size of the economic pie that the result can be grinding poverty. The corruption that has plagued a number of African economies demonstrates this. In earlier times, when military means were used to effect redistribution—with the spoils to the winning army—the results of the battle for share could be seen in ravaged land and in massive loss of life. World history, unfortunately, is littered with too many examples of this form and outcome of redistribution: when Rome and Greece ruled the world, throughout the Renaissance, and through much of the twentieth century.

Unfortunately, there are no magic recipes for minimizing unproductive entrepreneurship other than to effectively outlaw clearly destructive criminal behavior that should be stopped. A society in which theft is not punished will soon no longer be a "society" but instead a disconnected set of individuals, each fearful of the other, a true "Hobbesian" state of nature. As for lawful rent-seeking, there is no way in a democracy to halt it, though certain measures may inhibit its growth.

Lest readers come away from this discussion with too much pessimism, it is important not to overlook the good news: though lawful redistributive activities continue to take place, they are less prevalent in the world's wealthier countries than they used to be. In the Middle Ages and the Renaissance and in China in the early twentieth century, warlords were powerful, acting essentially as robber barons who kept society in turmoil, often destroyed outputs, ravaged crops and communities, and engaged in large scale murder and mayhem in order to extract ransoms, capture properties, and garner the wealth of others in any other ways they could devise. Although the warlords may still hold sway in places such as parts of Afghanistan, in much of the world this kind of lawless activity has been effectively curbed. Similarly, once kings could be expected to reward their favorites with patents of monopoly, lands, and even marriage forced upon wealthy widows, but between the Magna Carta and the Statute of Monopolies of 1623 such practices were largely eliminated in England, with other now-wealthy societies soon following suit.

It is reasonable to infer that this narrowing of the scope for redistributive entrepreneurship played an important role in the birth of the innovative societies of the past two centuries. As the doors to the unproductive path to wealth acquisition were (partially) closed, the enterprising were driven toward more productive avenues. If it is correct, as we argue below, that wealth-enhancing institutions become stronger as societies grow richer, then there is hope that this virtuous process will continue in economies that are now rapidly growing.

Keeping the Winners on Their Toes: Playing the Red Queen Game

It is not enough to induce innovative entrepreneurs to form businesses if we want entrepreneurial economies to keep growing. Once entrepreneurs succeed, it is vital that they or, more likely, the managers who succeed them be induced to keep innovating, rather than turning to rent-seeking to protect themselves from competitors, especially disruptive technologies (such as electricity or the Internet) that can quickly and radically change the competitive landscape.

This is the fourth condition for growth at the cutting edge. In Lewis Carroll's felicitous phrase, the aim should be to ensure that the winners in the competitive race run as quickly as they can in order to stand still. Or, as one economist has put it, entrepreneurial economies must ensure that their firms are constantly engaged in a "Red Queen game," in which every player's success depends on his or her ability to match or exceed the current efforts or expenditures of rivals, so that each is forced by the others to bid ever higher (Khalil, 1997). Where this kind of competition does not occur, winners are likely to be content to rest on their laurels. If they do, innovation slows down or even ceases, as will growth itself.

An analogy to military arms races is instructive. In medieval times, every king seemingly was forced into an arms race in which the ante was constantly raised, with innovation relentlessly raising costs. Stone castles replaced wooden castles and were not only more costly to build but far more costly to besiege. Gunpowder and artillery in the mid-fourteenth century increased the cost of fortification. The sociopolitical innovations that led the kings to become less dependent on vassals to man their armies forced them to pay their military, often purely mercenary troops, which added significantly to royal expenses. The predictable consequence of this military Red Queen game was that the kings were almost always seriously short of funds. For whenever they did manage to scrape up enough to proceed on military enterprises with little financial hindrance, this merely invited ratcheting of the arms race up yet another notch, so by the inherent character of the "game," any amount that seemed sufficient on one day was sure to be woefully inadequate in the next.

Thus monarchs found themselves perpetually underfinanced, heavily in debt and unable to find willing lenders, and reduced to distasteful expedients, to beg for a bit here, wheedle or extort a bit there. Indeed, much of medieval history is a story of battles—not the supposedly glorious clashes of arms, but battles between the kings and the subjects from whom the monarchs hoped to draw their funding. As some historians have put it, they were "pauper kings."

Fortunately, there is a happy and peaceful ending to this (truthful) parable about military Red Queen games. One consequence of the unceasing chase for money was that kings desperate for funds were forced into recognizing the rights of the individual. This process began in England and spread to the United States and eventually to much of Europe. To be sure, the process was a gradual one. Rights first were granted to the magnates (the fewer than ten earls and less than one hundred barons in England at the time of the birth of parliament), and then to towns and the commons (the upper middle class, the knights, the landowners, and the wealthier town residents). Furthermore, some kings found it necessary to turn to commerce rather than funding themselves with taxes and wartime booty. This made commercial activity—indeed *entrepreneurial activity*—respectable for members of the English nobility.

All of this helped lay the foundations for the future free-market economy and its remarkable productivity and record of growth. Indeed, the evolution of the rule of law—which predated the evolution of democratically chosen representatives—arguably was the single most important contribution to the birth of entrepreneurial capitalism. But the rule of law by itself does not guarantee that Red Queen game scenarios will continue to play out in modern economies, especially since they could not function without having large, established companies operating alongside the new, entrepreneurial firms that are more likely to be the agents of true economic change.

How then can the winners of the competitive race be motivated to keep innovating, whether incrementally or radically? Or, at the very least, how can society prevent the winners in one round of economic competition from thwarting the next generation of entrepreneurs who threaten to topple the previous winners? We consider here two institutions that would seem essential for this task: antitrust law and enforcement and openness to international trade and investment. We will take up a third important institution referred to earlier—the law and practices surrounding the transfer of new technology out of university laboratories and into the marketplace—in chapter 8, where we look ahead to ways to keep winners on their toes in all capitalist economies.

ANTITRUST Ask many microeconomists (and many plaintiffs' lawyers) how society can best assure continuation of Red-Queen-style competitive races in markets where only a few winners are left standing, and they will utter four words: "enforce the antitrust laws." We will not digress here to discuss these laws, which have become common throughout the developed and much of the developing world (though unevenly enforced), in great detail. For our purposes it is sufficient to highlight three common themes that run through these laws: that competitors should not be allowed to fix prices (except in rare circumstances where joint activity is necessary for products or services to exist, such as common royalties for copyrighted works); that mergers between firms already dominant in concentrated markets ought not to be allowed; and that firms with "market power" (those with the ability to set prices on their own rather to accept the impersonal verdict of the market) should not be allowed to abuse that power through exclusive arrangements and other behavior having no legitimate business purpose that cements their market position.[12]

These objectives are important, but we add our own caution from experience: it would be a mistake for nations, and for those who lead their economies, to place too much faith in antitrust laws as a way to ensure that Red Queen innovation races continue.[13] To be sure, antitrust law remains important to prevent naked price fixing among competitors and to halt mergers that would unduly concentrate certain markets. But antitrust is much less effective when it comes to keeping the true "winners"—*those who earn a position of market dominance or even monopoly*—in the competitive race.

In theory, of course, the antimonopolization provisions of the antitrust laws (Section 2 of the Sherman Antitrust Act in the United States) are supposed to ensure this outcome by preventing current monopolists from abusing their market power or would-be monopolists from attempting to monopolize their markets through conduct that has no efficiency justification. If the provisions work, monopolists should not be able to nip competition in the bud, though the laws cannot force monopolists to devote their extra profits to innovative activities. Indeed, if monopolists enjoy their market power because of economies of scale or because the economies of networks drive the market toward a single competitor—as long appeared to be the case with landline telephone service, for example—then they may be able to live a "fat and happy life" for many years. But eventually technology changes or consumer tastes change, and monopolists must innovate or die. That is what wireless telephone service has done and is currently doing to the local landline telephone providers. And if homegrown technology does not come along, foreign technology may be needed prod to monopolists to change their lazy habits.

Can antimonopolization antitrust enforcement do any better in the meantime? We are skeptical based on the U.S. experience with these efforts over the past several decades. During this time, the Justice Department has mounted four major antimonopolization cases: one each against AT&T and IBM and two against Microsoft. The IBM case was dropped after thirteen years of investigation and trial. The government settled the AT&T and first Microsoft case and "won" the second Microsoft case after a trial and several years of litigation over the appropriate remedy.

Academics and policy makers may debate for years the value of these cases. We each have our views on these cases but do not seek to settle scores here. Rather, we make only a simple point: that even in the cases the government won or settled, it took many years to reach that outcome—

eight years for AT&T, five years for the first Microsoft case, and another six years for the second one. These are not short spans of time. In each case, administrations and lead prosecutors changed and so did their approach to pursuing the cases, and technology marched on, and that was far more likely to undo the target monopoly than any legal action. AT&T's monopoly in long-distance telecommunications, for example, ultimately would be undercut by wireless telephone service. Microsoft's operating systems monopoly remains intact in the personal computer market, but it is being undone by "open source" technology for servers.

Did antitrust speed up change? Probably yes, but antitrust also had its costs, and not just in time and effort spent or in attorneys' fees on both sides. In each case, mangers of the target of the antitrust action became heavily focused on the litigation and almost certainly gave shorter shrift to their business in the meantime. The management of IBM was so diverted that by the time the case was dropped, the company looked to be deeply off track. (It was perhaps not a coincidence that during this period the company did not get an exclusive license to the personal computer operating system then being marketed by a little-noticed upstart named Microsoft.) All this is to say is that policy makers would be mistaken to count on antimonopolization enforcement alone to ensure that monopolies are forced to play Red Queen games.[14]

WELCOMING TRADE AND INVESTMENT If antimonopolization legislation and enforcement have limits in rich countries that have the resources and expertise to apply to the exercise, as well as large markets that render a limited role for "natural monopolies" (those for which, due to economies of scale or network effects, the most efficient industry structure is a monopoly), then antimonopolization efforts are likely to be less important for motivating winners in smaller, less rich countries. Fortunately there is an alternative and, we believe, ultimately more effective policy, not only for smaller, less developed economies but for larger, richer ones as well: openness toward trade and investment.

Competition from imports can prod domestic firms that may be getting lazy to actively participate in Red Queen–like innovation. For proof, just look to the American auto industry, which after World War II was dominated by three large companies (and one little one). In those days, consumers were lucky if their cars lasted more than three years because they weren't built to last, nor were they built to economize on fuel. When the first oil crisis jolted the world in 1973–74, the American consumer was only too ready to embrace the once-looked-down-upon Japanese imports, which were far more fuel-efficient and, as it turned out, superior in many other dimensions as well. Japanese imports woke up the U.S. manufacturers, who began improving the quality and fuel efficiency of their cars.

But the U.S. auto companies also engaged in the time-honored practice of rent-seeking in response to the Japanese threat, persuading U.S. policy makers (the free-market Reagan administration no less) to put "voluntary restraints" on Japanese imports during the 1980s. If the automakers thought this would take off the competitive pressure, they were sorely disappointed. Faced with curbs on their exports, the Japanese auto companies established their own plants here. The incoming foreign direct investment, which thank goodness U.S. policy makers did not stop, kept the pressure on the domestic manufacturers to continue improving their products.

The welcome sign to FDI did even more. When the Japanese manufacturers came here they brought with them their now famous "just in time" (JIT) production system that cut inventories of supplies and in the process shaved costs off the production of cars. The Japanese also brought their "quality circles" that encouraged line workers, and not just managers, to make productivity-enhancing improvements. American companies across the economy, not just the auto companies, took the lessons to heart. Dell Computer, for example, eventually became the country's leading PC manufacturer, largely on the strength of its JIT production system. And General Electric's famous "six sigma" quality campaign, endlessly promoted by the company and a bevy of management consultants ever since, essentially was borrowed from the emphasis on quality that the Japanese, ironically, had been taught by an American "quality advocate," Edward Deming (who was a prophet without honor in his own country for a long time).

The United States' experience, in other words, demonstrates that even economies at the so-called technological frontier can benefit significantly from open borders—to goods, ideas, and people. If the developing world needs a similar example from the ranks of its own, it need look no further than Hong Kong, a once poor city-state without any natural resources that on a per capita basis has become one of the world's economic powerhouses (even after it was absorbed by mainland China in 1997). Hong Kong achieved its success by attracting FDI primarily in the financial sector, and in the process it has become the financial hub for Southeast Asia. Ireland has followed a similar strategy, becoming not only a financial gateway to continental Europe, but also a research and manufacturing outpost for some of America's leading high-tech companies. The challenge that countries built on FDI face in the future is to take the next step and develop their own home-grown entrepreneurs.

Yet openness as a policy instrument has its limits too. Just as the potential losers from antimonopolization enforcement efforts tend to do all they can to resist, taking advantage of every trick in the legal book available to them to delay the outcome and outlast the prosecutors (as Microsoft essentially did), the "losers" from an open trade and investment policy do not sit back quietly either. As we will discuss in chapter 8, their efforts may be blunting the force of foreign-based competition to stimulate the Red Queen games of the future. That is why effective safety net policies for dislocated workers due to all sources are important, if not critical. This is another theme we previewed in the last chapter and will develop further in our concluding chapter.

Other Factors—or the "What Abouts?"

In addition to the four broad ingredients reviewed above, four other factors have been or might be asserted as essential for economic success at the frontier: culture, education, macroeconomic stability, and democracy. We do not dispute that each of these factors can enhance growth, but we do not include them in our list of basic factors for either or both of two reasons. First, none of these supplemental "what abouts" are essential for implementing each of the four basic ingredients. Indeed, some of them—such as culture and democracy—may be outcomes of the four basic institutions rather than their antecedents. Second, none of the four "what abouts" are unique to either big-firm or entrepreneurial capitalism, or, ideally, the right blend of the two.

Culture

In his masterful survey of all of the factors that have contributed to economic growth around the world and through history, David Landes, one of the world's leading economic historians, eventually reaches a disarmingly simple conclusion: "If we learn anything from the history of economic development, *it is that culture makes all the difference.* (Here Max Weber was right on.)" In other words, some countries grow more rapidly than others because their cultures are more conducive to growth. By implication, this must mean that culture is the defining characteristic for entrepreneurial success. As Landes continues: "Witness the enterprise of expatriate minorities—the Chinese minorities in East and Southeast Asia, Indians in East Africa [Landes could have added the United States], Lebanese in West Africa, and Jews and Calvinists throughout much of Europe" (Landes, 1999, 526). In her own thoughtful book on a related topic (globalization), Amy Chua adds Korean expatriates in the United States and Jews in Russia and the United States as additional examples of how culture matters (Chua, 2003).

The "culture-is-everything" view is deeply pessimistic for policy makers because it essentially implies that there is nothing they can do in their relatively short tenure to influence long-run growth. A country's people either work hard or they don't. Either they are creative, inventive, and entrepreneurial, or they are not. And there essentially is not much, if anything, that government can do about it.

Fortunately, we believe history is inconsistent with this policy pessimism. There are too many examples of countries turning their economies around in a relatively short period of time, a generation or less, and certainly shorter than the cultural view would imply: China and India over the past two decades (for many, though admittedly by no means all of their populations); Ireland over roughly the same time period; and over somewhat longer periods, much of Southeast Asia. These successes cannot be squared with the cultural-is-everything view. Indeed, at various points the same culture that allegedly contributed to growth was blamed for disappointing economic performance in China (Confucianism was said to be inconsistent with entrepreneurship and hard work) or, more recently, for contributing to the Southeast Asian financial crisis of 1997–98 (apparently the "Asian values" that up to that point had been so successful also led to "crony capitalism," which some observers blamed for the crisis).

Indeed, by pointing to the success of certain ethnic groups outside their home countries, Landes and Chua unwittingly demonstrate that culture is *not* everything, that the institutional environment clearly matters. Indians and Chinese were not successful in their home countries until relatively recently because governments there did not reward entrepreneurial success; to the contrary, they stifled it. When given the opportunity, Jews have left countries where they were oppressed and have migrated to places that offer them routes to economic success. And Arab Americans have significantly outperformed their brethren in their home countries. Indeed, as Moises Naim reports, Arab Americans are better educated and wealthier than average Americans (Naim, 2005a).

This isn't to say that culture is unimportant, for clearly it can matter. We nonetheless have not added culture to our list of defining characteristics of entrepreneurial economies because cultural characteristics clearly have played a role in enhancing the growth of state-guided economies as well, such as those in Southeast Asia or China. Even the state-favored firms in these countries have been run by entrepreneurial individuals who, though they may be more replicative than innovative, clearly have a strong work ethic and an eagerness to learn from other economies. Similarly, the large firms of Japan and Europe have benefited from what seems to be a cultural commitment to quality and craftsmanship that have made their goods so prized throughout the world.

But cultures favoring craftsmanship or replication are not equivalent to those that prize risk-taking, and so it still may be true that an "entrepreneurial culture" plays a distinctive role in entrepreneurial economies. Columbia University economist Edmund Phelps, in particular, has argued that one reason for Western Europe's sluggish economic performance over the past several decades is that its culture is not sufficiently conducive to risk-taking. As for Europe's success after World War II, Phelps attributes this to the transfer of American technology, noting that when that process was more or less complete, European growth slowed down and has never recovered. At bottom, Phelps wonders whether the anti-entrepreneurial culture is so embedded in Western Europe that it would resist transformation by any institutional reform.[15]

Phelps may be right about Western Europe, but it may also be premature to assume that future policy changes would have so little effect. After all, there is evidence from other parts of the world where culture can be and has been heavily influenced by institutions (or, as economists would say, that culture is "endogenous"). In particular, people once thought to be lazy and ill-suited to entrepreneurial endeavors suddenly can be looked on as industrious and creative once incentives reward those virtues. Look at the turnaround in Eastern Europe or at the postwar history of the Southeast Asian economies. Or consider the somewhat remarkable shift toward entrepreneurship in Russia, a country where enterprise was thought to have been snuffed out by more than seven decades of communist rule. In a survey taken of a random sample of entrepreneurs and nonentrepreneurs in Russia over the 2003–4 period, a team of scholars found that Russian entrepreneurs were more than twice as likely to have had family members running a business (in the 40–50 percent range) than other Russians (Djankov et al., 2005). We find this a clear demonstration of how in a society where formal entrepreneurship was not allowed until 1986, entrepreneurial activities have taken root in less than two decades through the same channel—family background—as one sees in highly entrepreneurial societies like the United States.

In short, we draw a different lesson from history than Landes. Policies and institutions matter; they can have a strong impact on "culture" in a period much shorter than a full generation. Put the right institutions in place, and people from all walks of life and backgrounds will respond, though admittedly perhaps because of history (so Phelps and presumably others would argue), some more than others.

Education

It seems obvious—perhaps especially to noneconomists—that as societies become more educated, or more accurately, as their labor forces become more *skilled,* they should grow faster. In the Solow growth model, for example, added skills in a society are implicitly reflected in additional labor. A highly trained technician, for example, may be the equivalent of two untrained laborers. So, economies should grow more rapidly as their workers gain more skills.[16]

Early economic research on the economic role played by education quantified the financial rate of return an individual could realize by spending additional time in school. In essence, "education" was defined by an "input," namely, the number of years spent in school, rather than as an "output," or how much workers actually knew. In any event, these studies, on the whole, demonstrated that, at least in the United States, the rate of return on time spent in school, specifically whether individuals went on to college, was quite low in the 1960s and 1970s. But starting in the 1980s, the gap in earnings between high school- and college-educated workers began to grow, so that the returns to a college education grew markedly. The conventional explanation for the turnaround is that technological advances drove the demand for skilled workers faster than the rate at which they could be turned out.[17] Other economists have pointed out that education yields benefits to society beyond those that can be captured by individuals themselves. More educated people are not only more informed citizens, thus improving the working of democracy, but a more educated society should produce more innovation, thus enhancing growth.

Economists in the United States have not been alone in extolling the virtues of education. Various multilateral organizations—UNESCO, UNICEF, the United Nations, and the World Bank—have all pointed to the important role that education has in reducing poverty and contributing toward stable, tolerant societies. Indeed, in 1990, the World Conference on Education, convened by most of these bodies, set universal primary education as a goal for every country by the year 2000 (a goal that has been missed by many countries) (Easterly, 2001, 71–72).

There is one problem with this emphasis on education as a key explanation of *different growth rates across countries*. When various economists have attempted to find a statistical correlation between the amount of schooling and economic growth (controlling for other factors affecting growth) in various countries, they haven't been able to find one (Easterly, 2001, 73–84; Bosworth and Collins, 2003). To be sure, other economists have come to a different conclusion (Mankiw, 1995), especially if skills are measured by proxies of educational *quality*, such as test scores (Barro and Sala-i-Martin 2004, 537). Nonetheless, our reading of the studies as a whole is that the statistical verdict on the contribution of education to growth is still out.

There is an old saw that defines an economist as someone who tries to prove that something that works in practice works in theory. Maybe the education-growth nexus is an example. Indeed, given our criticisms of cross-country regressions in chapter 3, it may not be surprising that the statistical studies that attempt to discern a link between education and growth are so mixed. Statistical studies cannot find what would seem to be obvious: that education matters for growth, period.

But then there may be a good reason for the murky picture. There are too many examples of highly educated countries where economic performance has been miserable. The former Soviet Union and the Eastern bloc countries boasted excellent primary and secondary educational attainment for much of their populations, but as the world has come to know since the Berlin Wall fell, those economies were in much poorer economic condition than many Western analysts had thought. Those nations were producing the equivalent of excellent parts for an economic engine that itself was fatally flawed. Without contract and property rights, there could be no entrepreneurs. In the end, the socialist economies essentially wasted the resources they poured into educating their populations (with the exception of space flight and certain military applications of scientific advance, where the Soviet Union was world class).

In his thorough study of economic growth, William Easterly points to another anomaly. As of 2000, when he finished his analysis, Easterly reports that while poor countries substantially expanded their education investments over the 1960–2000 period, the median growth rate of these countries steadily declined over these years (Easterly, 2001, 74). Literacy may well have improved in many of these countries, but corruption and military violence, among other factors, can offset any growth-enhancing impact of education.

We do not want to be misinterpreted. We are not asserting that education is irrelevant to growth or to improving the workings of national societies (whether or not they are governed democratically). Education indeed may have contributed to growth in the past in some countries, but that only proves that education is a *necessary but not sufficient condition for economic advance*. The institutions must be right for education to work its magic, just as the most brilliant baby will not grow up to be a brilliant adult without appropriate nutrition and training. Moreover, if education has spurred growth in certain parts of the world, that does not make it a peculiar feature either of entrepreneurial or big-firm capitalism. Economies that have been guided by the state have also benefited greatly from having better educated workforces.

We have two other observations on this subject. Assuming that, under the right institutional conditions, education is an important factor for a growing economy, an open question is whether economies earn a greater return overall from concentrating their educational investments among the elite, or whether a more universal approach is better. India has followed the former model, most other Southeast Asian countries the latter one. India's approach is responsible for its great and growing success in information-technology-related businesses, but this sector accounts for only about 2 percent of the country's output and labor force, though some forecasts have it accounting for as much as 7 percent by 2008 (Srinivasan, 2005). Hundreds of millions of Indians remain poorly educated. In contrast, Southeast Asian countries like Korea and Taiwan put greater emphasis on providing universal primary education when they were at similar stages of economic development. This strategy equipped much larger fractions of their labor forces with skills to work in labor-intensive manufacturing facilities, which several decades later have become not only state-of-the-art, but fountains of innovation. Clearly, the universal education strategy is more equitable than the targeted approach followed by India. It will remain an open question for some time whether the targeted approach produces greater gains in national income.[18]

Our second point is that, whatever one may believe about the contribution of economic growth under any capitalist system so far, education is likely to become even more important a factor for growth in the future, especially in economies at the frontier. Until as late as the 1970s, the proverbial inventor in a garage without an advanced education could come up with commercially useful innovations, some of them quite radical. The greatest American inventor of all, Thomas Edison, did not complete high school. Even into the 1970s it was possible for two high school graduates, Steven Jobs and Steven Wozniak, to build a personal computer quite literally in a garage.

But there is reason to believe that those days are gone. The founders of some of the leading Internet-based companies—Amazon, eBay, Google, and Yahoo—all were college graduates; some had graduate training. Looking ahead, it seems far-fetched to believe that future commercially applicable advances in biotechnology, nanotechnology, or information technology will be made by high school–trained, garage-based inventors. To the contrary, innovations in these sectors, along with others, are likely to be developed either in university settings or by individuals with advanced university training. Since, for reasons already explained, entrepreneurial economies are more likely than those guided by governments or managed by large firms to generate the radical innovations that will spawn great leaps in future living standards, it follows that the future innovative entrepreneurs, as well as those running the big enterprises that successful entrepreneurial firms eventually will become, will be highly educated. In the future, therefore, education is likely to be more critical for economic success than ever before.

Macroeconomic Stability

As we implied in our first chapter, of all the advice that many countries have received about running their economies, the Washington Consensus set of remedies has commanded the field. Yet most of the consensus suggestions are concerned with stability first, then growth. The notion is that if countries get their macroeconomic policy house in order, they will be less susceptible to seemingly periodic financial crises. And without crises, they have a much greater chance of growing.

We do not dispute these basic propositions—indeed, they are essential—but they are not unique to any particular form of capitalism. Any capitalist economy, however it is structured, should want stability and the best way to assure this is through some combination of budgetary discipline (small deficits, if any, in relation to GDP), noninflationary monetary policy, and since the Asian financial crisis, some degree of exchange rate flexibility (or, failing that, a buildup in foreign exchange reserves).

But good macroeconomic policy grades do not assure economies will grow at their maximum rate in *the long run*. For that, we submit that our four conditions are far more relevant. Using a distinction often made by many economists, macroeconomic stability is essential to keep aggregate demand close to or equal to a society's maximum potential output, but the four preconditions play a larger role in determining how fast that potential output will grow.

Democracy

There has been a long bipartisan tradition in the United States favoring democracy—free election and the rule of law—as the best form of government. In the early twentieth century, President Woodrow Wilson wanted to make the world "safe for democracy." President John F. Kennedy urged the nation to "pay any price, bear any burden" in pursuit of democracy (and in fighting its nemesis, autocratic communism). President George W. Bush justified the war in Iraq, in part, on the need to establish democracy in the Middle East. The United States has not been alone in this quest for democracy. The European Union requires new members to have functioning democracies before they integrate economically.

Yet is democracy essential for the establishment of the four key ingredients for growth at the cutting edge? That democracy can be important for growth is difficult to deny. Political freedom is likely to enhance economic freedom and, in particular, to insulate the rules favoring entrepreneurship from removal at the whim of an autocratic leader who may change his or her mind about what is best for an economy.[19] Furthermore, well-functioning democracies are likely to reject oligarchic capitalism, since leaders of oligarchic societies cannot survive if they serve larger slices of a shrinking pie to only a few. Instead, democracies are driven by the need of their leaders to remain in power to expand the pie itself—that is, to enhance economic growth.

But is democracy *necessary* for these rules? Experience suggests otherwise. The remarkable economic growth of China attests to the fact that entrepreneurship can and has flourished under autocratic rule. Would China grow faster under democracy? Probably yes. Indeed, one recent study argues persuasively that, on average, democratically ruled countries, even those that are less developed, tend to grow more rapidly than autocracies (Halperin et al., 2005). But even this study does not demonstrate that democracy is *essential* for growth (though it effectively rebuts the opposite view, expressed by a number of analysts, that autocracy is a precondition for economic development, up to a certain point).

Now, ask the question the other way around: does economic growth lead to democracy? Certainly the experience of South Korea, which for decades after World War II was essentially a benevolent autocracy but eventually became a democratic form of government, supports this view (Glaeser et al., 2004). As incomes grow, so does a country's middle class, which is more likely and able to demand political freedom. Conversely, there is ample evidence that countries already democratic are likely to backslide from that form of government when their economies perform poorly. It is striking, for example, that three-fourths of the collapses of democracies since 1977 were preceded by stagnant growth.[20]

But skeptics remain about the inevitability of democracy following strong economic growth. China has become a flash point. To some, continued growth in China may only strengthen the hand of the state and make it easier to deny political freedom (Bueno de Mesquita and Downs, 2005). Or as China gains economic strength, it will have more resources to pursue expansionist military objectives. At this point, of course, it is impossible to know whether the optimists or pessimists will prove to be correct about China. Our own view is that the odds are with the optimists—namely, that economic growth eventually will help democratize China, as it will other countries—but there can be no guarantee of this result.

One reason for being optimistic is to look to America's early history and especially the experiences of many of the country's founding fathers, which demonstrate that business skills can hone the talents needed to achieve and maintain self-governance. Benjamin Franklin, one of the authors of the Declaration of Independence, left copious writings describing how he had developed his diplomatic skills in the course of establishing himself as a printer. Paul Revere, a silversmith, was a consummate networker who used business contacts to coordinate the revolutionary effort. Alexander Hamilton, who managed a clerical office while still in his teens, later applied those skills to organize the Department of the Treasury. Even Thomas Jefferson, Hamilton's adversary, who argued that America should remain a nation of farmers, was hardly the stereotypical rustic at the plow. He managed a sizable plantation and sought more scientific ways to cultivate it. In short, he was much like the best American entrepreneurs: a striver and learner, often brimming with ego and unconventional opinions, but civic-minded and, in the end, a farsighted philanthropist. In short, the experience of economic freedom seems to breed both the skills and the inclination for political freedom.

China's business leaders may not be able to steer their country in the same way. But does that possibility mean that other countries—the United States, in particular—should do their best to thwart economic growth in China (or in other autocratically ruled countries, for that matter)? In our view, such a course is a recipe for a much more dangerous world. Autocrats who are shunned by rich countries would thus be given easy scapegoats for their countries' poor economic performance. The politics of "blaming foreigners" has a long and unfortunately successful history. Why give autocrats such easy ammunition?

We believe the better course is to urge autocracies at least to recognize economic rights—in particular, the ability to start a business and to be rewarded if successful. The odds, in our view, suggest that political rights eventually will follow.

Conclusion

In this chapter, we have laid out what we believe are four essential ingredients for maximizing growth by economies at or near the frontier. In other words, these conditions need to be met if an economy wants to maximize the odds that it will generate and commercialize radical innovation. In brief, governments must make it easy for entrepreneurs to form businesses; they must see to it that these entrepreneurs stand to earn handsome rewards if they are successful; they should heavily discourage unproductive "entrepreneurship"; and they should see to it that entrepreneurs or their successors are not allowed to rest on their laurels but instead are motivated by continuing Red Queen games to continue innovating and commercializing. If political leaders are able to ensure the presence of these preconditions, they are likely to generate the blend of big-firm and entrepreneurial capitalism that we believe will best enhance growth in the long run.

This isn't to say that other factors—culture, education, macroeconomic stability, and democracy—will not also enhance economic growth. Clearly they will. But in our view, these other factors are not unique to big-firm or entrepreneurial capitalism. Governments that want to guide their economies can benefit from having each of these factors in place. Furthermore, some of these factors—culture and democracy, in particular—are just as likely to be the products of the four basic preconditions as they are to be their precursors.

We also do not mean to imply that the four preconditions apply only to big-firm and entrepreneurial capitalism. Countries whose economies are heavily guided by the state can benefit from having institutions in place that promote entrepreneurship and Red-Queen-style competitions. Indeed, we believe that state-guided economies eventually must find ways of transitioning toward a blend of big-firm and entrepreneurial capitalism for a simple reason: at some point, the opportunities for imitation, the predicate for state guidance, will have been exhausted. At some point, economies must innovate rather than simply replicate. That is when state guidance will have run its course.

6

UNLEASHING ENTREPRENEURSHIP
IN LESS DEVELOPED ECONOMIES

Readers of this book surely have seen the horrifying depictions of famine and disease in Africa on television and very likely are aware that despite the amazing record of economic growth in much of the world, more than two billion individuals spread across the world still live on the equivalent of less than $2 per day. The striking failure of governments in these countries, as well as of international agencies that have tried to help them, to remedy this should haunt us all and caution those, like us, who seek ways to do better.

Nevertheless, suppose you are called in to advise the leaders of a developing country who aspire for it to grow. What can you tell them with any degree of conviction? In essence, the purpose of this chapter is to offer answers to that question, but with an appropriate degree of humility. We take our cue largely from the nations that have *not* failed to grow and, perhaps incidentally, whose success in at least some cases was achieved without planning, with little or no central direction, and via the happenstances of history, working through the powerful incentives emanating from the impersonal workings of the marketplace. Although the lessons from these experiences admittedly are not entirely clear and unambiguous, they do appear at least to tell us that one indispensable ingredient of success was entrepreneurship and an environment that encouraged its activities, offered it security and incentives, and minimized the obstacles to its exercise. This chapter, in short, focuses on steps that offer hope of transforming economies in which the arrangements and the rules of the game impede or even preclude the work of the productive entrepreneurs toward new regimes where these elements have been reversed.

In setting out our argument, our central focus, unlike other prescriptive books on the general subject of growth, makes no attempt to lay out a comprehensive set of steps that should be undertaken by an informed and responsible government that is hunting for ways to accelerate economic progress. Rather, much of the discussion will be about broad approaches to attaining a regime that can be relied upon to move matters in the required direction. We pay particular attention to how economies whose course is determined by government ministries or powerful oligarchies can transition toward new regimes in which economic developments are driven primarily by market forces and the activities of productive entrepreneurs.

We preview our argument here before delving into the details. First, regardless of the state of their economic development, all less developed countries can benefit by promoting entrepreneurship, of both kinds we have so far outlined: *replicative,* in the sense that technology should be borrowed from abroad, typically by accepting foreign direct investment; and *innovative,* through so-called bottom-of-the-pyramid product and service innovations adapted to the unique circumstances of individual developing economies (and for countries at later stages of development, through adaptation of cutting-edge products and services currently designed for rich country markets, firms, and consumers).

Second, it is unrealistic to expect the more successful state-guided developing economies, including the former developing countries that used state guidance to approach living standards of the industrialized world, suddenly to embrace all the principles of entrepreneurial capitalism outlined in the last chapter. Nonetheless, there are opportunities for these economies to introduce these policies *at the margin,* or *incrementally,* in fashions we discuss here.

Third, growth is most difficult to accomplish in oligarchic economies, some of which are very poor and others that are richer on average, but where incomes are highly unevenly distributed, as discussed in chapter 4. The simple reason is that for countries to grow, it is essential for their leaders to want that result and to be prepared to work for it. Since, by our definition (and most likely theirs too), oligarchs do not give the highest priority to economic growth, there are realistically only two broad options available for such countries: revolution from within or outside pressure from other countries to induce constructive change, which is tantamount to encouraging revolution. As it turns out, recent decades have provided several examples of peaceful, even quasi-democratic, revolutions. Some have resulted in economies that have entrepreneurial characteristics; others have moved their countries toward some variation of state guidance. Ironically, the more recent "populist" revolutions in Latin America, in particular, have their seeds in opposition to the United States, both its foreign and economic policies. We do not view these developments as unequivocally undesirable, however, since it may be necessary for countries that were once oligarchic to adopt some form of state guidance as a way station toward more entrepreneurial forms of capitalism. It is still too early to judge.

Fourth, though there are good theoretical reasons why foreign aid may be able to raise growth rates, especially among the poorest nations of the world where starvation and disease are regrettably all too common, in practice, the evidence for this proposition is decidedly mixed. If, and this is a big if, foreign aid for public goods—such as health systems, sanitation, roads, and communication infrastructure—can, in fact, be delivered in a way that promotes these ends, then it has a constructive role to play. But even then, aid must be viewed only as a short-term development strategy. Eventually, developing countries, even the poorest ones, must find ways to *grow on their own*. This will require the kinds of institutions outlined in the last chapter; the more quickly these are developed, the more rapid will be the alleviation of human suffering that prompts the well-intentioned call for more foreign aid to jump-start growth.

Finally, the growth of so-called micro-credit financial institutions throughout the developing world (and even in some parts of the developed world) in recent decades is a significant phenomenon whose importance cannot be ignored and that illustrates the sort of measure that can be sought as an effective means to facilitate the development process. Micro-credit has enhanced the formation of many small businesses, especially those owned by women, that otherwise would not have been formed. But as should be clear to readers from our previous chapters, these small businesses overwhelmingly are more replicative than innovative. Nations that spawn thousands, if not millions, of such small businesses may find this to be a useful strategy for alleviating poverty and, indeed, for jump-starting the growth process. But businesses backed by micro-credit are unlikely to be major engines of sustained economic growth, especially if the micro-lenders themselves continue to be subsidized primarily by funds from governments or nonprofit organizations. Micro-businesses launched by micro-loans, by definition, are too small to realize the economies of scale that only larger enterprises, whether home-grown or foreign, can achieve. The ultimate challenge for developing countries is to encourage larger, more established financial institutions to lend to enterprises that have a chance of growing to be larger firms—in other words, to move beyond the "micro" stages of lending and business formation.

Before outlining the logic that lies behind each of these broad conclusions, it is instructive to begin by defining terms: what is meant by a "developing country"? We explain next why a steadily stronger dose of entrepreneurship is necessary if developing countries are to achieve sustained economic growth and maximize the rate at which they close the gap in living standards with richer countries. We then examine a number of different models that developing countries can pursue. We close this chapter with some thoughts on how foreign aid and the new apparent silver bullet in development circles, micro-credit, can and cannot contribute to the catch-up process.

What Is a Developing Country?

The notion that some countries are "developed" and others are not has been with us for some time, at least since the end of World War II, after which many nations formed a specialized entity—the World Bank—with the specific mission of furthering the economic development of most of the countries in the latter category. Over the years, various words (at least in English) have been used to describe countries where average living standards of the population are far below those of rich countries like the United States. The terms include "developing" or "less developed," or simply "low income" or "poor."

Over the past sixty years, much has changed. Many of the countries that were once "poor" or "developing" are no longer so, having climbed the "ladder of economic development." Familiar examples, of course, are those in Southeast Asia, especially Japan, which was economically prostrate after the war. Indeed, so was Western Europe, which today boasts living standards close to those of the United States, where the median family income as of 2005 was roughly $45,000. In addition, economists today now speak of a host of "middle-income" or "emerging market" countries—those with per capita incomes typically in the $4,000 to $15,000 range. Examples include many of the "transition economies" in Eastern Europe, Turkey, and Chile. Some analysts group both middle- and low-income countries together as "developing countries" (World Bank, 1993), while others preserve the distinction between the categories, and indeed pay special heed to the poorest of the low-income countries, those where average purchasing power is less than $2 per day (Sachs, 2005).

Whatever the term, the typical metric used to evaluate where countries stand on the ladder of economic development is per capita income. To take account of different currencies, the income measures are typically converted to their dollar equivalents, using either market exchange rates or market rates adjusted for differences in purchasing power within countries (so-called purchasing power parity, or PPP, exchange rates). Table 10 provides an illustrative list reporting where a sample of different countries can be found on the economic development ladder, as of 2003, based on PPP exchange rates.

While we recognize that per capita income levels are significant measures of economic progress, they are not the only ones. For one thing, they do not account for factors that affect life but are not traded in markets—such as the quality of the environment, the stability of families, personal safety, or health. In addition, per capita measures, by definition, are averages. They do not reveal anything about how evenly or unevenly incomes or wealth are distributed among populations.

Of most importance to us here, however, are the paths by which countries that are not at the economic frontier can most rapidly catch up to those that are. In this chapter, we will focus on the countries that are furthest behind—those that are "developing" or "less developed." This category includes both those in extreme poverty—many of the countries in Africa, for example—as well as such rapidly growing economies as China and India, where hundreds of millions of residents still live in extreme

Table 10 Per Capita National Incomes (Purchasing Power Adjusted, 2003 Dollars)

Country	Per capita $US 2003
High	
Australia	28,780
Belgium	28,920
Canada	30,040
Finland	27,460
France	27,640
Germany	27,610
Japan	28,450
Switzerland	32,220
United Kingdom	27,690
United States	37,750
Near high	
Greece	19,900
Israel	19,440
Korea, Rep	18,000
Kuwait	19,480
New Zealand	21,350
Portugal	17,710
Slovenia	19,100
Middle	
China	4,980
Costa Rica	9,140
Gabon	5,500
Mexico	8,980
Peru	5,080
Philippines	4,640
Poland	11,210
Russian Federation	8,950
Saudi Arabia	13,230
Thailand	7,450
Argentina	11,410
Low	
Bangladesh	1,870
Cambodia	2,000
Cameroon	1,990
India	2,880

Source: World Bank, 2005 World Development Indicators (Washington, D.C.: International Bank for Reconstruction and Development/ World Bank, 2005).

poverty. We will also draw lessons from some countries that were once in this category but have since grown to middle-income status or higher.

The Many Paths to Economic Development (or Lack Thereof)

Americans or many Europeans who might have read our book (had it been written) in the eighteenth or nineteenth centuries probably would have had difficulty understanding our typology of capitalisms, though they probably would have understood what we mean by "entrepreneurship" (or at least the terms "adventurer" or "undertaker," which were the corresponding terms then in use). Most economic activity was agricultural, and those who tilled the land typically owned it (save for the slaves in America and serfs on the other side of the ocean) and thus were classic replicative entrepreneurs. So too were the owners of the retail shops and manufacturing firms located in the heart of urban areas. There were few big firms of the kind that are so prominent in the economic landscape today. And although governments handed out licenses or charters, they did not "guide" their economies in the sense in which we have used the term—by favoring specific industries and firms over others, explicitly for the purpose of advancing growth.

In short, in America and through much of Europe up to the twentieth century, entrepreneurial capitalism was the order of the day—not because of any government design, but rather, more or less, by accident. Entrepreneurial capitalism emerged from scratch, as it were, since neither what we have labeled "state-guided" nor "big-firm" capitalism had yet emerged. (Although some countries that recognized property rights also had high concentrations of wealth and were governed by an elite, and thus their economies could have been characterized as early examples of oligarchic capitalism.) Other examples of countries that are rich or near rich today, which one could say also started as entrepreneurial, include Canada and Australia, not coincidentally both offshoots of Great Britain (like the United States). But like the United States and Western Europe, both of these countries were at or close to the economic frontier before the Depression and, later, after World War II.

Perhaps most important for our purposes is that in all of the rich country models where entrepreneurship flowered from scratch, the formation of the requisite institutions—enforceable contract and property rights to ensure that entrepreneurs would keep the fruits of their risk-taking, legal and other institutions to curtail corruption, and the development of human and physical infrastructure (education and public roads, in particular)—evolved gradually and incrementally. There wasn't some "big bang" event that instituted all of these preconditions at the same time. Nor did the technologies and methods of production that the entrepreneurs developed suddenly emerge all at once. Instead, like Isaac Newton's observation that scientists in each generation stand on the shoulders of giants, the technological frontier moved out incrementally, at different rates in different years, but cumulatively at such a pace to enable living standards to double about every twenty-five or thirty years.

Things changed radically after World War II, a war that had horrific human consequences and also devastated much of the world, except for the United States. After the war, the world divided ideologically between those countries that were on one side of the "iron curtain," and whose economies practiced some form of capitalism, and those on the other side, where economies were centrally planned. Coincidentally, some but not all of the capitalist economies were also democracies (others were authoritarian and only later developed democratic forms of government), while the centrally planned economies all were authoritarian and dominated by a single communist party. Readers, of course, know that, throughout much of the postwar era, the leaders of these two camps, the United States and the Soviet Union, competed for allies, hoping to persuade countries that had not already committed to one form of government and economic system to adopt its model. Readers also will know that capitalism and democracy ultimately, largely won. (We say "largely" because today there are not only two holdout communist countries, Cuba and North Korea, but a number of countries in the Middle East that remain authoritarian, though capitalist in some form, as well as other "failed states" that effectively have no government and where the economic order is, at best, "precapitalist.")

Our interest here, however, is in the various forms of capitalism that seem to have been adopted in the postwar period by countries that did not follow or were not forced to follow the central planning model of the Soviet Union and China. Roughly speaking, they fall into the four broad categories we outlined in chapter 4:

- Countries that chose some form of state guidance, principally the Asian "Tigers" and India;
- Countries that have exhibited some form of oligarchic capitalism, or much of Africa, Latin America, and the Middle East;
- The rare countries, like Taiwan, that encouraged entrepreneurial capitalism and largely (like the United States) eschewed state guidance, except to promote broadly the development of industries or sectors that offered opportunities for exports;
- The Western European and Japanese economies, which initially embraced entrepreneurship and welcomed foreign investment after the war but eventually tolerated and even nurtured the growth and later dominance of large firms.

In addition, after the Berlin Wall fell, the centrally planned economies of Eastern Europe, the former Soviet Union, and China moved at different speeds toward different types of capitalism. All seem to be works in progress, with different combinations of state guidance (principally state ownership of banks), large firms favored by the state (or subunits of the central state government, such as provincial or local governments), foreign multinationals, and domestic entrepreneurs.

The Misplaced Lure of State Guidance

Looking across all these models, it is tempting to conclude—based largely on the superior growth records of the Asian Tigers but also, more recently, on the remarkable growth record of China—that developing countries that want growth (oligarchs are an important exception to this, as we will discuss soon) should embrace some form of state guidance if they too want to catch up rapidly to the rich-country frontier. Indeed, the very presence of richer countries seems to invite some form of state guidance by poor countries, which seemingly need only to replicate the promising targets provided by those richer economies: activities or industries that are labor-intensive and thus susceptible to competition from firms in locales with access to workers who accept much lower wages but are easily trained and strongly motivated, provided the domestic firms can gain foreign technologies and the necessary capital equipment. Guidance by the state also is attractive to ruling elites and government bureaucrats not only because their power is elevated when they seem to be or actually are "running" the local economy, but also because permission to launch and conduct business, when required by the state, opens up opportunities for bribes, providing an additional source of income for them. But before leaders of developing countries embrace state guidance as a silver bullet to the growth challenge, we urge them to consider several caveats.

First, the evidence does not support the view that detailed economic guidance by the state—that is, directing aid or providing appropriate approvals to some sectors and firms and not others—adds to growth, above and beyond what can and has been generated by high domestic savings and generally sound government policies that support growth (such as the provision of universal education, prudent macroeconomic policies, and protection of rights of property and contract) without attempting to "pick winners." In fact, in one of the World Bank's more widely known studies of this subject, this is just what a team of its economists concluded in seeking to explain the remarkable growth through 1993 of the countries in East Asia, including the so-called Four Tigers (Hong Kong, South Korea, Singapore, and Taiwan), China, and the three "newly industrializing countries" (NICs) of Southeast Asia (Indonesia, Malaysia, and Thailand). As the report stated: "Private domestic investment and rapidly growing human capital were the principal engines of growth (in these countries). . . . In this sense, there is little that is 'miraculous' about the [East Asian] countries' superior record of growth." But as the report acknowledged, these fundamental policies "do not tell the entire story." The report emphasized the importance of institutions—strong property and contract rights—but was skeptical that targeted state interventions appreciably increased growth, despite widespread belief to the contrary. It concluded: "Some important government interventions in East Asia, such as Korea's promotion of chemicals and heavy industries, have had little apparent impact on industrial structure. In other instances, such as Singapore's effort to squeeze out labor-intensive industries by boosting wages, policies have clearly backfired. . . . *On the basis of an exhaustive review of the experience of developing economies during the last thirty years, [a previous World Bank re-*

port, in 1991] concludes that attempts to guide resource allocation with non-market mechanisms have generally failed to improve economic performance" (emphasis added) (World Bank, 1993, 5, 9–10).

Second, since the World Bank's landmark study, the growth experience of India, in particular, provides strong evidence that state guidance can be more of a hindrance than a stimulant to growth and that random or accidental events—so often characteristic of entrepreneurial success stories— can fuel the expansion of a world-class entrepreneurial sector and, in turn, advance growth of the entire economy. Partially as a legacy of British colonial rule and partly as an outgrowth of the economic philosophy of its first leader, Jawaharlal Nehru, India's economy for several decades after independence was a model of detailed, intrusive guidance by the state. For almost every type of economic activity—not just opening a business, but buying and installing a rudimentary piece of equipment—some sort of government approval was required. Information technology (IT) related fields, such as software coding and development and later international call-center operations, were an accidental exception to this pattern, and in retrospect many Indians surely must be thankful that they were.

But India's rise to IT prominence could not have occurred without a series of deliberate decisions and "accidental" events whose ultimate consequences, in each case and especially in combination, would have been difficult if not impossible to have predicted at the time. For example, in the 1950s and 1960s India's leaders wanted to produce more home-grown scientific and engineering talent, and they did so by establishing and supporting what eventually became some of the world's finest schools of engineering, now turning out tens of thousands of highly trained Indian engineers a year. But it is doubtful that the policy makers who created these schools could have foreseen where they would eventually lead: the creation of entrepreneurial enterprises in the computer software, data-processing, and call-center businesses (such as Infosys and Wipro) that rank with the best of the world. Perhaps just as impressive are the large numbers of Indian expatriates who have gone on to found many high-tech companies in the United States. One indication: whereas Indians ran 3 percent of Silicon Valley start-ups in the 1980–84 period, they were running 10 percent of those launched between 1995 and 2000 and probably an even higher share since. Several Indian expatriates have become leaders of the

Silicon Valley venture capital industry, and in recent years they have been active in helping to launch similar enterprises in their home country. Although critics note that the Indian IT sector—and the cities associated with its growth, Bangalore, Hyberadad, Mumbai, and New Delhi, to name a few—accounts for a small fraction of the country's GDP and employment, India's Ministry of Finance projects that the value added by the IT sector will account for as much as 25 percent of India's economic output by 2020 (Srinivisan, 2005).

Other factors, even more accidental in nature, have contributed to the "Indian miracle." Perhaps most important has been the rise of the Internet, a development whose ramifications have yet to be fully realized and appreciated and whose consequences were not recognized, as late as the mid-1990s, even by Microsoft cofounder Bill Gates. Yet except for call-center operations, virtually nothing in India's IT sector would have been possible without the instant communications capability afforded by the Internet. Another factor is that for the most part, the Internet's common language has been English (although this is gradually changing and will continue to change in the future). Indians speak, write, and communicate in English and so were well positioned to take advantage of the opportunities afforded by the Internet when they arrived.[1]

To be sure, India's apparent success is not without its skeptics. Domestically there are complaints that now that the IT sector has grown so rapidly, the Indian government should pay more attention to the growth of the rest of the economy, manufacturing and agriculture in particular. Indeed, it is far from clear whether India would have done better had it followed the Southeast Asian model with respect to education—ensuring universal primary education rather than concentrating on a relatively small elite, focused around IT. Whatever one may believe the answer to be, there is little doubt that extending primary education throughout the country, along with building infrastructure, will be India's main economic and social challenge going forward.

Taiwan's postwar success also illustrates how a broader trust in entrepreneurship paved the way for that country's remarkable growth record after the Chinese civil war of the late 1940s. Taiwanese leaders recognized the need for growth but did not attempt to pick specific industries or firms to promote. Instead, they took the view that the best way for the government to assist growth would be to promote the growth of firms in *export industries,* through financing, tax incentives, and an exchange rate policy (carried out by central bank purchases of the U.S. dollar) that has kept the Taiwanese dollar undervalued relative to foreign currencies. The government also made it relatively easy for new firms to start and grow, and it subsidized the education of its talented students to study abroad, principally in the United States, where they could pick up the know-how to help run entrepreneurial ventures upon their return home. With a cheap currency, and a policy environment conducive to the formation and growth of new ventures, largely component manufacturers supplying foreign multinationals, Taiwan has become a vibrant hub of manufacturing and innovation. Indeed, over time, some of these manufacturers have moved up the development ladder to design and produce entire products themselves, marketing them elsewhere under global brands. Eventually some of these companies probably will become global brands themselves and no longer will need direct connections with foreign multinationals.

Meanwhile, the country's central bank has used the export revenues generated by successful Taiwanese companies to buy U.S. dollar debt, keep the value of the Taiwanese currency low, and thus facilitate the virtuous circle of export-led growth. By 2005, Taiwan's central bank held nearly $300 billion in foreign currency reserves (invested largely in U.S. securities). The country's per capita income stood at roughly $28,000 per year, putting it close to the level of leading countries of Western Europe and Japan.

Even mainland China's rise to economic power during the past two decades does not support the view that detailed state guidance is necessary for economic success. On the surface, this admittedly does not appear to be the case since China looks like the quintessential state-guided economy, one where the central government seems to allocate investment funds, through the country's main state-owned banks, to favored enterprises in selected industries. Furthermore, there are some sectors of the Chinese economy, notably energy and agriculture, which are directly managed or owned by the government and thus continue to be centrally planned, to the widespread detriment of the population. In the case of energy, state control means that the country's citizens have no control over the temperature in their residences, schools, or places of work and thus live and work much of the year in either uncomfortably cold or hot surroundings. As for agriculture, the Chinese government still leases rural land for up to thirty years and thus has not given its peasants clear title to their land, which reduces incentives for investment and improvements in agricultural productivity. It also contributes to the widening income disparity between the urbanized half of the country in the bustling and growing cities and the other half of the population living in rural areas mostly in poverty.[2]

Nonetheless, Chinese leaders over the last two decades have found a unique way to introduce and encourage entrepreneurial activity in an economy that once was centrally planned. Whether by design or by necessity, Beijing has decentralized economic and political decision-making to the provincial and municipal governments, which in turn have used their expanded freedom to engage in productive ventures as well as to grant licenses, incentives, and other favors to certain local privately owned "champions" (which are often purchased with "side-payments," or less politely, bribes) (Segal, 2005). Importantly, however, at the same time, Chinese government officials have tolerated the formation of countless numbers of other entrepreneurial ventures that have sprung up largely in the eastern, richer half of China, and by at least one measure, small- and medium-sized enterprises by 2003 accounted for half of the economy's GDP.[3]

The Chinese model may be a unique case, however, since other developing countries (with the outlying exceptions of Cuba and North Korea) do not have a legacy of central planning. In addition, China has advanced despite not fully having two of the ingredients for a successful entrepreneurial economy that we highlighted in chapter 5: effectively enforced property and contract rights, and a financial system that affords entrepreneurs access to capital to finance their ventures. The Chinese legal system is still a work in process, to put it charitably, and formal financial institutions—mainly the official state-owned banks—do not lend to new ventures, but instead have continued to funnel money to state-owned enterprises (though this should change as state banks will be privatized in 2007 as part of China's commitment to join the World Trade Organization). As a result, Chinese entrepreneurs typically borrow from informal lenders or investors (including families and friends) to back their enterprises (Dam, 2006). Below, we will suggest that informal law and finance eventually will reach their limits and that for Chinese entrepreneurship to move to the next stage, the country will have to develop more formal ways of doing business. Already foreign investors have demanded greater formality, and as more Chinese firms do business with them, formal law and finance should gradually spread to the rest of Chinese enterprise.

Indeed, China owes much of its economic success to the welcome mat its leaders have put out to foreign investors. And investors have responded, pouring ever-increasing sums, talent, and know-how into the country. By 2004, China had become the leading destination in the world for foreign direct investment (FDI)—that is, "sticky" investments in plant and equipment or at least significant minority stakes in domestic firms—attracting more than $60 billion in that year alone. One of the amazing things about China's success in this regard is that foreign investors have continued to rush into China, although legal protections for contracts and property, and the courts that support them, are far from ideal, and corruption reportedly is pervasive (Wei, 2001). The best explanation we can give for this oddity is that China's large and rapidly growing domestic market makes the country "too big to pass up" so that investors appear more than willing to wait for the legal and institutional systems to improve. China's agreement to make necessary changes, and to open further parts of its economy that have been sheltered from foreign investment (notably, financial services), as part of its entry into the World Trade Organization gives investors reason to believe that their hopes will be realized (although in 2006 there were disturbing signs of a potential backlash against foreign investment, especially takeovers of Chinese firms by foreign investors).

Somewhat ironically, poor countries that want to emulate China's success in attracting foreign direct investment will have to take measures that, as a by-product, should foster domestic entrepreneurship in their own countries. Foreign direct investment has long been very unevenly distributed around the world, being concentrated in rich countries and in only a selected handful of developing or emerging market economies. For developing countries that have not been prime destinations for foreign investment to have any chance at cracking into this select circle of destination countries, their governments will have to take steps to make foreign investors feel welcome. At the top of this list are such essentials as enforceable rights of contract and property and a minimum of corruption. Having a suitable supply of trained labor, made possible by widespread primary and secondary education, also is necessary. As it turns out, these elements are also essential to promoting domestic entrepreneurship.

In short, the examples of India, China, and Taiwan provide striking evidence supporting the World Bank's finding that state guidance is not the silver bullet for accelerating economic growth that some of its advocates may believe. Rather, economies grow because individuals and the firms they form are the engines that turn labor, capital, and technology into products and services that consumers, inside countries and beyond, want and are willing to pay for. Firms, in turn, just don't appear from nowhere. They are started and nurtured by entrepreneurs, who take on often seemingly unimaginable risks. Countries that want to grow cannot overlook this simple but powerful fact.

We want to be clear that our critique of detailed state guidance does not mean to include state efforts to attract foreign direct investment, either broadly or of a particular type. As we note at various points in this book, foreign investors can accelerate the growth of the countries to which they commit their funds, both by adding to the capital stock of those economies and, perhaps even more importantly, by transferring skills and know-how to the residents of those economies. It takes a sound legal system, some amount of physical (or increasingly, communications) infrastructure, and a reasonable degree of political stability for foreign investors to be interested.

But not all foreign investment is the same, and countries that have made efforts to attract it have had very different strategies and impacts, as Georgia Tech political scientist Daniel Breznitz has recently demonstrated (Breznitz, 2006). Most destination countries in the developing world (and in developed economies, for that matter) have concentrated on attracting foreign companies to build manufacturing plants, which employ, relatively speaking, large numbers of local residents and which over time often lead to process innovations in the host country. But only when efforts are made to encourage those plants, once built, to buy components and services from other domestic companies, as has happened in Taiwan, will local governments rapidly spur the development of local entrepreneurs. In contrast, Israel has pursued a very different strategy for attracting foreign investment, seeking not so much manufacturing but rather for foreign companies to locate their research and development activities within

Israel, while these companies (American in particular) manufacture elsewhere (either at home or in other locations). Breznitz argues that this knowledge-intensive FDI strategy leads more to product than process innovation, and relative to the manufacturing strategy, employs fewer people. As a result, the product innovation approach is associated with greater income inequality than is the process approach. Nonetheless, the Israeli strategy seems to put the country on the cutting edge, perhaps because of spillover benefits of enhanced R&D within the host country. India and China are making great efforts to attract foreign R&D activities to their economies as well and at this writing seem headed toward success.

The Benefits of Entrepreneurship for Poor Countries

For poor countries today, the examples of countries that have succeeded without state guidance or that have expressly abandoned it may not seem relevant for any number of reasons. India or China, for example, with their billion-plus residents and potentially huge markets for rich-country multinationals, may seem unique. Or Taiwan may seem like a special case because of its close ties to the United States. Or leaders (and residents) of countries where incomes are so low that they seem to be caught in a "saving trap"—a term coined by Columbia's Jeffrey Sachs—may see little hope for spawning locally based entrepreneurs who can power their economies' growth. Such despair, to the extent it exists, certainly is understandable, but it is also misplaced. Even in poor countries, facilitating entrepreneurship is a sound strategy—and arguably the best strategy—for accelerating economic growth.

Perhaps more than anyone else, management scholar C. K. Prahalad has made a powerful case that ample opportunities exist for entrepreneurs in or from developing countries to design and sell products and services specifically tailored for their residents (Prahalad, 2005). Among the many examples of bottom-of-the-pyramid innovations and successful commercial enterprises are cheap mobile telephones and service, countless brand-name consumer products that are sold in small units easily purchased by poor residents, and "smart" automated teller machines that enable individuals who cannot read to access financial services.

One especially successful bottom-of-the-pyramid entrepreneur whose activities are beginning to attract notice is Iqbal Quadir, a native of Bangladesh, who emigrated to the United States and eventually became a (presumably well-paid) investment banker and, now, an academic scholar. Quadir helped started GrameenPhone, a joint venture with Grameen Bank. Grameen-Phone allows for multiple users of a single cellular phone, which makes it inexpensive for many poor Bangladeshis to use. Quadir argues that by allowing Bangladeshis to avoid wasted trips, by making it easier to look for work, and by widening peasants' access to markets, cellular phones are contributing as much, if not more, to Bangladesh's GDP than any foreign aid channeled to the country. Quadir is not alone in his optimism about the benefits of mobile phones and their use in developing countries. According to researchers at the Progressive Policy Institute, by 2015 the continent of Africa should have more mobile phone users than the United States.[4] Meanwhile, at this writing, Quadir is attempting to use similar bottom-up and inexpensive technology to generate electricity and to provide clean water, at a more rapid pace and less expensively than if attempted top-down by government.[5]

Quadir's entrepreneurship may not have been ignited had he not left Bangladesh for the United States, which illustrates one way rich country economies can indirectly contribute to bottom-of-the-pyramid development strategies. A more direct route occurs when multinational companies headquartered in rich countries develop versions of their products for developing country markets. And that is exactly what an increasing number of them have been doing. Procter & Gamble and Unilever are two consumer products companies, for example, that have successfully introduced mini-versions of their various consumer brands—even poor residents in developing countries are highly brand conscious (no doubt due to global communication and advertising)—in numerous developing countries. If Prahalad is right, more global companies, especially those marketing information technology equipment and software, should be following similar strategies with their products in the future (Mohuiddin and Hutto, 2006). Indeed, the race is on among numerous manufacturers and entrepreneurs to develop inexpensive personal computers or "thin clients" (that would work with servers) for purchase or lease by the billions of residents of developing countries.

Bottom-of-the-pyramid strategies are inherently focused on developing products and services for domestic consumers residing in developing countries. But another, not mutually inconsistent, form of innovation looks out to manufacture or provide services primarily for foreign purchasers. In the standard development story, those countries that have been successful in doing this—and there are many, the Asian Tiger economies being prime examples—have been powered either by multinational companies that locate their plants or offices in developing countries and use them as export platforms, or by home-grown entrepreneurs who license or just copy foreign technology and use domestic, lower-cost labor to export to third country markets. As we discuss shortly, this formula requires hospitable domestic institutions to attract foreign investors or to encourage domestic entrepreneurs to launch and grow their enterprises, and it seems to be key to the success enjoyed by the Asian Tigers in lifting their people out of poverty.

In fact, in recent years, some entrepreneurs in such developing countries as India and China have moved beyond simply replicating products or services developed abroad and are now designing their own process and product innovations destined for markets in richer countries. An increasing number of multinational companies have taken notice of this turn of events and are now moving their own R&D functions to India and China, to take advantage of the talent pool these countries have to offer, at a substantially lower cost than using research staff in rich country locales. Recent advances in computing and telecommunications make this far easier to do than in the past. India's software centers, for example, are famous for processing huge volumes of data while Americans and Europeans sleep. And researchers throughout the world use the Internet to collaborate with each other, accelerating the design and production of new products and services.

In sum, the rapid development of India and China is not irrelevant to poor countries today. The Indian and Chinese experience provides a powerful lesson to all developing countries: sooner or later, economic development, even in supposedly poor countries, eventually requires a healthy dose of entrepreneurship.

Summary

We trust readers are by now convinced, or at least are sympathetic with the view, that state guidance is not the silver bullet for growth acceleration that some advocates seem to believe it to be. But even those economies that may have pinned their growth strategies on some forms of state guidance, and believe that this has been successful, have several reasons for wanting eventually—we believe the sooner the better—to facilitate the emergence of home-grown innovative entrepreneurs.

For one thing, governments that guide their economies and attempt to pick "winners" (firms or industries) in the process often get it wrong, for any number of reasons. Firms (and their governments) in other countries may do a better job. Or the firms in the industries chosen by governments practicing state guidance may prove unable to turn their state-provided advantages into commercial success because their activities are constrained by bureaucrats with little market experience. Furthermore, states that may, for a time, successfully steer their economies can't guide everything. There are sectors or industries that grow up without direct government support, and, indeed, the more such sectors there are and the more successful they become, the faster any economy—even one where state guidance plays a significant role—will grow. India's rise to prominence in information-technology-related activities provides one highly visible example.

In short, like parents who eventually must let their children leave home and fend for themselves, governments must sooner or later let the businesses that develop, with or without government support, fend for themselves in the global marketplace. The challenge is how to do this—that is, what specific steps are required and how fast should they be adopted?

Moving Away from State Guidance

The advantage of state guidance, where it is present in some form, is that at least the government and its leaders are apt to have some interest in promoting economic growth. To be sure, they also have or eventually acquire other motives as well: protecting the "turf" of their ministries or agencies, their power, and their jobs, among other objectives. This is why even a well-intentioned set of leaders who want to improve the living standards of their citizens nonetheless may be reluctant to abandon old practices, especially those they (strongly) believe to have been successful to date.

Nonetheless, presuming that some change is desired, for the reasons already advanced or because it has become clear that state guidance no longer is working or not advancing growth as rapidly as in some peer countries, two obvious questions arise. First, what specific steps are required to move an economy in an entrepreneurial direction? Second, at what pace should change proceed?

Elements of Reform

It will be no surprise to readers to realize that the main required elements of reform are the preconditions for entrepreneurial capitalism we outlined in the last chapter: a minimum of impediments or regulatory requirements to starting and expanding new businesses; incentives for productive enterprise; disincentives for unproductive entrepreneurship; and measures to ensure that successful entrepreneurs and, later, the larger firms they establish continue to innovate. In addition, entrepreneurial capitalism, like other forms of capitalism, is likely to be more successful the more extensive the provision for public goods, including education, roads and sanitation, and a functioning legal system. Here we use the basic framework of preconditions outlined in chapter 5 but focus on a few more concrete measures that seem particularly relevant to economies that can be characterized as primarily guided by the state.

LOWERING BARRIERS TO BUSINESS FORMATION The first and perhaps one of the more important lessons to be drawn from the experience of the recently successful economies is that productive entrepreneurs cannot be expected to appear and function unless they are allowed to—that is, only if the widely prevalent bureaucratic and other handicaps that beset the creation of new firms are significantly reduced. For several years the World Bank has been collecting detailed data on the costs of forming a business in countries throughout the world and reporting them in its annual *Doing Business* report. Although the figures change from year to year as the Bank obtains more data and as countries make efforts to reduce these costs (a commendable and important trend the Bank highlights and applauds), the Bank's findings from its 2006 report showing the countries where it is least and most costly (as a share of a country's GDP per capita), respectively, to register a business are illustrative of the problems that developing countries still have to surmount (see table 6).

Virtually all of the countries where it is easiest to start a business are developed, but all of the countries where it is most difficult are still developing if not very poor. Perhaps more disturbing is that for the second year in a row, the Bank reported that the start-up gap between rich and poor countries had widened. "Since 2003 rich countries have made business start-up 33 percent faster on average, cutting the time from 29 days to 19 days. They have cut the average cost by 26 percent. . . . Meanwhile, poor countries have reduced the time required by only 10 percent, from 62 days to 56 days. The cost remains a staggering 113 percent of (those countries' low) income per capita, and the minimum paid-up capital 299 percent of income per capita—10 times the level in OECD countries" (World Bank 2006, 11).

These are no small matters. It is not realistic to expect a substantial share of an economy's labor force to devote itself to entrepreneurship if that activity is systematically beset by impediments and booby traps. Yet the World Bank's reports illustrate how easy, at least in principle, it is to reform: eliminate the involvement of courts in business registration; do not require publication of the registration in a newspaper; introduce standardized and streamlined registration forms, with a fixed (and modest) fee; and impose a nominal or zero-capital requirement (unless the public interest unquestionably requires it, as in a newly established bank or provider of insurance). Furthermore, as telecommunications improve, allow online registration.

Taking some or all of these steps can quickly lead to results. The World Bank's 2006 *Doing Business* report documents sharp jumps in the numbers of businesses registered and increases in business investment in countries that have streamlined their business registration systems. Furthermore, as barriers to conducting business come down, informal firms no longer need to hide from the authorities and thus are able to grow to more efficient sizes, hiring more workers. Since formally registered enterprises also pay taxes, they help to fund government programs. It is thus clearly in the interests of local and national governments, as well as the wider society, to make it easier for entrepreneurs to do business.

FORMALIZING LEGAL SYSTEMS It is important not only for governments to smooth the way for enterprise formation, but to ensure that the institutional framework—and specifically the legal protection of contract and property rights—is secure. This proposition has become so well established that we feel no need to discuss it further, except to note that it is more difficult to achieve than commonly supposed. A well-functioning legal system requires an effective judicial system, including independent judges who are well trained and cannot be bribed. It also requires an effective law enforcement system, since law is nothing unless individuals and firms expect that the rulings of courts always be enforced. It is not necessary that developing countries adopt any particular set of legal institutions, whether those in the Anglo-Saxon tradition (where much, but not all, law is "common" and tends to evolve over time through successive judicial rulings), those based on Civil Code countries (where law typically is made only by some kind of legislative action or official edict), or institutions arising from some other cultural source, although there is a running academic debate over which legal system is most conducive to economic growth.[6] The key, in our view, is that whatever set of institutions is in place must be stable and viewed widely by residents and foreign investors as trustworthy, so that all parties can reasonably expect to know what the rules are when they conduct business or go about their private lives.

Getting to this point is not something that happens with a wave of the hand or through some official pronouncement; it can take decades if not generations to establish (although the Russian experience of entrepreneurial values being handed down through family relationships in less than a generation is an encouraging sign that the transition can be much shorter). This isn't to say that growth cannot happen until this occurs, just that the circle in which commercial transactions take place can widen only when parties at both ends of any bargain have a common understanding of the rules. Since growth occurs largely through trade, which permits the specialization of labor, the more rapidly this circle of trust widens, the greater will be the opportunities for growth. In effect, trust can substitute for formal legal rights, and where it works, it can be a lot less costly than reliance on detailed legal documents (Fukuyama, 1996). This helps to explain why China, which has lacked a formal legal system, has been able, so far, to defy conventional wisdom and grow as rapidly as it has.

But, as Chinese leaders are learning, trust goes only so far. As the distance between parties grows—so that seller and buyer do not know each other or may not be engaged in repeat transactions—trust becomes an inadequate substitute for law. In a world of strangers, law must be present to provide comfort and confidence to the parties that their deals will be honored and that their disputes, if they arise, will be resolved amicably, or at least fairly, through some kind of legal process. Foreign investors, in particular, will not do business in a country unless they not only know the rules of the game, but also have confidence that the rules will be enforced fairly, consistently, and expeditiously. This is why, among other reasons, China has agreed to beef up and further formalize its legal system and its courts as part of its agreement joining the World Trade Organization. The same legal institutions and protections that are developed for foreign investors inevitably must apply to domestic parties, so over time it is unlikely that China will continue to defy the conventional wisdom about the importance of reasonable and well-enforced contract and property rights for maintaining economic growth. China's legal system will become more formal, not just in name but also in enforcement (this includes the protection of intellectual property rights, a sore spot in China's relations with other countries, especially the United States).

IMPROVING ACCESS TO CAPITAL Perhaps the most visible indicator that an economy is characterized by state-guided capitalism is that much of its financial system—and specifically its banks—is government owned. There has been much progress in recent years toward the privatization of state-owned banks in many countries, developing and already developed, although there is still a long way to go in this regard. As of 2004, for example, state-owned banks served a majority of individuals in developing countries and were most dominant in China (which is well known) and also in India (which is not as well known, but where government-owned banks account for about 75 percent of all banking assets, although this share seems likely to decline with the rise of new domestically owned private banks).[7]

In principle, additional privatization should move countries further in the entrepreneurial direction, and thus we clearly side with those who encourage this. Privately owned banks are far more likely than government-owned institutions to base a decision to lend solely on the basis of commercial considerations, and for this reason they are more likely to back entrepreneurial ventures, not so much at the new firm's start-up stage (since even banks in developed countries do not do much of this) but for firms that have demonstrated some success and are poised for growth. Furthermore, as states wean themselves off government ownership of banks, they are less likely for political reasons to prop up poorly performing commercial enterprises, which will open up their economies to competition from new firms.

But the difficulties of privatization of government-owned financial institutions should not be understated. For one thing, there are the political challenges of getting such a program started. Governments used to owning banks are reluctant to give them up, as are the favored borrowers who benefit from their special access to funds. As persuasive as the substantive arguments are to us—that privatization should improve growth by steering money toward firms with better commercial prospects and away from borrowers whose easy access to money has insulated them from the competitive pressures to keep innovating—governments long engaged in state guidance are much more likely to be moved, if at all, to privatize by the potential and immediate financial gains that can be realized when the shares of the state-owned institutions are sold. In addition, in a rare case, the desire to gain broader access to global markets can push governments toward privatization. Thus, as part of the conditions for joining the World Trade Organization, China had to agree to privatize its large state-owned banks by 2007. Other countries may be tempted to sell interests in state-owned financial institutions to foreign interests as a way of gaining access to the know-how (in this case, that associated with running banks) that typically comes with foreign capital.

But there also are practical difficulties entailed in privatization itself. At the top of the list: should the government auction off the shares of the bank to the highest bidder(s), and if so, which bidders should be allowed in the auction? Clearly, domestic banks already in operation should be allowed to bid, unless the acquisitions would lead to an undesirably high degree of concentration of local banking markets (which would deprive depositors and borrowers of significant choice among institutions). Permitting nonfinancial firms to bid reduces the risk of concentration but could lead to the problem of "connected lending," or the channeling of bank funds to the subsidiaries or affiliates of commercial owners, which led to unsound loans in the run-up to the Asian financial crisis of the late 1990s. Allowing foreign financial institutions to bid would enhance competition in local banking markets and open the gates to cutting-edge technology, but it can for any number of reasons trigger significant political criticism from domestic interests who fear selling of their country's "crown jewels" to foreign interests (criticism that is not restricted to developing countries). Indeed, criticism of just this sort has begun to emerge in China, and the leadership has responded.[8] Meanwhile, if the shares are not auctioned but simply distributed to the residents of the population—much as the shares of former state-owned firms in Russia were distributed—enterprising, but potentially nefarious, individuals or groups can gather up the shares and concentrate ownership in an elite group, which may not only lead to the connected lending problem already noted, but trigger the kind of backlash against capitalism seen in Russia. In short, although we encourage governments that continue to own financial institutions to turn them over to private interests, we do not underestimate the political and practical difficulties of accomplishing the transition.

Accordingly, governments interested in promoting entrepreneurship should not limit their horizons to privatizing existing financial institutions. They should be open to the licensing of new ones, whether owned by domestic or foreign individuals or firms. Indeed, precisely because foreign firms are likely to have more experience and cutting-edge know-how and technology than domestic residents, governments should be especially welcoming to them.[9] Governments concerned about undue political opposition to foreign acquisitions of existing institutions can minimize this problem if foreign institutions are allowed to enter developing country markets only by establishing new firms or branches of their home offices. An objection may be raised that foreign banks traditionally have not shown much interest in financing local entrepreneurial ventures, preferring instead to lend to the local operations of home country firms or to larger companies in the countries they enter. This criticism does not take account, however, of the strong interest foreign banks are likely to display in consumer credit card lending, a market that has yet to be significantly developed in emerging economies. Many credit card borrowers in developing country markets can be expected to use their credit cards to start businesses, just as they do in the United States and other developed economies.

Of course, developing countries must have the capacity to oversee the safety and soundness of newly chartered banks, in particular, skills that even bank regulators in developed countries still have not mastered (though there has been much improvement since the rash of bank failures in the United States and other developed economies in the 1980s and early 1990s).[10] Since the financial crises of the late 1990s, the International Monetary Fund and World Bank have worked together closely to provide technical assistance to aid developing countries in this essential endeavor.

EDUCATION Finally, although an educated workforce is not a magic answer to the growth puzzle, it is a necessary (though not sufficient) condition for rapid growth. After all, in the standard neoclassical growth model, for example, education increases economic output by enhancing "human capital," but only if the right institutional conditions are present to ensure that firms have incentives to make use of the additional skills. As for the link between education and entrepreneurship, to the extent there is one, it works through at least two channels. Education that both imparts knowledge and gives students the ability and confidence to recognize and act on commercial opportunities may well, eventually, lead more of them to be entrepreneurs at some point in their lives, again assuming the institutional incentives are in place for this to happen. Furthermore, by equipping students—and then adults—with the ability to read, to reason, and to solve problems, education makes individuals more productive on the job throughout their lives, which gives local entrepreneurs an available local pool of labor to draw from and thus greater incentives to start and grow their entrepreneurial ventures.

Countries have fundamentally two ways in which they can educate their citizens, either "widely" or "deeply." Because the resources of developing countries, especially the poorest ones, necessarily are limited, they are likely to be able to pursue only one of these strategies. Only later, as their level of prosperity rises, can they afford to pursue both.

The "wide" or "universal" approach seeks to provide roughly the same basic education—ideally through the equivalent of high school—to a country's entire population. Public or private funds may support universities, but this is not where the country puts its main emphasis, at least initially. Instead, some countries that have followed the universal model have essentially outsourced university-level or graduate education for their best students by subsidizing them to attend universities abroad—historically in the United States but increasingly in institutions elsewhere (Australia, Canada, and Europe).

In contrast, the "deep" approach concentrates on educating the most talented individuals at home, in domestic universities, while giving somewhat less attention to universal education (perhaps by limiting the number of years of basic instruction made available to students of lesser ability). To do that, the universities themselves must be funded, their physical facilities must be constructed, and their faculties must be developed, either at home or through education abroad. For poor countries, the most efficient course, at least initially, is to send a core group of their most talent potential faculty members for training abroad (with monetary incentives to ensure their return) and then have the initial cohorts train new cohorts.

It seems reasonably clear which countries have followed each of these two very different approaches to creation of human capital. Asian and Eastern Europe countries have pursued the universal model, seemingly quite successfully. Students in primary and secondary schools in these countries generally rank quite high in international tests of mathematics and science achievement. Literacy rates for these countries also are among the highest in the world. In contrast, India provides the best example of a country that has pursued the "deep" or "elite" educational approach. Although it has taken several decades to accomplish, India has managed to create some of the finest engineering universities in the world. Access to them is strictly based on merit, and the annual examinations of high school students for placement into the top schools are major life events not only for students but also for the schools, neighborhoods, and cities in which they live. India also took the gamble that by letting some of its most highly educated individuals emigrate to the United States, some of them eventually would return to found or fund businesses in their home country. Although it took several decades for the results to come in, by now they have. The gamble has paid off, and many returnees are helping to build the Indian economy (Saxenian, 2006).

The Chinese approach to education stands somewhat between these two extremes. The country does an outstanding job educating its most innately talented students, especially in technical subjects, in primary and secondary schools, and it is investing heavily in university-based education, though its graduates do not yet seem to rank with those from the best Indian establishments. It is quite possible that this will change in coming years, although much may depend on how rapidly the Chinese government moves away from its authoritarian model, since scientific advances are more likely to flourish in environments that promote freedom of thought and expression. In this respect, India will continue to have an advantage over China because of India's embrace of democratic institutions.

Both the universal and elite educational models have been quite successful in stimulating aggregate economic growth but with very different distributional outcomes. As one would expect, if educational opportunities are to be afforded widely, then earnings should be distributed more evenly than in societies where educational resources are concentrated on a limited portion of the population. This helps explain the contrast in the relatively flat income distributions in the Southeast Asian economies, on one hand, and the much wider disparities found in India and China, on the other.

At the same time, some degree of income inequality is necessary to encourage entrepreneurship, especially its more innovative forms that typically entail more risk. India, in particular, has had more entrepreneurial success, at least in the high-technology sectors, than the Asian economies, arguably in large part because of the excellence of its universities.

Whether the universal or elite approach to education produces *greater* growth, however, is not yet resolved. This is because as economies grow richer, they can better afford to pursue both approaches simultaneously, and it may be difficult or indeed impossible to determine unequivocally which approach has contributed more to growth. For example, perhaps the greatest economic and social challenge now confronting both India and China is the need to spread growth to the large parts of their populations that have not benefited from the rapid advances in living standards enjoyed in the dynamic regions and among the more educated portions of their populations. Both countries have experienced social unrest because of this, although in China, continuing unrest is also related to demands for greater political freedom. The leaders of both countries seem committed to expanding educational opportunities more widely. At the other end of the spectrum, one can expect Southeast Asian and Eastern European economies to devote more effort to upgrading the quality of their universities. The major life sciences initiatives in Singapore and Korea are evidence that this is already happening.

It is not easy for even richer countries to master commitments to both universal basic education and excellence in higher education. For a time, the United States seemed to be successful at both, but despite high college attendance rates, it has had continuing problems ensuring that students from low-income backgrounds graduate high school and do so with the skills they need to earn adequate incomes. At the other extreme, Western European countries and Japan have long had excellent primary and secondary educational programs that top the international rankings, but they have had not the same success with their universities. Israel seems to score well on both dimensions—at the primary and secondary level and in developing world class universities—but some of its success may reflect the uniquely large (relative to the native population) immigration of highly educated former residents of the Soviet Union during the 1990s. It remains to be seen whether its educational success will continue in the twenty-first century.

So what does all this imply for parts of the developing world—notably much of Africa, Latin America, and portions of the Middle East—where literacy rates are relatively low and educational opportunities are less than universal? In particular, should these countries attempt to emulate the Southeast Asian/Eastern European universal model or the more elite Indian model? Many developing countries, even the poorest, have elites who currently send their children abroad for university education, as did the elite class in India's highly regimented caste system as that country's educational system was being established. In India's case, the country was able to build university faculties from the pool of children educated abroad who returned as adults. Other developing countries probably do not have a large enough population to pursue a similarly meritocratic approach, nor do they have the advantage India did of a broadly English-speaking populace that can easily fit into the global commercial system. Furthermore, an elite educational strategy that inherently leads to greater income inequality can aggravate existing social grievances, with which other countries may not be able to deal. For all these reasons, we are inclined to side with the conventional wisdom that encourages developing countries to make basic education universally available, to follow in the footsteps of the

Southeast Asian and Eastern European countries (though without replicating the state guidance of their economies) rather than to copy India's elite approach.

None of this will be easy to do, especially in the poorest countries in the world where disease rates are high, health is generally poor, and food is hard to get. For example, there are currently more than 100 million primary-school-aged children throughout the world who are not enrolled in school, 70 percent of whom reside in South/West Asia and sub-Saharan Africa (UNESCO, 2005). In 2000, the average sub-Saharan African had completed just 3.5 years of school, compared to 9.8 in advanced countries.[11] Of 155 developing countries, only about half have built enough schools to educate all of their primary-school-aged children (Bruns et al., 2003). And even in many of these schools, the facilities are not adequate. For example, more than 90 percent of sixth graders in Tanzania attend schools where no books are available, and two-thirds of the schools in Chad do not have latrines (UNESCO, 2005).

There are many reasons why primary-school-aged children in the developing world do not receive an education, including the cost of tuition and the distance they must travel to school. Gene Sperling, director of the Center on Universal Education at the Council on Foreign Relations, points out that "the decision whether to send children to school often falls to parents living in extreme poverty, for whom the costs of schooling may appear to outweigh the benefits" (Sperling, 2005, 105). In addition to the monetary cost of attending school, many families in developing countries face even larger opportunity costs, such as giving up of time spent collecting firewood and water or time spent earning an income. In many families, an important part of a family's income is earned from the labor of primary-school-aged children, and more than 11 million children under the age of fifteen in sub-Saharan Africa have lost at least one parent to HIV/AIDS (UNESCO, 2005). Clearly, these are huge problems to overcome.

Pace of Change

If we know what steps must be taken to accelerate economic growth, then why not do it all it once? That, in essence, was the question that was asked and answered in the affirmative by those who advised Eastern Europe and the former republics of the Soviet Union to embrace some form of "shock therapy" after the fall of Berlin Wall. The feeling was that the chasm between central planning and a market economy could be crossed only in a single jump, and that historical circumstances had provided a crucial moment, a narrow window of opportunity for substantial and lasting reform. Any intermission in that process arguably would provide an opportunity for opposition to form and thus to defeat the effort.

The main argument against shock therapy is that it may not be politically viable, either at the outset or over the sustained period required for it to work. Not only are government officials likely to be wedded to the old system—whether it be central planning or its more benign cousin, state guidance—but so will those firms and their workers who have benefited from or are protected by the existing regime. Predictably, they will oppose change at the outset. But if the circumstances are right, as they were throughout much of the Soviet Union and Eastern Europe after the Berlin Wall fell, opposition at the outset may be too weak to prevent even radical change. The question, then, is whether after shock therapy has been applied, will the "patient"—namely, the citizens who must make their living in the economy—accept or reject the therapy.

As it turns out, events in Russia have provided a test of the political viability of shock therapy, and the test results have not been encouraging. Privatization was handled in such a way that a vastly disproportionate amount of the ownership of key productive facilities went to the oligarchs. This, in turn, led to a backlash from the Russian polity and the state, with the result (so far) that Russia's president, Vladimir Putin, has moved the country back toward state guidance. On the surface this may not appear to be a bad outcome, with Russian GDP growth averaging 7 percent since 2000 (Bush, 2006). An upper class, and even a middle class, bent on buying a rash of Western consumer goods is rapidly developing in the country. But the Russian economy remains heavily dependent on the prices of the commodities it sells on world markets, especially oil, and no doubt owes a large amount of its recent good fortune to the large run-up in oil prices since they hit rock bottom in the late 1990s. Inequalities in income, meanwhile, appear vast and growing. Over the intermediate to longer run, Russia must find a way to move away from state control and toward a better mix of entrepreneurial capitalism if it wants to diversify away from a commodity-based economy to ensure lasting growth that benefits the wider population.

Indeed, that is the central challenge that other economies that have relied on state guidance—principally in Asia, but also in India—face. If the Russian experience with shock therapy is any guide, then moving all at once is not likely to be the best option, even for economies where performance has been poor and one would expect political support for radical change. This was the case in Russia, and yet political support for shock therapy quickly wilted when the winners were so few in number and their profits so large. It might be claimed that things would have turned out differently if time and care had been taken to ensure that ownership was widely dispersed. But even if such a goal were achieved, success might well have proved to be temporary, since some owners could have been expected subsequently to invest heavily and gather larger shares in their enterprises, which would reconcentrate ownership. In short, the lesson we take away from the Russian privatization experiment is that capitalism, with its vast rewards to the successful, inevitably entails considerable inequality and that a great deal of inequality can spark a backlash.

If shock therapy for developing or emerging market countries may not generally be sustainable, what is the alternative? Our suggestion is some form of incremental change, or entrepreneurial capitalism *at the margin*. The notion is to encourage entrepreneurship *while not necessarily dismantling the part of the economy that is dependent on state guidance.*

China's move away from central planning provides perhaps the best example of this incremental approach. Rather than privatizing all of its state-owned enterprises (SOEs), including its banks, all at once—in much the way that was done in Russia—Chinese leaders have so far let the SOEs remain in business, supported by continuing loans from state-owned banks. At the same time, however, the central government has permitted provincial and municipal governments as well as individuals to launch their own enterprises. The not-so-hidden strategy is to let the seedlings of new enterprise grow while tending to the forest of the existing SOEs, with the hope that the new ventures eventually will become more important to the economy than the SOEs. That is exactly what has happened, apparently with great success. Whereas virtually all of that country's GDP as recently as the early 1980s was produced by state-owned enterprises or on state-owned land, by 2005, nearly two-thirds of China's output was generated privately.[12] The country's remarkable rate of output growth over this period is without parallel anywhere in the world (although Ireland and India have been close).

Israel provides another example of a once-poor country, without natural resources, where the state, in combination with the country's labor unions, guided the economy during part of the postwar period and yet has successfully moved away from state guidance over time. Perhaps without knowing or acknowledging it, Israel followed China's example. It, too, focused on spurring growth at the margin in various sectors—agriculture, chemicals, electronics, and information technology. The Israeli government helped this process along by permitting, if not encouraging, technology transfer from its vaunted military to private uses. In addition, the country had the unique benefit in the 1990s of being a prime destination for a massive (relative to the size of the preexisting population) influx of highly educated immigrants from Russia and other former states of the Soviet Union. Although it took some time to absorb all of this talent, eventually the Russian immigrants helped fuel a boom in high-tech entrepreneurship, primarily as employees of firms started by Israelis but in some cases as entrepreneurs themselves.

Israeli government policy—beyond welcoming immigrants by providing Hebrew-language training and temporary housing and other living support—has facilitated the start-up and expansion of high-tech entrepreneurial ventures, in particular, through a government-supported venture fund that provided seed capital to enterprises that already had some private sector backing. In his exhaustive review of this program, Professor Dan Breznitz of Georgia Tech has concluded that this matching requirement, coupled with the nimble decision-making by the fund's leaders, made government support successful (Breznitz, 2005). Although it is difficult to know with precision how many companies have prospered as a result, the overall picture of entrepreneurial success is unmistakable: Israeli companies have been remarkably successful in "going public" on the New York Stock Exchange.

So how exactly can governments wedded to state guidance ease their way into more entrepreneurship? To begin with, they must be motivated to initiate change in the first place, and this is not likely to happen unless their economies are mired in recession or have posted lackluster economic performance for an extended period, either in absolute terms or relative to countries their people and governmental leaders view as peers or rivals (such India and China with respect to each other, for example). In principle, authoritarian leaders should be expected to adopt reform measures less quickly than their democratic counterparts, since they do not face the same prospect of losing their jobs if national economic performance proves disappointing. Of course, there can be and are exceptions to this general tendency. China's authoritarian leaders, after all, did initiate that country's move away central planning, at least in large urban areas, although they have not been as enthusiastic about embracing free markets in the vast poor rural areas of the country. In contrast, although democracies may have the virtue of forcing leaders to recognize the need for change, strong vested interests in democratically governed countries may block effective reform that poses a threat to the jobs and incomes of specific, well-identified groups.

For these reasons, any reform strategy of moving away from state guidance is most likely to succeed if it facilitates entrepreneurship without at the same time transparently and immediately threatening large vested interests, in both the private and public sectors. Over time, however, as new ventures form and become successful, economic and political power naturally will gravitate in their direction, and the power of the previous regimes will wane. Pressure from outside sometimes can encourage change; indeed, Japanese leaders who want change often have welcomed pressure from abroad (especially the United States), which they can use to justify internal reforms. The desire to play in a larger, global arena can also provide a powerful impetus for change, as China's willingness to lower its trade and investment barriers and to improve its legal institutions in return for membership in the WTO attests.

The World Bank's annual publication *Doing Business* has provided for the first time a global yardstick for nations to measure their progress. A plausible inference from the fact that a number of nations have lowered the costs of starting and growing a business in recent years is that some governments take their rankings seriously and want to avoid the global embarrassment of being singled out every year as lagging in these efforts.

By the foregoing logic, therefore, several of the elements of the instruments for entrepreneurial success already identified would seem to have the highest priority. In the short run, measures to reduce the costs of opening and growing new businesses should top any list. Although in principle new businesses can and will challenge existing enterprises, the large established companies that have benefited from state favors and guidance in the past may not view these start-ups as a significant threat because they are so small (at least at first). Furthermore, because lower registration costs should substantially reduce the degree of business informality, it should increase government tax collections and thereby give government officials a vested interest in reform. Indeed, astute governments may be able to use some of the additional revenue to lower business taxes generally, muting potential business opposition to reform efforts.

Similarly, if privatization of state-owned banks is deemed too risky politically for the reasons already discussed, a policy of chartering *new* banks, coupled with permission for foreign banks and financial institutions to enter local markets de novo should be welcomed even by existing enterprises, some of which may find that such moves lower their borrowing costs and enhance the availability of funds.

Educational reforms also should encounter little political resistance, and yet these efforts at the margin promise what are perhaps the greatest long-run benefits of all. A central problem in any effort to raise educational attainment, of course, is how to finance it. In this regard, an "elite" strategy is likely to be far less expensive than the "universal" approach, although as we have discussed, we are somewhat skeptical that other countries can be as successful as India has been with an elite approach. Moreover, a universal strategy would be significantly more equitable. Although in principle foreign assistance targeted toward education could help address the financing problem, monies directed through governments often do not reach their destination. Or recipient governments may use the foreign funds provided for one purpose (education) to reduce their funding of other necessary public services (such as health and sanitation). We will discuss these hurdles to effective foreign assistance below. But even if they can be overcome—in particular, if recipient governments actually use any additional funds to expand educational offerings rather than divert them to other uses—no developing country can or should count on such aid for any extended period. For this reason, the revenues for any program to expand educational opportunities must be found largely internally, which is yet another reason to drop barriers to business registration: to generate additional tax revenue to fund education. Even a universal program that is incremental in nature—adding additional grades to the universal program as the funds become available—can lead, over time, to revolutionary change, as the remarkable growth records of the Southeast Asian economies in the postwar era attest.

Transition Away from Oligarchy

It is one thing for governments that have long engaged in state guidance but want to move in a more entrepreneurial direction to begin the job, as difficult as it may be. It is quite another to expect oligarchies to change direction. After all, the central problem with oligarchs is that they normally are happy with the way things are, so they have little interest in stimulating growth, which can threaten to upset their comfortable positions. So how can the residents of the societies they rule—and there are plenty of them, throughout Africa, Latin America, and the Middle East—get them to change?

One can hope for the equivalent of a religious conversion, but this, of course, is hardly likely. Indeed, we do not know of any leader of what can plausibly be described as an oligarchic economy who has voluntarily taken steps to change it to some other form of capitalism. The pressure for significant—indeed, revolutionary—change, then, must come from either within or without the country, through some form of external pressure.

By "revolution" we do not mean replacing an existing regime by force, but preferably by peaceful, constructive change. Indeed, the most dramatic series of relatively peaceful economic and political revolutions to occur during our lifetime (or for that matter, in any lifetimes) are the transitions of the formerly centrally planned economies and authoritarian societies of Eastern Europe and the Soviet Union toward mixes of state-guided and entrepreneurial capitalism and democracy during the late 1980s and since. Each of these transitions responded to internal forces—citizen protests and demonstrations that eventually led to ouster of the authoritarian regime—but they also were heavily influenced by each other. In particular, it was not an accident that the transitions in Eastern Europe and the former Soviet Union occurred at roughly the same time. The dominance of the latter over the former meant that when the Soviet Union and its political and economic systems unraveled, the Eastern Europe societies were destined to follow.

To be sure, the centrally planned economies of Eastern Europe and the Soviet Union were not strictly examples of oligarchic capitalism, but they nonetheless were all oligarchic societies in a fundamental sense. In each case, the members of the governing regime typically enjoyed monetary and nonmonetary privileges denied to other citizens. Power and wealth were concentrated in the hands of a relative few. The major difference between these economies and the oligarchic capitalist societies of Latin America, Africa, or the Middle East is that in the centrally planned economies the government directed all resources and prohibited the ownership of private property. But the ruling elites at the top certainly had the functional equivalents of private property, since they directed how state-owned property could be used, often to their own benefit.

That many of Eastern European and former Soviet economies are now moving, albeit at different paces, toward some form of capitalism that at least tolerates, if not encourages, entrepreneurship can only be counted as a major success, for them and for those in the rest of the world who care about economic progress. Ironically, the one major disappointment is Russia, the heart of the former Soviet Union. There, the central planning regime was almost immediately replaced by true oligarchic capitalism. Indeed, the very term "oligarchs" has come to be taken as synonymous with the handful of Russian billionaires who quickly assumed ownership and control of Russia's former state-owned enterprises (Gazprom, Russia's giant energy company, in particular), as well as the new firms in banking and various natural resource industries. But oligarchic capitalism in Russia has been short-lived and, at this writing, seems to have been replaced by a state-guided economy accompanied by an authoritarian political system overseen by President Vladimir Putin.

Recent history provides other examples of popular uprisings against oligarchic regimes, with similarly disappointing outcomes. The elections of Hugo Chavez in Venezuela and Evo Morales in Bolivia brought to power two leaders who have brought stronger state control and ownership to their economies. Argentina's Nestor Kirchner and Brazil's Lula da Silva ("Lula") have moved in a similar direction. In the Middle East, meanwhile, electoral democracy has yet to deliver positive economic news. We do not dwell on the obvious but controversial case of Iraq, where democratic elections have been made possible only by U.S. military intervention, and where the outcome for democracy and for the economy is likely to be unclear for years. Rather, we point to the case of Palestine, where the oligarchic rule of the Fatah party under the leadership of Yassir Arafat gave way, again through democratic election in early 2006, to the extremism of Hamas. From what we can tell, Hamas came to power largely if not solely because the Palestinian people were fed up with the corruption and the economic failure of Fatah, and that this played a far more important role in its electoral victory than Hamas's terrorist past (and possible future) and its refusal to recognize the State of Israel. But because of its extremist "foreign policy," Hamas has forfeited the support of the United States and Europe and has had to turn to Iran and other sources for financial assistance. The country's economic prospects, at this writing, therefore do not look good even though the former oligarhic rule of Fatah has been overturned and even if Hamas is successful in reducing the corruption with which it was associated.

We draw what we believe are two significant lessons from all this. One is that democracy does not ensure that governments will allow or encourage pro-growth forms of capitalism. The democratic revolutions in Latin America in the 1970s and 1980s, and in many African nations in the 1990s, brought ruling elites to power who quickly established or perpetuated oligarchic capitalist systems—that is, economies that benefited the few and not the many. Indeed, although many Latin American countries introduced market-oriented reforms after they adopted democracy, their economies and governments still were tightly controlled by these elites, whose firms had licenses and other privileges not available to the many informal enterprises that operated in these economies. And, as noted, the populist backlashes of the past decade have only replaced one set of oligarchs with another, all of whom have handed out subsidies to satisfy their populist base of support but done little or nothing to encourage the formation and growth of new enterprises.

The failure of democratically elected regimes around the world to advance economic growth should give pause to policy makers in the United States who have sought to make the promotion of democracy the most important foreign policy objective of the nation. Not only has it become apparent that free elections alone are insufficient to produce substantively democratic government—with the checks and balances of its different branches—but elections have elevated to power individuals with little or no commitment to encouraging economic freedom and independence.[13] This certainly suggests a revision of foreign policy goals, one that takes a broader view of democracy itself, beyond just elections and also includes the promotion of an entrepreneurial sector, principally via the means we have just discussed. Entrepreneurship is not just a key to advancing growth in other economies, for the benefit of local residents. It is also more likely to generate public attitudes that are friendly, or at least less hostile, to the wealthier economies. Entrepreneurs and their employees who need and can benefit from the capital equipment, technology, and know-how provided by American and other developed-country firms, through trade and direct foreign investment, are likely to view their suppliers, investors, and trading partners more favorably, probably far more so than those who may be working at state-owned companies whose managers owe their positions to leaders who whip up nationalist opposition to foreign firms and their governments as a way of distracting electorates from their poor economic conditions.

Our second lesson is one of realism: it may be that transition from oligarchy will sometimes or often entail a detour—perhaps a long one—toward some form of state guidance, as has occurred in Russia and seems to be occurring in some Latin American nations, before the countries have governments that are ready to embrace an entrepreneurial form of capitalism without the heavy hand of state guidance. People who are used to being ruled by governments dominated by a narrow group of elites, even if they are disliked, may not be ready to support new leaders who are willing to trust the market more than the guidance of the state. It may take another bout of economic stagnation, or worse, for voters to demand the greater economic rights and freedoms that are associated with more entrepreneurial economies and societies. Or, if the people are lucky, some of the new leaders may recognize this on their own.

What, if anything, can or should rich countries do to encourage peaceful revolutions against existing oligarchies and thereby produce more entrepreneurship and less state guidance if and when change actually occurs? The traditional foreign policy tool kit contains more sticks than carrots, or typically sanctions against countries that are violating some widely shared norm. But it is well established that sanctions are not effective without widespread support (Elliot et al., 1990), and this is not likely to be forthcoming unless the behavior is deeply offensive, such as the Apartheid once practiced by South Africa or the construction of facilities for production of nuclear weapons in the case of Iran. It is highly unlikely that a large number of nations—even rich ones—will ever agree that the practice of oligarchic capitalism, even assuming it could be well defined, evokes sufficient moral outrage to justify sanctions of any type.

Another foreign policy stick short of sanctions is the "conditionality" the International Monetary Fund typically imposes on its loans to borrower countries—that is, the special requirements the borrowers must satisfy before loans will be granted to them. Certainly, many oligarchic economies have borrowed or continued to borrow from the IMF, and thus it is conceivable, in principle, that the Fund could condition its future lending on the kind of measures we have just surveyed for promotion of entrepreneurship. But the Fund's record of success in pursuing conditionality in the past is mixed at best (Goldstein, 2000). Moreover, in the wake of the strong criticism the IMF received during and after the Asian financial crisis for the many detailed conditions it imposed on its loans, the Fund appears to have returned to its traditional concentration on macroeconomic conditions, fiscal and monetary prudence. It is unlikely that the national directors of the Fund will impose such detailed conditions any time soon, however defensible they may be as a way of encouraging long-run growth.

This leaves policy makers to come up with some kind of imaginative "carrots" to induce oligarchic leaders or, more important, those who successfully replace them to move their economies in a more entrepreneurial direction. One possibility is for the United States to use its new conditional approach to foreign aid—carried out through the Millennium Challenge Account (MCA)—to channel aid to countries pursuing policies that promote entrepreneurship. Although we are skeptical of foreign aid as a way to encourage sustained growth, it is possible, at least in theory, for a conditional approach of this type to work, and for that reason we urge that it at least be tried.

Foreign aid always will have its limits, however. In addition, if countries are to promote entrepreneurial behavior on a consistent basis, there must be popular support for doing so, especially in the "democratic" oligarchies. One way the United States, in particular, can help to generate this support over time is to sponsor the equivalent of "reverse Fulbright" scholarships/internships for college students and recent graduates to come to the United States to take an entrepreneurship practicum at a leading university and to then serve as interns in entrepreneurial companies.[14] The program could be available to foreign residents from developing countries, though special efforts and perhaps additional slots would be open to residents from countries that are deemed highly oligarchic or, more broadly, the countries of Latin America, Africa, and the Arab Middle East. Exposing increasing numbers of impressionable, potential entrepreneurs to the ways of doing business and, specifically, starting and growing a business would not only impart useful knowledge, but also instill an appreciation for entrepreneurial endeavors and what legal, institutional and other environmental conditions are required to make them flourish. Indeed, it could also be useful, if the governments of the sending countries were so willing, to expose government officials to such experiences (though they may be more difficult to place with entrepreneurial companies).

We strongly believe that U.S. entrepreneurial companies would welcome the opportunity to build human bridges to developing-country markets. Indeed, it is quite likely, in our view, that other rich countries might copy the program, although they would probably be successful in competing against the United States program only to the extent foreign applicants believed that they could gain equivalent entrepreneurial opportunities and training in those counties. But even alone, the United States program could build constituencies among potential future leaders in oligarchic developing countries for entrepreneurially driven economic change. Ideally, their experiences and outlook would spread like a virus—a healthy one to be sure—in their home countries. Like investments in education generally, which have long payoffs, this program might not offer easily seen returns for many years, perhaps a decade a more. Then again, it took nearly fifty years of fighting the cold war to bring success, though it has been replaced by a new ideological struggle between the West and fundamentalist Islam. Governments that are threatened by the spread of such fundamentalism might find an entrepreneurial scholarship/internship program for their young adults to be an especially important way to counter the influence that fundamentalist schools and clerics have exercised.

As for the United States, we believe that such a program, if scaled properly, could be as effective or more effective than any monies the government now spends on public relations or the marketing of United States–style freedoms and values. The best marketing device is a true entrepreneurial experience, which is, after all, the comparative advantage the United States still maintains relative to the rest of the world.

Aid, Savings, Investment, and Economic Growth

One of the keys to growth is a high level of savings, which makes possible high investment—both in physical and human capital. But what if the people are too poor to save on their own, needing what meager incomes they have simply to survive? The obvious answer, it would seem, is to attract savings from abroad. But what if the people in these countries also suffer from disease and poor health, and governments have insufficient resources to control, let alone prevent and treat them? To compound the problem, what if the countries are located in regions of the world near the equator where the heat and humidity are stifling for much of the year, or if they are landlocked and thus cannot cost-effectively import necessary raw materials nor export any semifinished products they somehow might be able to manufacture for sale abroad? In such environments, foreign investors are unlikely to commit funds, fearing that they will be unable to earn a return on investment that will compensate for the risks involved.

Welcome to much of Africa and, more distressingly, to much of the entire developing world, where several billion people live on less than $2 per day. Also, welcome to the arguments that have sustained several decades of foreign governmental assistance, from rich countries and the multilateral development banks they fund, to poor countries so clearly in need of such aid. On humanitarian grounds alone, it would seem cruel not to agree and, indeed, to oppose efforts to increase the amounts of foreign assistance the rich world currently provides. Rich country governments have put themselves on record in the 2000 Millennium Declaration as calling for annual aid equivalent to 0.7 percent of their countries' annual GDPs, even though nearly all of them (including the United States) currently fall far short of this admittedly arbitrary goal. More concretely, at the G8 meeting in Scotland in July 2005, leaders of the rich countries of the world agreed to increase annual aid flows to developing countries by at least $50 billion by 2010 and to write off the foreign debts of eighteen of the world's poorest countries.

But does foreign assistance really help the economies of recipient countries? By the preceding logic, the answer would appear to be a compelling "yes" since external capital should add to the meager levels of domestically generated savings to fund both private and public investments. Yet out of the many empirical studies conducted on this subject and that control for the many other variables that may contribute to (or detract from) growth, the answer is mixed at best. Columbia professor Jeffrey Sachs has laid out perhaps the strongest, or at least the best known, case for the proposition that aid improves growth. In his book *End of Poverty*, Sachs makes out a seemingly powerful argument that by improving human health and education and by facilitating the construction of critical public infrastructure, aid can markedly improve the lot of hundreds of millions of people around the world currently trapped in poverty.

But other empirical studies, using the same cross-country regression model approach that Sachs and other aid defenders have followed, have reached a different conclusion. New York University economist William Easterly not only fails to find that foreign aid advances growth, but reaches the same conclusion with respect to other sources of capital (Easterly, 2001). A prominent 2005 study by the (then) chief economist of the International Monetary Fund and a colleague also found no statistical linkage between aid and growth (Rajan and Subramanian, 2005).

There are several reasons why aid may not succeed in enhancing growth, though it may save lives or provide other benefits to recipient countries.[15] At the top of the list is the fact that foreign aid provided by rich country governments or multilateral development institutions almost uniformly is or must be distributed through *governments of poor countries*. The leaders of the recipient governments, in turn, may misuse or appropriate the aid or allow the aid to reduce growth-relevant spending they might otherwise have undertaken on their own (the so-called substitution effect). Aid can be and probably is often misdirected, supporting investments in roads or infrastructure that do not necessarily achieve high social rates of return.

Whatever the reason, it should give policy makers some pause before they casually accept the all-too-plausible conclusion that more *government-to-government* aid is an effective way to enhance growth.

Even if the problems with government distribution could be solved, the beneficial impact of aid can be offset in other ways. In particular, the influx of aid dollars can push up a country's exchange rate and thereby make its exports less competitive on world markets. In fact, one study has documented a clear statistical linkage showing that in countries that receive more aid, labor-intensive and export-oriented industries grow more slowly than in other countries, controlling for a variety of other factors (Rajan and Subramanian, 2006).

It is quite possible, of course, that the cross-section time series regressions are misleading, that they simply are ill equipped in data and method to determine whether an aid-growth nexus exists, and if so, of what magnitude. After all, we ourselves discussed the limits of the statistical technique in chapter 2, suggesting that it either omitted or poorly measured the contribution of the difficult-to-quantify but important institutional and legal factors we have emphasized throughout this book. Perhaps the cross-country regressions also are missing an important, unmeasured contribution of aid. Or aid may fail the statistical tests because much of it is provided for *noneconomic* reasons, but instead to reward allies or to influence the foreign policies of donor countries. If it were possible to identify only those countries and time periods where enhancing economic growth was the primary or sole motivation of aid, maybe a statistically significant link between aid and growth would show up.

We will not attempt to resolve the statistical debate here, suspecting that it will continue long after this book is published and as long as aid continues to flow. Rather, we want to make three simple but important points that are relevant to the theses that have been offered here.

First, even if aid does somehow manage to jump-start the economic engines of poor countries, aid cannot *sustain* economic growth. As one analyst has concisely observed, "just spending more money is not going to build the long-term functional economies that will create the employment and wealth creation to get Africa and other poor countries out of their poverty trap."[16] Sustained growth will occur only if the institutional environment is modified so that it becomes conducive to growth. State guidance, at least initially, may prove to be the key institution in many countries, as some continue to believe to have been the case in Asia. But over the longer run, state guidance must give way to some form of entrepreneurial capitalism, with incentives for innovative as well as replicative entrepreneurship, if growth is to continue.

Second, in theory, the Millennium Challenge Account program initiated by the Bush administration recognizes that U.S. governmental aid can be most effective or, indeed, effective at all if it is awarded primarily, or even exclusively, to countries that have adopted and are effectively carrying out growth-promoting economic policies. The MCA conditions (one of which explicitly relates to entrepreneurship) are listed in table 11. Such a precondition structure for an aid program may work where it is vigorously adhered to, though aid-supplying policy makers themselves may still find ways to circumvent the policy by continuing to channel aid funds in a manner that adheres to the traditional military or foreign policy reasons that have long influenced U.S. foreign aid policy. In any event, even if the conditional approach is strictly followed, it may find only a few recipients who qualify for aid, which would limit aid's reach (and clearly make it impossible for donor countries to meet the 0.7 percent of GDP target set in the 2000 Millennium Declaration).

Third, ultimately more thought must be given to processes by which aid can be delivered directly to the intended beneficiaries—the sick, children in schools, and so forth—immunizing it from the influence or direction of local governments. This would reduce the "leakages" in the aid pipeline associated with corruption, inefficiency, or substitution. The Gates Foundation, for example, is committing huge sums to preventing and fighting diseases in third world countries, and it is doing so directly, not through government intermediaries. Circumventing the distorting influences of local governments is more difficult to do with monies provided for education or to build infrastructure, which are inherently governmental functions. [17] We leave it to those more expert than ourselves to see whether aid supplied privately nonetheless can be delivered directly toward these uses.

Despite these obstacles, it is conceivable that aid has enhanced growth in countries where the institutional/legal and macroeconomic environments have not prevented economic progress. Certainly, the statistical studies whose results are so critical of the aid programs are not so far be-

Table 11 Millennium Challenge Account Conditions

Develop just governance
• Secure individuals' civil liberties, including political rights
• Sustain free and fair elections
• Maintain the accountability of the national government by fulfilling the will of its citizens
• Maintain an acceptable rule of law and control corruption, including bribes and graft
• Limit government power by holding periodic popular elections, creating an independent judiciary, and allowing freedom of speech and press

Invest in people
• Provide all citizens with primary education and guarantee a high completion rate by reducing child labor, increasing teaching quality, and allowing girls to attend schools
• Allocate funds to fight malaria, tuberculosis, diarrhea, and other illness that reduce the "productive strength" of the people
• Maintain high vaccination rates in order to address the basic health needs of the poor

Promote sound economic principles
• Develop and maintain laws that encourage economic freedom of individuals
• Support sound monetary and fiscal policies
• Create a fair and transparent regulatory system
• Decrease the length of time required to obtain government approval of private sector business activities and the creation of new businesses
• Open markets to foreign competition and increase international trade
• Create systems to properly manage foreign investment and avoid investing national funds in overly risky markets

Source: Schaffer, 2003.

yond criticism as to allow us with a clear conscience to forego all aid, particularly aid directed to immediate and dire crises, such as famine or infectious disease epidemics. But history suggests that generous aid programs are not the only path to economic advance, nor can they assure its result. There are many examples of now middle-income or rich countries that did not get to where they are because of foreign aid. The United States is a prime example, and it is at least arguable that aid was not the prime contributor to economic advance in the Asian Tiger economies. Although none of these economies had as many strikes against them as the impoverished lands of Africa, which are too poor to save and invest on their own, it should not be forgotten that Europe and Japan, while rich today, were virtually prostrate after World War II. Although Marshall Plan aid was not inconsequential, this aid was not provided universally to the countries in question, which did much to help themselves.

In the end, however, it doesn't really matter whether one is an aid optimist or pessimist. Even most pessimists will concede that if aid is used well, it can help in the short run. Indeed, one really doesn't need statistics to recognize that aid can be useful for a while to do the things that Sachs calls for—provided one can ensure that the aid will actually get to those in need. But there remains much truth in the proverbial story that while giving fish can stave off starvation, the only way to continue to do that is to teach recipients how to fish. Thus, less developed countries need entrepreneurship to advance growth precisely because they have low savings. Even in the rich world, the evidence indicates that investment contributes only a small part of overall growth. Where savings and investment are limited, more emphasis on enterprise and innovation becomes indispensable, as the one way for those who have little to make do today, and to do better tomorrow. Once incomes grow above a certain level, saving and investment can increase—Southeast Asia demonstrates that—but, still, substantial progress always entails a need for innovation. Later, after success arrives, big firms can and need to contribute, just as they do in rich countries.

What Role for Micro-Credit?

Our focus in this book is on the critical role of entrepreneurship for economic growth and the attendant opportunity to reduce or eliminate poverty. Toward that end, we have offered various measures to promote this goal to protect the legitimate interests of prospective entrepreneurs and to enhance the opportunities for their activities. Noteworthy in this list are suggestions to provide prospective entrepreneurs with funding, without which they cannot hope to launch their new firms. An example of this is a funding arrangement that has recently attracted much favorable attention, showing the legitimate grounds for hope that it appropriately offers and, simultaneously, the limitations and obstacles it has, at least so far, been unable to avoid. In these two sides of the matter this topic is not alone. We know no proposed remedial measures that are immune from handicaps and that offer a sure and easy path to growth.

Specifically, we refer to policies to promote "micro-credit," or lending of small amounts ($1,000 or less) to start-up businesses.[18] The founding of the micro-credit movement—and that is what it has become—is generally credited to Muhammad Yunus, an economist-turned-banker from Bangladesh, who established the Grameen Bank in 1976, although two other nonprofit micro-lenders (Opportunity International and ACCION International were established a few years earlier). Yunus and Grameen are most famous for providing credit to groups of women entrepreneurs, typically no larger than five, who in turn rotate loans among their members. As the initial borrowers repay their loans, the funds are reloaned to the members next in line. A key feature of the lending contract is that all members are *jointly liable* for the debts of the group; that is, if a member of the group doesn't service her loan on time, the others are responsible for payment. Why women? Because Grameen concluded that women are more willing to join such groups or are better credit risks than men—or both. The Grameen lending model has been copied in some form by many other lenders around the world, not just for women but also for men, enabling millions of people around the world to start businesses that they otherwise would be unable to launch.

Micro-lending has now been widely embraced by developing countries, by rich countries, and by multilateral lending institutions, such as the World Bank. During 2004, for example, development agencies reportedly committed $1 billion to microfinancial institutions around the world. Former President Clinton expressed his verbal support of the concept throughout his presidency and made numerous visits to micro-lenders while on foreign trips. Two international Microcredit Summits have been held, the first in 1997 and another in 2002, and have attracted leaders from around the world. Yunus won the Nobel Peace Prize in 2006.

Since financing is important for entrepreneurs and micro-lending seems to be filling an important vacuum in the marketplace, it would appear to be an essential ingredient in policy makers' toolbox for encouraging growth in developing countries. But the reality is more complicated.

Grameen Bank and other micro-lending institutions got their start and still operate with the aid of subsidies from nonprofit organizations (such as foundations, initially the Ford Foundation, in particular), governments, and multilateral lending institutions. There are signs that a few and perhaps an even growing number of micro-lenders have since become profitable,[19] but clearly the good work of micro-lenders will remain limited as long as they are forced to rely on subsidies. There is not a bottomless well of nonprofit or government support for this activity, however noble.

The hope, of course, is that the nonprofit micro-lenders will induce more conventional lenders to participate in the market, either directly by lending to customers or indirectly by lending to other micro-lenders. It is too early to tell whether and to what extent this will occur, although there are a few promising signs. Citigroup, ABN-Ambro, and ANZ (a leading Australian bank), among others, have mounted ambitious efforts (Barr, Kumar, and Litan, 2007). Similarly, a Latin American investment pool, Profund, has successfully invested in a number of micro-lenders in the region, achieving a 6 percent annual return—low, given the risks, but providing some profit nonetheless. The key to Profund's apparent success, however, is that the lenders it finances charge their customers interest rates that reflect market risks, and these rates can be as high as 100 percent per year. These seemingly exorbitant rates of interest (certainly to readers living in more developed economies) reportedly are still well below interest rates charged by "informal" lenders. Nonetheless, high market rates limit the ability of new firms to get started.

Another question surrounds the ability of micro-lending, even if subsidized, to produce sustained economic growth. Micro-borrowers use their credit overwhelmingly, if not exclusively, to create what we have labeled "replicative" firms, or enterprises that simply reproduce what many others have done or are currently doing. Economies can grow only so much through replicative activity. Growth is capped when all those who otherwise would not be employed are engaged fully in replicative activities.

For economies to enjoy further growth, one or both of the following must occur. Some not insignificant portion of the replicative enterprises must grow substantially larger, to realize economies of scale and thus to achieve the productivity gains that ultimately drive improvement in living standards. Or some firms must begin or transform themselves into innovative enterprises, selling new products or services or existing ones that make use of innovative and productivity-enhancing inputs or modes of organization. As we have suggested, some form of innovation is indispensable for all economies if they want to grow at a more rapid rate.

It is not yet clear, however, to what extent micro-lending has contributed or in the future is capable of contributing to either of these developments: marked growth of replicative enterprises or the launching of innovative ones. For both of these outcomes to occur, more conventional lending, at lower rates of interest, will be required. Indeed, one of the other large players in the micro-lending market, ACCION International, has learned that over time the more successful businesses in any group need more funding than the overall group can obtain. Those businesses *must* graduate to the conventional loan market or else find their opportunities for further growth constrained.

In short, the most important long-run contribution of the micro-lenders is that they have demonstrated how it is possible to enable millions of the poor to reach the first rung on the ladder to economic success. But the acid test is whether countries have the laws and institutions that will enable those who make it to the first rung to climb higher and, in the process, drive economic growth for their entire economies. This requires much more than micro-lending, although microfinance increasingly looks like it might be one good way to start.

Conclusion

In this chapter we have avoided presenting a set of well-specified recipes that any government of a less developed country with ambitions for growth can follow in detail, confident that it will lead unerringly to that goal. We have offered no such detailed formulae because we are convinced that no such dependable instructions exist.

Instead we have discussed the broad means that may be able to move countries from regimes of state guidance or oligarchic capitalism, the foundation of the poverty of so many societies, toward the ultimate goal of more entrepreneurial economic systems that we believe will be more conducive to sustained growth. As an intermediate arrangement, we have also posited that governmentally directed capitalism may be helpful, but even this latter arrangement eventually will run out of steam as a growth engine, and so the way to further transition toward more entrepreneurship is unavoidable if catch-up is to be achieved.

We have emphasized the difficulty of carrying out such transitions and have discussed in broad, general terms what the rest of the world can do to help the process along and what approaches are likely to prove disappointing. But even if a country has succeeded in inaugurating a regime of entrepreneurial capitalism, the state will continue to play a role in setting up and monitoring the rules of the game that provide the appropriate incentives. Here the discussion of what should and what should not be done must become more specific, more systematic, and more exhaustive. Unfortunately, disappointing experience shows that no one is yet in a position to provide such a definitive elaboration of these matters. But we hope the next two chapters can take us a good part of the way, describing the actions, rules, and institutions that can produce a combination of entrepreneurial and big-firm capitalism that experience shows to be capable of doing the job.

7

THE BIG-FIRM WEALTHY ECONOMIES:
PREVENTING RETREAT OR STAGNATION

In 1979, Ezra Vogel, a professor at the Harvard Business School, published a highly acclaimed book, *Japan as Number One*. The book, and its compelling title, seemed to capture the fears of the country during the traumatic decades of the 1970s and 1980s, which were punctuated with the deepest U.S. recessions of the postwar era, followed by a recovery accompanied by (then) historically large federal budget and trade deficits, both in absolute terms and relative to GDP. A good portion of the U.S. trade deficit was with Japan, whose companies and their owners used their export earnings to invest in new manufacturing plants in the United States and, in some cases, to buy "trophy" real estate, such as the Pebble Beach Golf Course and Rockefeller Center in New York. Many politicians, and many American citizens, feared that Japan would soon displace America as the leading economic power in the world.

Readers of Vogel's book, of course, now know that these fears proved to be without foundation. A decade after the book was published, the Japanese stock market, where share prices had soared, came plummeting back to earth with a massive thud. Japanese banks, which had expanded largely on the back of the rising prices of the shares they held, lent too much money to many ill-founded projects and borrowers and eventually experienced the worst losses of any banking system on record. At one point in the 1990s, it is conceivable that had the assets and liabilities of the country's largest banks been "marked to market," all of them would have been insolvent in economic terms. The sluggish response of Japan's political leaders to the banking crisis contributed to that country's deep economic funk, which lasted for more than a decade and from which recovery is still incomplete. So shaken was the confidence of Japanese consumers and businesses that even the extraordinary fiscal and monetary stimulus applied by the Japanese government and central bank did not seem to work. Only by the time we began writing this book, in 2005, was Japan's economy showing any signs of recovery.

After Japan fell from its economic pedestal in the late 1980s, similar fears were soon expressed in some quarters in the United States about what was projected to be the next great economic challenge: that posed by Western Europe (especially by the countries on the Continent). Lester Thurow, former dean of MIT's Sloan School of Management, penned a best-selling book in the early 1990s, *Head to Head,* in which he forecast, among other things, that the Western Europe economies, fueled by the strengthening and expansion of the European Union (EU) and the likelihood (then) of a common European currency, could soon overtake the United States. In fact, the common currency, the Euro, became a reality in 2002, and the EU itself has enlarged from its initial fifteen member countries to more than twenty today, but the economic "threat" from the continental economies never materialized. Throughout the 1990s and well into the first decade of the twenty-first century, Western European economies have grown less rapidly than that of the United States, while unemployment rates have hovered near or in some cases above double digits. Throughout Western Europe one hears calls by political leaders for fundamental economic transformation aimed at catching up to the United States, though without some of the undesirable features of the U.S. economy (such as greater income inequality).

Readers of this book today, particularly those in America who by now have become accustomed to warnings about the economic threat posed by China, India, and the more advanced Southeast Asian economies (such as Singapore and Taiwan), would do well to remember that the previous alarms about both Japan and Western Europe proved to be off the mark. Furthermore, as we will discuss in our concluding chapter, although the underlying premise behind these alarms—that Americans are somehow engaged in an "economic war" with other countries—may have its political uses in accelerating the adoption of policies that are conducive to economic growth, the military analogy is fundamentally misplaced. The global economy is not a "zero-sum game" where some countries "win" and others must "lose." The objective for any country is to do its best to improve living standards of its own citizens, and this objective can be furthered if other countries grow as well.

In fact, the economies of Japan and Western Europe have achieved remarkable success on this score, literally rising from the ashes of World War II to approach the per capita income of the world's leading economic power, the United States. Indeed, by some measures—such as quality of life, access to health care, and amount of leisure—average standards of living in continental Europe, in particular, arguably exceed those in America.

Nonetheless, when measured in economic terms—such as output or income per capita—the economies of Japan and Western Europe (excepting Ireland and the United Kingdom) have grown more slowly in recent years than that of the United States, as shown in table 12. No longer does it appear that either economy will soon overtake the per capita income level of the United States, as Americans feared and perhaps Japanese or Europeans anticipated as recently as the 1980s or early 1990s.

Indeed, analysts from around the world, including the United States, worry about the long-term prospects for the economies of continental Europe and Japan. Both parts of the world face daunting demographic challenges, arguably more difficult than those the United States must confront

Table 12 Growth Rates of GDP per Capita

Country	1990–2004	1995–2004	2000–2004
France	3.45	3.67	3.17
Germany	3.31	3.02	2.60
Ireland	7.68	8.24	5.56
Italy	3.39	3.30	3.03
Japan	3.38	3.20	3.67
United Kingdom	4.18	4.34	3.96
United States	3.96	4.14	3.56

Source: World Economic and Financial Surveys, *The World Economic Outlook Database, 2005* (Washington, D.C.: International Monetary Fund, 2005), available at http://www.imf.org/external/pubs/ft/weo/2005/01/data/index.htm.

in this century. The possible future stagnation of continental European and Japanese economies clearly is not in anyone's interest. Not only have both regions historically been major contributors to global growth and purchasers of goods and services from the United States and other countries, but economic stagnation can lead to untoward political consequences. A less economically confident Europe or Japan is more likely to be protectionist, anti-American, and less likely or able to meet the requirements of future global security, environmental, health, and economic challenges.

Accordingly, a number of economists in recent years, both outside and inside Europe and Japan, have called upon European and Japanese leaders to adopt radical and immediate change to make their economies more flexible and productive, that is, to undergo the more up-to-date equivalent of the "shock therapy" that was urged upon the former Soviet republics and Eastern Europe after the fall of the Berlin Wall in 1989. Although we are broadly sympathetic with the need for major changes, we have a somewhat different perspective on their nature and the pace at which they can or should be carried out and will devote this chapter to explaining how and why. A quick preview of our argument follows.

First, the standard prescriptions for improved economic performance in both Japan and continental Europe, which look very much like the "Washington Consensus" prescriptions for developing countries, lack a central organizing principle. Precisely what kind of capitalism do the proponents of the standard prescriptions envision for these other countries? Our answer to this question, again not surprising to readers who have made it this far, is that continental Europe and Japan, as perhaps the leading exemplars of big-firm capitalism, need a healthy dose of what we have called "innovative entrepreneurship." Although some large firms in these parts of the world have been truly innovative—Toyota in Japan or Nokia in Europe, to take two examples—the United States experience teaches that the most reliable source of radical innovation (and that is what is required to step up growth) is to be found among new, vibrant firms that do not have a vested interest in preserving their current markets. Ironically, the European and Japanese economies were built by entrepreneurs and still have many smaller firms, indeed so small in some cases (Italy being a prime example) that they are unable to take advantage of economies of scale necessary to match the low prices coming out of China and other low-cost producing nations or find it difficult to grow.[1] Nonetheless, the industrial makeup of these economies is far more stable—and stagnant—than that of the United States where the names of companies in any list of "top" enterprises changes from decade to decade. Thus, we find it fair and useful, though admittedly convenient, to characterize the continental European and Japanese economies as leading exemplars of big-firm capitalism and to suggest that only by renewing the innovative entrepreneurial spirit that once helped build these economies can each reasonably expect to grow more rapidly in the future.

Second, and of equal importance, any reform program aimed at enhancing growth over the long run must take account of fundamental political realities in both parts of the world: that abrupt, radical change is unlikely to be embraced by the majority of voters or, even if initially embraced, is not likely, given current realities, to be maintained for a sustained period. Instead, if any reform package is to have a chance at producing an enduring and constructive impact, it probably must be incremental in nature. The model we suggest here draws on the way in which China has gradually embraced capitalism, as opposed to Russia's sudden turn from central planning to something akin to Wild West capitalism.

The Need for Growth

In chapter 2 we made the case for economic growth, aiming largely at American readers. But the arguments we laid out there apply with equal force to all countries, their governments, and their citizens. As the output of economies grows, so do average standards of living, something that all surely want.

Economic growth is also useful, if not essential, if countries want to make good on their costly promises to their citizens: promises to pay for their health care, their retirement, to cushion the economic pain of unemployment, and so forth. While European governments have promised their citizens more protection than those of most other countries, including Japan, these two parts of the world share a common demographic challenge—population aging—that will be far easier to meet with faster growing economies. Figure 5 should make this clear. As recently as 1995,

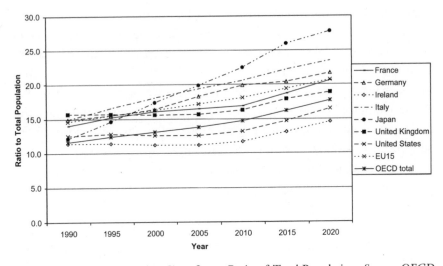

Figure 5. Population over Age Sixty-five as Ratio of Total Population. *Source: OECD Factbook 2005: Economic, Environmental, and Social Statistics.* Paris: OECD, August 2005.

the share of the population represented by those over sixty-five was pretty much the same—roughly within two percentage points of 15 percent—in Western Europe, Japan, and the United States. By 2005, however, the share of the elderly in Japan had soared to 20 percent, while the share in the United States remained flat at 13 percent. By 2020, all rich countries will have aged to the point where the share of the elderly will be approaching 30 percent in Japan, 20–25 percent in Western Europe, and 17 percent in the United States. By 2030, it is predicted that there will be only one worker for every retiree in Italy, and a ratio of 1.3 workers to each retiree in Germany (Baily and Kirkegaard, 2005, 16). Feeding, clothing, and caring for retirees will therefore require a very large and increasing share of what employed persons produce in total.

Population aging in these societies will have certain unavoidable implications. As the share of the population over sixty-five increases, the ratio of those working to those not working—and receiving pension and health care benefits in retirement—will steadily fall. Only if workers become increasingly productive, that is, only if economic output per employed person grows, will workers experience the rising living standards their parents enjoyed, unless of course retirement benefits are cut, which is highly unlikely as elderly citizens comprise an ever larger share of voting publics. More than generational warfare is at stake. If wages do not continue to rise, then those most able to leave—those with the skills necessary to prosper in an increasingly global and technological economy—will do so, making it more difficult for the economies they leave to support aging populations. Indeed, many of continental Europe's "best and brightest" have already crossed the English Channel to work in the more thriving economies of Great Britain and Ireland, or the Atlantic Ocean to reach the United States (to the extent they are able to do so given the more restrictive immigration policies pursued since the September 11 terrorist attacks).[2]

In principle, Japan and Western Europe would find it much easier to manage their aging challenge if they adopted substantially more liberal immigration policies, but this, too, is highly unlikely. Japan has a long history of not accepting immigrants, and for cultural reasons it is not likely to change course despite the growing fiscal pressures implied by its rapidly aging population. Meanwhile, many European countries already face considerable difficulties in absorbing their existing immigrant populations, which, as shown in table 13, are substantial in a number of nations, and which in some countries constitute a greater share of the populations than is the case in the United States, which is widely known for its welcoming attitude toward immigrants. But as the 2005 riots among Islamic immigrants living in France and the ongoing tensions between the native and immigrant Islamic populations in historically tolerant Netherlands illustrate, many European countries have had a hard time fully accepting into the economic, political mainstreams of their societies immigrants who are often less skilled and hold different religious beliefs. As a result, immigrants typically suffer much higher unemployment rates and earn lower wages than natives, who already have their own substantial unemployment problems (Great Britain and Ireland excepted).

For these reasons, therefore, neither Japan nor the European countries are likely to be able to reduce significantly the financial burdens of their aging populations by accepting more immigrants. Both regions must find a way to grow more rapidly in the years ahead or else face wrenching generational warfare over the generosity of retirement benefits. In some ways, this challenge will be more difficult for the countries to meet at this time

Table 13 Immigrant Population in Selected Countries, as a Percentage of Total Population

Country	1990	2002
Denmark	3.7	6.2
Netherlands	8.1	10.6
United States	—	11.8
Austria	5.9	8.8
Belgium	9.1	8.2
France	6.3	—
Germany	8.4	8.9
Ireland	2.3	4.8
Japan	0.9	1.5
Norway	3.4	4.3
Spain	0.7	3.1
Sweden	5.6	5.3
United Kingdom	3.2	4.5

Source: OECD Factbook 2005: Economic, Environmental, and Social Statistics (Paris: OECD, 2005).

than following World War II, when both parts of the world were flat on their backs and citizens worked hard simply to survive. Furthermore, the nations then were too poor to support a broad economic safety net—for those no longer working or those still in the labor force who were looking for work. Today, however, residents of both Western Europe and Japan are largely comfortable economically—at least the healthy majority who have jobs—and they perceive no immediate crisis, even though many of their children cannot locate suitable employment. The central question both parts of the world face is how soon their citizenry will wake up and realize the magnitude of the economic challenge before them and whether, when they do, a crisis already will be at hand.

Entrepreneurship and the Transformation toward Big-Firm Capitalism

One of our central themes in this chapter is that both the countries of continental Europe and Japan have drifted too far in the direction of what we call "big-firm" capitalism and are now sorely in need of the kind of innovative entrepreneurship that has sparked a reawakening of their European cousins across the English Channel and the remarkable resurgence over the past decade in productivity growth in the United States. But the capitalisms of both regions of the world were not always so dominated by large firms. In the nineteenth century and into the early twentieth century, the companies that are now synonymous with big-firm capitalism—Daimler Benz in Germany, Fiat in Italy, Toyota and Mitsubishi in Japan, to name just a few—were, after all, started by entrepreneurs.

And it is not just the entrepreneurs who championed entrepreneurship. Intellectual leaders, at least in Europe, also praised the virtues of individualism and enterprise, thereby providing important role models for entrepreneurial thought in the United States. For example, as Edmund Phelps has pointed out, as early as the eighteenth century, the French economist Jean-Baptiste Say (the father of "Say's law," that "supply creates its own demand") extolled the importance of entrepreneurs in constantly reinventing economies. Similar, and perhaps even better known, are the writings of British political economist Adam Smith, who first explained how supposedly self-interested businessmen, actually entrepreneurs in his day, were forced by market pressures to serve the broader social interest by focusing on what they did best.

> As every individual, therefore, endeavours as much as he can both to employ his capital in the support of domestic industry, and so to direct that industry that its produce may be of the greatest value; every individual necessarily labours to render the annual revenue of the society as great as he can. He generally, indeed, neither intends to promote the public interest, nor knows how much he is promoting it. By preferring the support of domestic to that of foreign industry, he intends only his own security; *and by directing that industry in such a manner as its produce may be of the greatest value, he intends only his own gain, and he is in this, as in many other cases, led by an invisible hand to promote an end which was no part of his intention.* Nor is it always the worse for the society that it was no part of it. By pursuing his own interest he frequently promotes that of the society more effectually than when he really intends to promote it. (emphasis added) (Smith, 1976, 351)

Despite this thought leadership, both Europe (including Great Britain) and Japan moved away from their entrepreneurial roots toward a very different sort of capitalism, one that focused on not only preserving large firms, but also actively promoting them through various forms of state guidance: subsidies, implicit or explicit directions to banks to support particular enterprises, and other kinds of state assistance (although there has been an active debate among academics for some time over the importance of these measures for growth). In Japan, this big-firm capitalism took the form of zaibatsus, or financial-industrial conglomerates, in which the countries' largest banks both loaned money to and invested in the equity of that country's emerging large enterprises. In Europe, too, banks took equity positions in large borrowers, but neither the firms nor the banks called all the shots. As Columbia University's Edmund Phelps has explained, a "corporatist" economic model evolved in the early decades of the twentieth century in continental Europe, South America, and East Asia, one in which property may have been privately owned but the fundamental decisions about how national savings were to be allocated were made by *social consensus*—including firms, labor unions, banks, and, we would add, government. (Phelps, 2006). This corporatist model was (and is) similar to the iron triangle of "big firms, big labor, and big government," minus the banks, so well described for the United States in the first two decades following World War II by the late John Kenneth Galbraith in his then-best-selling work *The New Industrial State* (a description that no longer fits the U.S. economy, as we have argued at various points in this book).

The corporatist model, especially the active involvement of organized labor in firm governance, flowered after World War II, especially in Germany, the home of "codetermination," or the practice of labor representatives sitting on corporate boards (often along with bank representatives). Before the war, labor unions struggled to gain the right to strike, both in Europe and in the United States. For a time, formal labor participation in firm governance in the postwar era was viewed favorably, even in the United States, as an important instrument for gaining labor's cooperation in productivity and quality improvements in firms while avoiding strikes. In more recent times, however, labor's involvement seems to have acted as a brake on innovation, especially changes that lead to job loss. To this extent, labor board representatives have a clear conflict of interest, since their main objective—protecting existing jobs—is not coincident with the central objective of the firm, which is to maximize its current and future profitability.

So how did this come to pass? That is, how and why did Japan and continental Europe seemingly move away from their entrepreneurial roots to embrace something very different? This is a complicated question and we clearly do not pretend to be able to answer it fully, but we do have some thoughts that are relevant to the answer. Furthermore, we believe it is important to understand the answer to this question both when analyzing why the two parts of the world later experienced significant slowdowns in their rates of growth and when thinking about ways in which growth may be accelerated in the future.

For one thing, there was no populist revolt—as there was in the United States, in the form of antitrust legislation—in either Europe or Japan against the emergence of large firms that may have dominated particular markets. To be sure, both parts of the world later adopted antitrust laws, and in the past two decades, in particular, European authorities (operating through the European Union) have become especially aggressive in this area. But until these recent developments, European and Japanese authorities have tolerated, and arguably encouraged, the growth of large enterprises.

In the postwar era, this attitude has been easy to understand. Coming out of the war, both the Japanese and European economies (and societies) were devastated. Once-large firms literally had to be resurrected at a time when American companies dominated the global arena. It would have seemed self-defeating for governments in either Japan or Europe to handicap their fledgling enterprises through antitrust constraints. A similar rationale would have applied to the prewar years as well, especially in the two decades following World War I, when Germany was flat on its back and Japan was only emerging as an economic force. Later, in the 1930s, with the world mired in depression, the last thing policy makers in either part of the world would have worried about would have been the consequences of allowing their large firms, which then were struggling to survive, to grow too large. The only remaining puzzle is why neither Japan nor Europe adopted some form of antitrust policy before World War I. Our educated guess is that in this period, the United States itself was just beginning to experiment with antitrust enforcement; indeed, the United States Congress did not prohibit anticompetitive mergers until 1914. The only antitrust law before that time, the Sherman Antitrust Act of 1890, prohibited restraints of trade and acts of monopolization, and prosecutions under this law, though notable (against the steel, oil, and tobacco industries), still were not yet significant in number.

Second, the financial systems in both Japan and Europe were especially conducive to the emergence and growth of big-firm capitalism. In both economies, banks have long been the dominant source of financing for business, and not just any banks—very large banks. Indeed, in Japan, following World War II, certain "main banks" developed in and around Tokyo, and government (through the Ministry of Finance) fostered their growth. As this occurred, banks assumed far greater importance in financing businesses than they had before the war, when the capital markets, both in the form of bonds and stocks, provided most business financing, even for medium-size firms (Hoshi and Kashyap, 2001).[3] In Europe, governments themselves owned some banks (as has been true in many developing economies). Furthermore, in both economies, banks were permitted to own equity in companies, which typically often borrowed money from the same institutions. In addition, these so-called universal banks were permitted to engage in a wide range of other financial activities, including the underwriting of securities and insurance.

The Japanese and European financial systems heavily favored well-established companies rather than start-ups or fledgling enterprises for two reasons. Banks naturally were more interested in lending to larger companies whose shares they had bought and could potentially trade. At the same time, securities markets developed more slowly in Japan and Europe than in the United States, an outcome that may have been an unintended consequence of advanced banking institutions in the former countries, which were not nearly as prevalent in the latter. In particular, it is possible, if not likely, that securities markets developed more quickly and more deeply in the United States precisely because commercial banks were prohibited from underwriting securities under the Glass-Steagall Act of 1933, enacted in the midst of the Depression. This prohibition ironically protected investment banks (that do underwrite stocks and bonds) from competition for more than six decades before Congress effectively repealed Glass-Steagall in 1999 (by enacting the Gramm-Leach-Bliley Financial Modernization Act), during which time several of these institutions (notably, Goldman Sachs, Morgan Stanley, and Merrill Lynch) grew into financial powerhouses. The same thing did not occur in Europe very likely because the large universal banks there already had easier ways to finance the activities of their large firm customers—simply by lending to them— than by underwriting their securities.

It is more difficult to explain the slower development of securities markets in Japan, where Glass-Steagall was imposed by the United States after World War II and therefore should have given a similar impetus to the development of strong investment banks and securities markets in Japan as it did in the United States. That this did not occur seems attributable to at least two factors. One is the poor condition of the Japanese economy coming out of the war. A second factor is that because the pattern of cross-shareholdings of commercial companies and banks that existed before the war continued thereafter, large Japanese corporate borrowers had little incentive to turn to securities markets for financing.

In any event, the slower development of securities markets in Japan and Europe, relative to the United States, biased the financing of companies in the former economies, both before and after World War II, toward large enterprises. Securities markets represent an alternative source of funds for enterprises and thus afford more opportunities for new entrants to support their growth, which can often come at the expense of established firms. In addition, securities markets offer a means of "exit" for venture capitalists, who played an important role in the early stage financing of many high-technology companies in the United States in the 1980s and 1990s (Gompers and Lerner, 1999). That is, investors in a start-up company that reaches a certain level of maturity and profitability can exit from that firm by simply selling their shares in the securities market. Other economies where securities markets are not as well developed have not been as successful in fostering the formation and growth of innovative companies, which inevitably has meant a larger role for more established firms.

Finally, big-firm capitalism was especially in vogue in both Europe and Japan after World War II for the reason already hinted at: governments there presumably thought this was the only way for their economies to compete with the powerful, emerging global companies from the United States. By the mid-1960s, for example, some Europeans voiced fears about the continuing and seemingly inevitable growth of U.S.-based multinational companies (Servan-Schrieber, 1968), much as Americans later (in the 1980s) came to fear what then seemed to be the juggernauts from Japan. Indeed, the European Commission, now the European Union, was born in the 1950s in part to counter the economic power of the United States. European governments also have encouraged the growth of national champions in certain industries (Airbus in airplane manufacturing being a prime example) more or less explicitly to counterbalance the rise of American companies.

A good case can be made that for its time, at least through the first two or three decades of the postwar era, big-firm capitalism served a useful purpose, though we will never know definitively whether the European and Japanese economies would have advanced more rapidly with a different mix of more entrepreneurial firms. As we discussed in chapter 4, large firms, with the ability to mobilize large pools of capital and labor, have an inherent advantage in mass-producing others' innovations or in imitating products and services developed elsewhere. Because they literally were starting over, firms in both economies were well positioned after the war to do little more than imitate or adopt American technology, either through licensing, joint ventures, or simply basic observation. And that is exactly what they did until a number of the more successful enterprises introduced incremental and in some cases radical innovations that outpaced their American counterparts. The development of fuel-efficient, reliable cars in Japan is one example. In Germany's case, Daimler Benz already had the expertise before the war in manufacturing high-quality automobiles, and this advantage continued after the war.

But a capitalist system that is good at imitation is not necessarily well suited for more radical (or even less-than-radical) innovation. By definition, innovation is a departure from what currently exists. Large firms are generally not enthusiastic about departing from what they are already making money at, and so radical, disruptive innovation is far more likely to come from newer companies. In particular, innovation has difficulty flowering in an environment where everyone needs consensus. There are exceptions to the rule, of course—Toyota and Honda perhaps are the leading examples. The problem is the rule, the subject we take up next.

Eurosclerosis and Japanese Stagnation

If imitation is the best form of flattery, then imitation has much to recommend it. From the ashes of World War II, continental Europe grew through the next four decades, to the point where by the mid-1980s, per capita incomes in the core European countries were roughly 80–90 percent of the United States level. Japan's growth was even more impressive, reaching a similar level but starting from a lower point.

Yet what happens when one runs out of things to imitate? That is essentially the problem that confronted both Europe and Japan at the end of the twentieth century. Since 1990, per capita incomes of European countries and Japan have slipped relative to the United States, as evidenced by slower rates of per capita GDP growth in these countries compared to America (see table 12). Slower growth has translated into persistently higher unemployment in regions of the world where unemployment rates traditionally had been lower than in the United States. For the past several decades, continental Europe has been plagued by unemployment rates that have hovered at or above double digits. In Japan, where unemployment rates of 2 percent or less had become the norm, the unemployment rate has held stubbornly in the 4–5 percent range for much of the past fifteen years.

Slow growth and high unemployment in Europe even has acquired a name: "Eurosclerosis." In theory, the closer integration of the European Union—in particular, the harmonization of different national rules so that goods and people can easily cross borders within the Union—was supposed to jump start European growth in the 1990s (Hufbauer, 1992). A similar growth spurt was widely expected following the decision by most of the EU countries in the early part of this decade to adopt a single currency, the Euro, which was supposed to make it easier for firms and consumers throughout Europe to trade with each other by eliminating the toll extracted in the form of currency conversion fees and uncertainty about the values of the former national currencies. In addition, a truly common

European market was supposed to enable European firms to realize economies of scale, the better to compete on the world stage. In combination, these effects should have accelerated growth.

In all likelihood they did, but any growth-enhancing effects of the move toward a single European market ran into strong headwinds from other forces (which we discuss shortly). Table 12 shows the result: while growth throughout continental Europe has continued, it has not accelerated or met the level of the United States, let alone the optimistic expectations of those who have backed closer European economic integration throughout the past two decades.

Economic problems in Japan are equally if not better known. Until 1989, Japan's postwar record of economic growth was stellar, the envy of the world. Then came the crash of that country's stock and real estate markets, the bursting of the so-called bubble economy, and with it the rest of the Japanese economy. From 1989 forward, Japan's GDP grew very slowly (see table 12), while its stock market languished and its banking system fell into disarray, requiring huge infusions of government funds to remain afloat. During the past fifteen years, Japanese authorities have tried an extraordinary combination of monetary and fiscal stimulus to raise GDP; the Bank of Japan has lowered short-term interest rates essentially to zero, and the government has variously pushed tax cuts and spending programs that have generated annual deficits of 5 percent of GDP or more, very high by Japanese (or any other country's) standards. Until 2005 or so, this extraordinary combination of fiscal stimulus had little effect, as Japanese consumers continued to save high fractions of their incomes (no doubt fearing worse times ahead, collectively a self-fulfilling strategy) and Japanese firms were reluctant to invest.

Clearly, in Japan's case, something structural in that country's economy has stunted growth, since it is difficult to imagine that any stronger macroeconomic stimulus could reasonably have been provided or, if so, that it would have more effect (Lincoln, 2001). Continental Europe, too, has structural problems, although restrictive macroeconomic policy there also has limited growth.[4] Indeed, the leaders of European governments essentially admitted their economic problems by embracing, at least in principle, a broad-ranged reform effort in the Lisbon agenda of the European Commission announced in April 2000.

So what are these "structural difficulties" and are they similar or substantially different between the two economies? Let's review some of the commonly mentioned obstacles and the evidence relating to them.

Taxes and High Social Welfare Spending

One barrier to growth in Europe that some Americans (and Europeans) point to is the substantially higher taxes in Europe. There is a reason for this, of course, and that is because continental (and Nordic) European countries typically have much more extensive government "safety net" programs—universal health insurance, child care, and unemployment programs—than are found in other rich countries. Indeed, the safety net programs are cited by some observers as making life too comfortable for Europeans, contributing to the fewer hours they work and ostensibly dampening incentives for them to start new businesses.

Whatever readers may think about these two subjects (and we suspect opinions will vary significantly)—taxes and the welfare states they support—the evidence is slim that they are major contributing factors to slow productivity growth, although generous unemployment programs, in particular, almost certainly do contribute to the persistently high unemployment rates in continental Europe (Phelps, 2006). If taxes and welfare-state programs were significant barriers to more rapid growth in Europe, then how does one explain the slowdown in productivity growth in Japan, where taxes are among the lowest (relative to GDP) of any of the rich OECD countries? Furthermore, throughout most of the postwar era, European countries have ranked at the top of the OECD's list of tax revenues, as shares of GDP, and yet Europe grew rapidly until the 1980s. If tax burdens were significant impediments to long-term productivity growth, their effects would have been evident much earlier.[5]

As for the welfare-state arguments, with the exception of unemployment insurance benefits, one would think that a generous government safety net—the support of health care and childcare, in particular—would *promote* rather than detract from growth. For example, if workers know that their health care costs are covered independent of their employment circumstances, then they should be more willing to establish their own firms than if, as in the United States, their health insurance is tied to their current jobs. While this effect may be at work and perhaps is reflected in the rates of self-employment in continental Europe that are higher than they might otherwise be, a strong government safety net nonetheless does not appear to have driven many Europeans to *be innovative* entrepreneurs.

Culture

Perhaps, then, the absence of innovative entrepreneurship in both continental Europe and Japan reflects a different cultural mindset than is found in other countries—not just the United States, but in India, China, and Israel, among others. For example, given the poor economic conditions from which Japan emerged in the first several decades after the war, it is possible that widespread lifetime employment opportunities available in large firms (and in the government), coupled with the related housing and other social benefits of working for large companies, over time created a cultural bias favoring employment by others rather than independent entrepreneurial activity, and that this attitude has been handed down to successive generations. Such an outcome appears to be reflected in the new business formation rate in Japan, which over the past quarter century, has ranged between a third to a half that of the United States (Cox and Koo, 2006). Furthermore, because the government does not provide as extensive retirement benefits as are found in other rich economies, many of those who reach the age of sixty or thereabouts and thus no longer work for large companies turn to self-employment, typically ownership of small retail establishments, as a means of providing for retirement. Thus, a culture of "replicative entrepreneurship" has developed in the postwar era that has nothing to do with what we have called "innovative entrepreneurship." To sum it up, a reasonably good case seems to exist for the proposition that Japanese culture does not support innovative entrepreneurship—by the young and middle-aged workers, or by those who supposedly are in retirement but in fact are engaged only in replicative entrepreneurship.

A different sort of cultural attitude against innovative entrepreneurship seems to have pervaded Europe. There, too, the trauma of the postwar years may have driven a generation of workers to embrace the comfort and seeming employment stability of working for larger firms and to transmit that attitude to their offspring. The problem that many young European adults now face, however, is that large firms have not been hiring in recent years, in large part because it is extremely difficult under the law for these firms to fire any new employees who turn out to be incompetent or irresponsible. In principle, one would think that the harsh economic environment would encourage many younger workers to seek entrepreneurial careers. But as Edmund Phelps has suggested to us, a generation of parents has sheltered its children (now adults) from having to earn money in their teen years, whether in school or over the summers, and this may have dulled their entrepreneurial drive and instincts. The risk aversion that is so inconsistent with entrepreneurship is perhaps most pronounced in France, where surveys in 2006 reported that most young French wanted civil service jobs for the apparent lifetime security they offered.

One other cultural attitude, shared among Japanese and Europeans, is an apparent hostility toward extreme income inequality (though not to inherited wealth). It is commonly observed, for example, that the differential between the pay of typical workers and senior executives at American companies is much wider, and growing more so, than in either Japan or Europe. In one sense, the narrower income disparities in the latter two economies may work to their economic benefit, since workers are more likely to see themselves in the same economic boat as their managers if their pay is more closely aligned, and thus be more likely to think of productivity improvements on their own (something for which Japanese companies are rightly famous) or to accept those introduced by management. But any such beneficial effect of narrow pay differentials, assuming it to exist, may also be more than offset by the hostility that those narrower differentials may generate toward entrepreneurs who earn extraordinary profits from their successful undertakings. Corporate legal theorist Professor Mark Roe of Columbia University has observed that Europeans, as individuals and through their elected officials, look askance on highly profitable ventures and presumably those who profit from them (Roe, 2002). From what we know about the consensus-driven culture in Japan, we suspect that similar attitudes can be found there as well.

Policies Underpinning Culture

As appealing as these cultural explanations for the absence of innovative entrepreneurship in continental Europe and Japan may be, it is important, in our view, to realize that certain *policies* underpin or, at the very least, have helped to shape these attitudes. The British and Irish experience, if nothing else, demonstrates that supposed "cultural attitudes" can sometimes be altered much more quickly than is sometimes surmised, particularly with the help of appropriate changes in government policies. As recently as 1980, both these economies were the laggards of Europe, especially Ireland, whose per capita income then was roughly half that of the Continent. Yet through major policy reforms—privatization of state-owned companies and freer product and labor markets in the United Kingdom, and substantially lower corporate income taxes, a well-educated labor force, and inducements for foreign direct investment in the case in Ireland—both economies grew much more rapidly in the ensuing twenty-five years than their continental counterparts. In the process, it has become much more socially acceptable, indeed desirable, to make money, not just by working for someone else but also on one's own.

Indeed, a quick look at both the Japanese and European economies reveals how certain policies have contributed to whatever cultural bias may exist against innovative entrepreneurship. For example, in Japan, tax policies permitting companies to deduct the costs of housing provided to their employees on the one hand reward employee loyalty, but on the other strongly discourage workers from going out on their own until they are forced to retire (much of the same can be said of U.S. tax policies that have allowed employers to deduct the cost of health care insurance provided to their employees). In addition, Ministry of Finance "guidance" that has supported the Japanese main banking system indirectly penalizes entrepreneurship by ensuring that banks finance large, existing enterprises rather than start-ups. Without access to formal financing to grow their enterprises, Japanese citizens who might otherwise want to start the next Toyota, Honda, or Mitsubishi are discouraged or effectively prevented from doing so. The increasing concentration of the Japanese financial system, especially its main banks, which Ministry of Finance authorities have encouraged in the wake of Japan's post-bubble banking problems, has further biased the banks toward lending funds to large enterprises rather than to less-well-established newcomers. This effect may have been partially offset by the unwinding of the banks' shareholding positions in their large borrowers, but the historical lending patterns favoring the funding of large companies still appear to remain the same.

Would-be European entrepreneurs also complain about a lack of access to capital, though the role of government policy on this issue is less clear. European governments do not guide private banks' lending decisions, but complaints about the lack of access to bank capital are more common than in the United States (European Commission, 2002). But in an age when credit card financing is widely available and is used in developed economies to finance start-ups, and many start-ups themselves do not seem to require much capital, it is not clear how significant a constraint access to capital really is, any longer, to the launching of at least some new enterprises (Hurst and Lusardi, 2004). For ventures that are more capital-intensive, however, the absence of early stage or "seed" capital is a problem that Europeans, and the French in particular, have raised as a significant barrier to innovative entrepreneurship. Later we suggest that to the extent that financing is a problem, it is closely related to other policies that inhibit growth of new enterprises in Europe.

Another policy-driven barrier to entrepreneurship is the cost and red tape entailed in business registration. The data presented in table 14 suggest that although the costs of registering a business are low in some European countries, in others they remain sizeable. Also it is much more difficult to hire and fire workers throughout Europe than in the United States. If it is difficult to start and, perhaps more important, to grow new companies, it should not be surprising to find that Europeans are less prone to engage in entrepreneurship than Americans.

In short, although cultural attitudes may now be discouraging would-be entrepreneurs from launching enterprises in both Japan and Europe, which helps to entrench the dominance of large firms in both economies, it is vital to realize that past policies have contributed to these attitudes while independently reinforcing big-firm capitalism in each of these areas of the world.

Eurosclerosis, Japanese Stagnation, and Big-Firm Capitalism

The recent decades of relatively slow growth in Europe and Japan attest to the weaknesses of big-firm capitalism (see chapter 4). One tendency of large firms, especially if guided or assisted by the state, is either to overinvest or to invest in the wrong projects. Japan's experience provides a striking example. Through much of the 1980s when Japanese companies

Table 14 Costs of Doing Business in the United States, Japan, and Europe

	Cost of starting a business (% income per capita)	Cost of registering property	Difficulty of hiring (index 0–100)	Difficulty of firing (index 0–100)	Cost of enforcing contracts (% of debt)
United States	0.5	0.5	0	10	7.5
Japan	10.7	4.1	17	0	8.6
Western Europe					
Austria	5.7	4.5	11	40	9.8
Belgium	11.1	12.8	11	10	6.2
Denmark	0.0	0.6	11	10	5.3
Finland	1.2	4.0	44	40	6.5
France	1.2	6.5	78	40	11.7
Germany	4.7	4.1	44	40	10.5
Greece	24.6	13.7	78	40	12.7
Iceland	2.9	2.4	33	0	9.3
Ireland	5.3	10.3	28	30	21.1
Italy	15.7	0.9	61	30	17.6
Netherlands	13.0	6.2	28	60	17.0
Norway	2.7	2.5	44	30	4.2
Portugal	13.4	7.4	33	60	17.5
Spain	16.5	7.2	67	50	14.1
Sweden	0.7	3.0	28	40	5.9
Switzerland	8.7	0.4	0	10	5.2
United Kingdom	0.7	4.1	11	10	17.2
Eastern Europe					
Albania	31.1	3.6	44	20	28.6
Bosnia & Herzegovina	40.9	6.0	56	30	19.6
Bulgaria	9.6	2.3	61	10	14.0
Croatia	13.4	5.0	61	50	10.0
Czech Republic	9.5	3.0	33	20	9.1
Hungary	22.4	11.0	11	20	8.1
Moldova	17.1	1.5	33	70	16.2
Poland	22.2	1.6	11	40	8.7
Romania	5.3	2.0	67	50	12.4
Slovakia	5.1	0.1	17	40	15.0
Slovenia	10.1	2.0	61	50	15.2

Source: World Bank, 2006.

were investing at a rapid rate, and the share of investment in Japan's GDP was well above that of the United States, there were many calls in the United States for U.S. companies to think longer term and for policy to encourage them to do so. It was said that the supposed obsession of U.S. stock analysts and investors on companies' short-term profits was leading U.S. firms to ignore the long term, and allegedly the strongest proof supporting this argument (or complaint) was the high investment rate in Japan. Some believed that Japanese companies were able to take a long-term view and to invest as much as they were doing because of their close relationships to their main banks through the ownership stakes enjoyed by these banks, which also supposedly had a long time horizon (encouraged by "administrative guidance" from government officials who ensured that they were doing the right thing).

In retrospect, these fears and the policy arguments that flowed from them look seriously mistaken. If anything, the cozy alliance between Japan's banks and its leading big-firm borrowers led the latter to *invest too much* and in the wrong ventures. All this became apparent when the bubbles in the Japanese stock and real estate markets burst, leaving Japanese companies that had invested so heavily with excess capacity. Japan's economic problems were compounded by the complicity of the large banks in this outcome. Because the banks could count a portion of their unrealized gains on their company shareholdings toward their shareholder capital, the banks looked much stronger than they actually were. In turn, the banks were eager to make loans to their borrowers, many of whom collateralized the loans with inflated property values. When the property boom turned to bust, property collateral values fell, as did demand for the products that the firms were producing. Furthermore, the sharp drop in stock prices wiped out much or all of the unrealized gains in the company shares held by the banks, which forced a sharp reduction of the banks' capital and thus their ability to lend. In combination, all these things—the bursting of the property and stock market bubbles and the downturn in demand— meant that the Japanese banks were in deep trouble on two accounts: their capital base had dwindled and their borrowers had difficulty repaying their loans. Meanwhile, many borrowers were stuck with excess capacity.

The Japanese government compounded these problems by failing to take prompt action to shore up the banks and force them to restructure their loans (and quickly recognize their losses). Instead, Japanese financial officials appeared to take their cue from U.S. financial policy makers during the 1980s, who when confronted with the insolvency of several thousand savings institutions engaged in "regulatory forbearance," hoping that economic conditions would improve sufficiently rapidly so that the officials would be spared from taking more aggressive action. Japan's regulators failed to enforce their own capital standards and allowed the troubled banks (and there were many of them) to continue lending to troubled borrowers by simply rolling over (or extending the maturity of) previously extended debt. This went on for more than a decade, not only delaying adjustment by many of Japan's leading companies to new economic realities, but depriving worthy borrowers of funds for expansion. Eventually, Japanese policy makers bit the bullet and injected government funds into the banks to help restore their capital positions, but unlike American policy makers—who ultimately allowed many financial institutions to close—Japanese regulators tended to force the merger of troubled financial companies with each other. (There were a few exceptions to this policy, and in one notable case, the failure of Long-Term Credit Bank, the regulators allowed an American company to buy the institution.)

As a net result of this failure to recognize reality, Japan's economic recovery was delayed, perhaps for years, and its economy was denied the benefit of companies that might have formed and grown had they had access to the capital that was instead channeled to troubled companies that were artificially propped up. Japanese taxpayers will be paying a heavy price—perhaps the equivalent of several hundred billions of dollars—for the years of delay in cleaning up the country's banking system (Hoshi and Kashyap, 2004). The government's fumbling also contributed to a loss of confidence by Japanese citizens in their political system, which more than likely made them less willing to spend, thus contributing to persistently high private savings rates, which counteracted much of the macroeconomic stimulus that Japan's fiscal and monetary authorities attempted to provide throughout this period. The persistent pattern of cross-shareholdings between the large banks and their customers, although it gradually began to unwind in the 1990s, also contributed to the sluggish reaction of the banks' to their borrowers' financial difficulties. So did the fact that mutual life insurers have been among the largest shareholders of the large commercial banks. Because mutual life insurers have no stockholders, only policy holders, they had weak incentives to bring pressure to bear on the banks to improve their performance (Fukao, 2004), which they could have done had they more aggressively cut their losses on existing loans and sought out more opportunities to lend to other firms. In short, the Japanese capitalist system, built around large companies and their banks— that, for a time, seemed primed to promote investment and growth among the economy's largest, most successful firms—contained the seeds of its own malaise, which did not become evident until the firms (and their financial backers) discovered that opportunities for imitation and incremental innovation had been exhausted.

Continental Europe, too, has suffered from problems related to big-firm capitalism, but these have a different origin and do not relate to the excessive investment that eventually led to the bursting of Japan's asset-market bubbles. But as in Japan, government policy shares in the blame, and in the future, change in policy will be required to correct the problem.

A shorthand summary of Europe's economic problems is that the continental economies are simply too rigid and do not facilitate or adapt well to change. This rigidity is reinforced by government policies that are inconsistent with the last of our four preconditions for successful entrepreneurial capitalism: "keeping the winners on their toes." Indeed, a number of continental European policies do the opposite, inhibiting entry by new firms (through restrictive zoning rules and in some countries excessive costs for registration of new businesses); subsidizing certain national champions, which tilts the competitive playing field toward the chosen firm(s) and away from potentially more efficient competitors; imposing various industry-specific regulations ostensibly for other purposes but with the net effect of sheltering existing firms from competition (as, for example, the German requirements relating to the water used in local beer production); and maintaining various sorts of tariff and nontariff barriers that thwart global competitors from enhancing competitive pressure on local firms (Baily and Kirkegaard, 2005).

European labor regulations also contribute to economic rigidity. In many European economies, layoffs and firings at all but the smallest firms are subject routinely to regulatory or court review. This system not only deters both existing and new firms from hiring new workers (see the ratings in table 14), thus dampening the demand for labor and raising the unemployment rate, but it indirectly works to the relative advantage of larger firms since it helps to insulate them from competition that otherwise new, rapidly growing enterprises would provide. Indeed, one significant finding of a study of OECD economies is that successful start-up enterprises in the United States add workers at a much faster rate than those in Europe (OECD, 2003). Certainly, the major reason for this must be the more restrictive labor rules in Europe. To make matters worse, generous unemployment compensation and health and disability programs that can provide payments to unemployed workers for extended periods dampen the supply of workers who are actively looking for work at any one time. Although this effect may lower the measured unemployment rate by reducing the measured labor force—which includes only those already working and unemployed individuals who are *actively* looking for work—it dampens total economic output and its growth.

Accordingly, contrary to what one would expect in a dynamic economy, where good firms grow and poorly performing firms do not, in several European countries the very opposite has been the case. As one study has documented, in these countries the companies in the bottom quartile of performance—the least productive firms—have grown more rapidly than the best-performing companies. As the study authors conclude, "the United States eliminates its least productive companies; the EU does not," a result they attribute to the oppressive combination of excessive product and labor market regulation and zoning rules that inhibit entry by more innovative firms (Baily and Farrell, 2006b).

The European Postwar Miracle: Can It Happen Again, and If So, How?

To their credit, European and Japanese political leaders and high-level bureaucrats are very much aware of their economies' structural difficulties and have announced plans to address them. In Europe, the Lisbon agenda is the principal reform vehicle, with an announced objective no less sweeping than to make the EU into the "most competitive and dynamic knowledge-based economy in the world, capable of sustainable economic growth with more and better jobs and greater social cohesion." The

European Council (an official body of the EU) has recognized that this will require a *"radical transformation of the (European) economy"* in order to create 20 million new jobs by 2010.[6] To accomplish this, the Council has proposed reforms that, in principle, would reenergize the continent's large firms while encouraging significantly more entrepreneurship.

As for Japan, as of this writing, Prime Minister Koizumi has been among the most vociferous champions of radical reform. Koizumi successfully ran for reelection in 2005 on a platform that, among other things, called for privatizing Japan's largest financial institution, its Postal Savings System. This would build on prior reform efforts that have helped to make Japan's economy somewhat more flexible and enhanced incentives for innovative activity. Among them: modestly lower taxes, lower barriers to imports, some crackdown on bribery of government officials, and some progress in lowering the costs off starting a business (Cox and Koo, 2006, 5).

Perhaps by local standards the Lisbon agenda and Koizumi's reform plans are radical, but they fall far short of what many American—and, indeed, some European and Japanese—observers have been advocating for some time. Typically, advocates of these more radical reform packages or suggestions urge that the various components be adopted *simultaneously*. In that sense, the recommended plans are roughly equivalent, at least in terms of ambition, in their expressed commitment to the "shock therapy" that a number of Western economists urged upon the former states of the Soviet Union and Eastern Europe after the fall of the Berlin Wall, on the conjecture that one can cross a chasm only in one large jump not in many incremental steps.

For example, with respect to reform in Europe, the former chairman of President Clinton's Council of Economic Advisers, Martin Baily, has outlined (with colleagues) a series of ambitious reforms that would go far beyond anything the European Council or EU member states have so envisioned (Baily and Kirkegaard, 2005; Baily and Farrell, 2006b). We focus on these proposals not so much because we endorse each and every one of them (though we are sympathetic to them) but because they are illustrative of the kinds of policy suggestions that a number of analysts, inside and outside the EU and including such official bodies as the OECD, have been urging upon Europe for some time.

The proposals, which are listed in table 15, fall into three broad categories. The first two are structural (aimed at enhancing productivity growth and the flexibility of European labor markets) and the third is macroeconomic (to allow greater flexibility of fiscal and monetary policy during economic downturns). Although the specific measures highlighted in table 15 may look very much American in character, the kind that could be found in any "Washington Consensus" set of reform proposals for less developed countries, Baily and colleagues argue, persuasively in our view, that the proposals are based on well-analyzed economic principles and represent what would work best to rejuvenate the European economies. That many of the proposals seem to draw on the American experience is not accidental, however, since U.S. economic performance over the past decade has been extraordinary (though the American economy can stand some improvement and faces its own set of significant challenges in the future).

Baily and his colleagues also argue, again persuasively in our view, that several reform proposals advanced by the European Council pursuant to the Lisbon agenda are not high priority items (because of their distant connection to productivity growth) and may even be counterproductive. These include tax reform to reduce the high marginal income tax rate on upper-income taxpayers (in light of evidence that these rates, as high as they are, are not as detrimental to growth in output and employment as high marginal rates on low- and middle-income workers, which do discourage labor force participation); large-scale public infrastructure spending (given the lack of evidence that more spending here would add significantly to long-term growth); or significant increases in training and education of labor (to which Baily and his colleagues give low priority in light of the already relatively high skills of European workers).

Over the years, analysts in the United States and elsewhere have called for similar reforms in Japan, but with some differences from the list in table 15. For example, labor markets in Japan, too, are inflexible, but this is not so much because of extensive government protections that inhibit firms from shedding workers if they need to, but because large Japanese companies have a practice of not hiring laterally, instead taking on workers at a young age and keeping them until they retire. This system of lifetime employment has changed modestly over the past decade on account of Japan's economic difficulties but remains largely intact, especially at the larger Japanese companies. Below, we offer one modest policy suggestion that might crack this system and encourage more Japanese to take the entrepreneurial plunge.

In addition, although the country's main banks have been gradually unwinding their shareholdings in nonfinancial companies (typically their borrowers), this process has a long way to go, but it could be accelerated by government officials through "administrative guidance" (without the need for formal regulation or legislation). Although there is some hope that this is already occurring,[7] until it happens on a wider scale, the Japanese banking system still will be heavily biased toward lending to the country's largest companies rather than to prospective or new, high-growth enterprises. If the Japanese Postal Savings Bank is successfully privatized, this will gradually free up capital that would have gone into the bank, allowing it to find its way toward other ventures, with potentially some amount for newer companies. But this, too, will take some time, since even the prime minister's proposal would not fully privatize the system for another ten years. Fortunately, one item in table 15—more macroeconomic flexibility—is not relevant to Japan. As we have already noted, the Japanese government and its central bank have tried every trick in the book to promote economic expansion in the country, and only after more than a decade of such stimulus has it appeared that this policy is finally having some success.

It may seem ideal for governments in continental Europe and Japan to embrace these reforms fully and introduce them as rapidly as possible—or, in other words, to adopt a "shock therapy" approach to economic reform. But we believe the chance that this will happen is remote. The vast majority of adults in continental Europe and Japan are employed, earning more than they probably ever expected to, believe that they will continue working at their current jobs (if they are in large firms) until they retire, and are expecting to have a comfortable retirement largely paid for by governments their taxes have financed. Under these circumstances, it is not hard to understand why there seems to be so little support for any set of reforms that may threaten these expectations, even if in some not-so-distant future governments find it difficult to meet their financial obligations and even though in the current environment the children of financially comfortable parents cannot find substantial, well-paying work in their home countries.

Several recent events and trends can be understood when seen in this

Table 15 Illustrative Proposals to Reform European Economies

To increase productivity
- Reform zoning rules to encourage location/formation of new businesses
- End government subsidies of poorly performing companies
- Abandon policies for promotion of "national champions"
- Remove industry-specific regulations that limit competition
- Remove or reduce barriers to the formation of new businesses
- Open EU markets further to global competition
- Remove artificial impediments to competition in the service sectors
- Move rapidly toward EU-wide standards for professionals
- Improve the market for corporate control by eliminating artificial barriers to efficiency-enhancing mergers and acquisitions

To improve work incentives and increase labor market flexibility
- Substantially reduce barriers to hiring and firing of employees
- Require companies to provide reasonable compensation for laid-off workers, but only at moderate and predictable levels that do not discourage workers from looking for new jobs
- Limit government benefits for unemployed workers in size and duration, but pair them with a new "wage insurance" program to cushion the impact of accepting a new job with lower pay
- Cut marginal tax rates on low- and middle-income workers
- Modify the wage-setting process to facilitate more localized bargaining (so that wages are not uniform throughout the EU, regardless of local labor market conditions)
- Reform government retirement programs by gradually raising the age for "normal" retirement
- Reforming government health programs by introducing more marketlike incentives for performance

To improve macroeconomic performance
- Allow for more flexibility in the targets for government deficits
- Establish a more flexible monetary policy

Sources: Baily and Kirkegaard, 2005; Baily and Farrell, 2006a and 2006b.

light. In 2005, French voters rejected the EU constitution in part, in our view, out of fear that a stronger EU could mean faster economic and political reform in France (and elsewhere), something a majority of voters did not seem to welcome. Several months later, German voters refused to give Angela Merkel's Christian Democratic Union a majority in their parliamentary elections of September 2005, very likely because they, too, feared too much economic disruption from the economic changes—especially those that would have loosened German labor markets—Merkel had promised or at least hinted at during the campaign. As a result of the vote, Merkel was forced to cobble together a multiparty coalition that has so far evidenced little appetite for Merkel's pre-election economic reform proposals. Indeed, by spring 2006, Merkel had become one of the most popular leaders in Europe in large part because she had *rejected* her pre-election platform (Walker, 2006b).

The reaction against any move toward freer labor markets in France has been even more negative. In early 2006, Prime Minister Villepen, in an effort to reduce persistently high unemployment rates among French youth, proposed a law that would allow employers to hire and fire at will workers under the age of twenty-six. The proposal sparked a wave of protest marches and even riots, which forced the French government to back down (and to propose instead a weak substitute, a subsidy to employers to hire younger workers). From where we safely sit—on the other side of the Atlantic Ocean—the hostile public reaction to any efforts to liberalize labor protections for any class of existing workers in the core countries of continental Europe appears to be even stronger than the opposition to "off-shoring" that has arisen in the United States (and which appears to have abated somewhat since the 2004 presidential election).

At this point, perhaps some critics, in rebuttal, may point out the willingness of Great Britain and Ireland to embrace significant reforms during the past two decades, which clearly have helped rejuvenate both economies, a prospect that once would have seemed fanciful. If these economies could pull themselves out of much deeper economic holes than those in which continental Europe and Japan now find themselves, why can't the latter economies embrace a set of radical reforms—even something akin to shock therapy? Or critics may point to the example of Denmark, which has scaled back its labor protections but introduced generous systems of retraining to take their place.

Our answer is that it is precisely because Europe and Japan are comparatively much better off than were Great Britain or Ireland several decades ago that their citizens are unlikely any time soon to see the need for their governments to adopt the economic equivalent of shock therapy. For example, as of the late 1970s, Great Britain stood as a prime example of state-guided and big-firm capitalism that had grown stale and fallen from economic grace, from a position of economic leadership among European countries following World War II to a highly visible laggard several decades later. Ireland, meanwhile, was widely looked on as one of the "poor men" of Europe. In neither country were the majority of voters happy about their circumstances, and thus they were more than willing to vote for political leaders who would implement radical, even disruptive, reforms that held some promise of igniting faster growth.

And that is exactly what each country got, although the details of the reform packages differed between the countries. In Great Britain, the form of shock therapy ushered in by Margaret Thatcher and her Conservative party colleagues in the Parliament consisted largely of privatizing state-owned companies and curtailing labor regulation, measures that led to major restructuring of British industry and subsequent productivity improvements. Over time, these changes, cemented during Tony Blair's tenure as prime minister, led to sharply lower unemployment and faster growth in an economy that many observers in Europe and elsewhere had written off. Ireland's reform process started earlier, with the introduction of free, universal primary education in 1968, and in the 1980s, the slashing of corporate taxes to the lowest level in Europe, just 12.5 percent. Ireland's political leaders also negotiated a new "social partnership" with the country's labor unions, which effectively capped wage increases while curtailing worker protections that had the effect of discouraging firms from firing and, therefore, from hiring workers. All of these reforms helped Ireland attract what eventually turned out to be a flood of foreign multinational companies, first in the computer industry (Intel, Dell, Hewlett-Packard, Microsoft, among others), and later in the financial services industry. The result was the "Irish miracle," or the most rapid growth rate in Europe, and one that has exceeded even the extraordinary growth performance of the United States (see table 12).

Although today they are comparatively much better off than either Great Britain and Ireland was several decades ago, and thus unlikely to embrace the kind of shock therapy that the latter economies were able to implement, the economies of continental Europe and Japan still can accelerate their growth through a less radical, more incremental strategy—one that not only has a chance of being adopted but being sustained.

Toward Innovative Entrepreneurship—At the Margin

Now that they are at or close to the technological frontier, both continental Europe and Japan have no choice, if they want to grow faster (as they should for reasons already outlined), except to foster more innovation. It is possible, of course, that through some combination of luck and good policy, existing large firms or perhaps foreign multinationals (large firms from abroad) will advance innovation to some degree. Yet as we have seen, large firms typically are better known for their incremental advances than for their radical breakthroughs. If the latter is what European and Japanese policy makers want, their top priority should be to promote the formation and growth of *innovative* enterprises.

On the surface, it might appear that European leaders have recognized this in their Lisbon agenda. In particular, the European Commission in 2003 issued a Green Paper on Entrepreneurship, which outlined a series of ways to promote small- and medium-sized enterprises, or SMEs. Japanese government officials also, from time to time, give a nod to the importance of SME growth.

But the very term "small- and medium-sized enterprises," or its acronym SME, reveals a fundamental confusion about the meaning of "entrepreneurship." There is a world of difference between what we have called "replicative" entrepreneurs and "innovative" entrepreneurs. Although replicative entrepreneurship offers those who undertake it a financial means of support, it is only through innovative entrepreneurship—commercial activities that embody some new product or service, or method of production or delivery—that societies advance their technological frontiers and thus their standards of living.

This distinction explains why self-employment data, for example, can be highly misleading, at worst, or of little use, at best, in assessing how successful economies are in promoting innovative entrepreneurship. As shown in table 16, Europe and Japan have plenty of self-employed individuals. In some European countries, the share of self-employed in the workforce exceeds that of the United States. But even more so than in the United States, we suspect (for there is no hard evidence, given the paucity of the data) that the vast proportion of the so-called self-employed entrepreneurs

Table 16 Self-Employment Rates for 2002

Country	Percentage of total number of workers
Austria	11.0 (2001)
Belgium	15.1 (1999)
Canada	9.6
Czech Republic	15.6
Denmark	8.3
Finland	12.4
France	8.7
Germany	10.0
Greece	34.7
Hungary	13.4
Iceland	16.4
Ireland	17.0
Italy	24.6
Japan	11.2
Korea	30.4
Netherlands	11.1
Norway	6.8
Poland	24.0
Portugal	25.3
Slovak Republic	8.5
Spain	17.8
Sweden	9.5
Switzerland	9.7
Turkey	37.8 (2001)
United Kingdom	11.5
United States	7.2

Source: David G. Branchflower, "Self-Employment: More May Not Be Better," NBER Working Paper 10286 (Cambridge, Mass.: National Bureau of Economic Research, 2004).

in Europe and Japan are replicative, owning small retail establishments or service firms. The challenge that continental Europe and Japan face is to find a way to spawn and grow their next Nokias or Toyotas or the next innovative, high-growth companies that can revolutionize their economies in the same way that Microsoft, Intel, Cisco, eBay, and Amazon and the rash of biotech companies are doing for the United States. Although the European Green Paper frequently mentions "fast-growing" or "innovative" firms, its recommendations are aimed broadly at promoting new enterprises generically and give no special emphasis to innovative entrepreneurship in particular. We are aware of no official Japanese document or government initiative that does this either.

Although it clearly is not easy to create and then foster the growth of innovative, new companies, the challenge in one sense does not require the political boldness of any reform package aimed at prodding large firms and their workers to make fundamental changes. By its nature, a reform program that is designed to promote something new must work *at the margin* rather than directly challenge existing vested interests. This should make significant reform more feasible and sustainable politically. The trick, as discussed in chapter 6, is for governments in Europe and Japan to remove barriers to new, potentially high-growth companies without directly challenging the way existing large firms do business or any protections their workers may now have.

To its credit, the European Commission has recognized the need for certain of these reforms for continental Europe (we know of no officially endorsed set of recommendations for Japan). For one thing, the EC's Green Paper rightly recommends that member states further reduce the costs and administrative delays in registering new businesses and adopt more streamlined bankruptcy procedures (which, as we discussed in chapter 5, can help to promote entrepreneurship by reducing the risks of failure). The Green Paper is also right to call for more entrepreneurship education in technical schools and universities. Here, especially, both Europe and Japan can take a page from the American playbook, where university-based entrepreneurship programs have flowered in the last two decades, in part from efforts by the Kauffman Foundation (with which each of the current authors is affiliated) to promote entrepreneurship across college campuses and not just within business schools, where the subject has been traditionally taught.[8] Although this is easier said than done, since there is a shortage of effective teachers of entrepreneurial skills even in the United States, universities in both Europe and Japan may find it especially promising, at least for some initial period, to promote entrepreneurship through joint ventures with American universities that are doing this effectively (just as many universities around the world are doing in other fields) and through programs that might place home country students in internships with entrepreneurial companies in the United States. Assuming the right incentives are in place in their home countries after they finish—and this is a critical subject—there is potentially an ample supply of prospectively highly innovative entrepreneurs in both Europe and Japan. We say this because both parts of the world have excellent primary and secondary educational systems that consistently turn out students that are well trained in such technical subjects as mathematics, computer science, and basic science, fields that are essential for innovative entrepreneurs to know and master in an increasingly technologically sophisticated global economy.

The EC's Green Paper also identifies the lack of access to capital as a significant barrier to entrepreneurial activity and recommends that governments launch or augment resources to provide seed funds, especially equity, to SMEs. In particular, the paper lauds the Finnish public program for providing micro-loans to its entrepreneurs and thus seems implicitly to endorse that concept for other governments, as well as government guarantees of micro-loans.

The EC's complaint about the shortage of risk financing for entrepreneurs has some validity, since banks in Europe have not traditionally funded entrepreneurs nor is there yet much of a venture capital industry in Europe, let alone anything that could be called angel investing. The same observations apply to Japan. We are skeptical, however, of the solutions to this problem outlined in the EC's Green Paper, for Europe and Japan. We know of no evidence that governments anywhere—including state governments in the United States that have established venture funds—can systematically and over sustained periods outperform private venture capital or private investors generally. Indeed, because there is always a danger that politics can infect the management of government funds, it is possible, if not likely, that such funds will underperform; that is, they will not yield returns that cover the government's own (low) cost of capital.

In principle, one way to minimize this risk is for government venture funds to invest only on a matching basis with the private sector. For example, the Advanced Technology Program administered by the Commerce Department in the United States in the past has provided funding only for those technology-related ventures that have also attracted private money. There is some evidence that this approach has been successful (National

Research Council, 2001). A similar story apparently can be told about government-funded venture capital efforts in Israel (see chapter 6). But even with a private matching requirement, it is still difficult to know whether the ventures funded by the government would have attracted other private funding had the government money not been available.

Meanwhile, the notion that more broadly based micro-lending will provide a significant stimulus to innovative entrepreneurs is fanciful. Micro-loans typically are made in small amounts, of $1,000 or less in developing countries and not much more in developed economies. While small loans may be enough to empower their borrowers to earn a decent living and, in the best of cases, to expand to the point of employing a few other workers, the enterprises they fund are not likely to become high-growth firms that lead to broader-based productivity gains for society as a whole. As we discussed in the last chapter, micro-lending may help to cure poverty, but it is not the promising source of funding for truly innovative entrepreneurs.

How then can the capital access problem be solved, and are there any other significant barriers to innovative entrepreneurship in continental Europe and Japan that must be overcome? In our view, the same answers help address both questions.

To some extent, the fact that until recently wealthy individuals in Europe and Japan have not invested to a significant degree in start-up enterprises, either through venture capital firms or as angel investors, reflects the culture in both societies. There is a strong tradition of family enterprise in both economies, and if family businesses generate profits, family members are likely to keep their money for any new venture "in the family." This pattern is one that is difficult for government policy makers to change, at least directly. In principle, governments could provide tax benefits for third-party equity investments in start-up companies, but given the cultural traditions in both Europe and Japan, we are not certain that this would work. It might backfire by providing incentives for tax avoidance analogous to various tax shelters in the United States that over the years have drained the United States Treasury without contributing to overall economic growth.

In fact, there is some evidence that the private equity markets, fueled by inflows of funds from foreign investors, may be moving on their own to address the capital access issue, at least in Europe. In 2005, approximately

$73 billion (60 billion Euros) was committed to private equity. Although most of these funds were targeted toward buyouts of existing European firms, this development is a good sign that some new blood—via capital infusions—is being poured into Europe's larger firms. Indeed, the roughly $15 billion (12 billion Euros) invested in true venture funds, where the money is more likely to be targeted toward start-ups or early stage companies, represents a 44 percent increase over the year before, clearly an encouraging result.[9]

One set of policies might boost these figures further by lifting one of the largest, if not the largest, barriers to the formation and growth of innovative entrepreneurial ventures: the legal and institutional hurdles that prevent all but the smallest firms (which some countries have exempted) from laying off or firing employees they no longer need or who are not performing satisfactorily. As we already noted, excessively strict protection of existing workers inhibits employers from hiring new workers. This effect is especially important, in our view, in explaining the shortage of new, rapidly growing companies in Europe. Why go to the trouble of forming a potentially innovative enterprise, let alone *fund* such a firm, if in the future when the firm needs more employees, it will become locked in to keeping them, regardless of their performance or changes in the market for the firm's goods or services? Indeed, we suspect one reason highly successful new European ventures like Skype (which pioneered Internet-based telephone calling) sell out to other companies rather than expand internally is that, especially in a rapidly changing technological environment, their founders don't want to incur the essentially fixed costs of a permanent workforce, unable to make an easy transition to other tasks and duties if market demands require it. Fear of the same future might also help explain why would-be European entrepreneurs (like Pierre Omidyar, one of the founders of eBay) move abroad—to the United States or across the English Channel to either Great Britain or Ireland—to start their companies rather than building them in their home countries.

The labor issue is different in Japan but no less of an important reason why venture capital has not taken off in that country. Again, as we have noted, large Japanese companies have traditionally used a system of lifetime employment, which strongly discourages existing employees, even those with potentially innovative ideas, from leaving to starting new ventures. If the undertaking fails, the former employee not only will be unable to rejoin his (or her) firm, but also will find it difficult, if not impossible, to gain similar employment at other firms. The same system also makes it very difficult for the rare entrepreneur to find suitable employees or partners to assist them in the venture. Knowing all this, why would potential sources of finance be interested in funding such ventures?

We do not believe, therefore, that culture, however important it may appear to be in contributing to the persistence of any practice or pattern, is immutable. To the contrary, changes in government policies—more labor flexibility for firms in Europe and perhaps innovative incentives for Japanese firms to allow or encourage workers to pursue entrepreneurial ventures—can, over time, lead to changes in attitudes of potential entrepreneurs and their potential financial backers. In particular, if more individuals are freed up to pursue their entrepreneurial dreams, and if some of these ventures prove successful, other would-be entrepreneurs and those who might fund them will see that it is possible make their dreams, too, come true.

We believe that such a virtuous cycle can be launched in part by drawing on recent developments in Europe and other parts of the world in an unlikely arena: philanthropy. Until very recently, the formation of foundations devoted to charitable purposes was, for all intents and purposes, an exclusively American phenomenon. With few exceptions, wealthy individuals in Europe or Japan bequeathed their wealth to their families rather than giving much of it during their lifetimes or through bequests at death to foundations. This supposedly "cultural" pattern has been changing, however, especially in Europe, as wealthy individuals there now see how their American counterparts are behaving ("Business of Giving," 2006). If the "culture" of giving away money can change, then so can the "culture" of investing it, for a profit.

How specifically can this virtuous cycle of innovative firm formation be launched in Europe and Japan? Our answer here is similar to the advice we provided in the last chapter for developing (and more advanced) countries wedded to state guidance: *reform at the margin*. Thus, in the case of continental Europe, in addition to the measures we have already favorably mentioned, European countries could exempt *new* enterprises—those legally formed after a certain date—entirely (or nearly so) from the current labor protections that apply to other firms. We suggest an exemption based on date rather than size, which is already present in the laws of a number of European countries, because a size threshold not only creates a "notch" at the threshold but also, for reasons just noted, a strong barrier to the formation of potential high-growth enterprises in the first place. Indeed, the EC's Green Paper on Entrepreneurship mistakenly suggests a lighter regulatory touch for small firms in general. But this is the wrong criterion. If a lighter touch is called for in any other regulatory sphere (beyond labor)—and we hold open the possibility it might be—it should be based on date, namely, one carved only for new firms, which would provide much stronger incentives for their formation than any special treatment based on size.

The political-economic rationale for exempting new firms from the current onerous labor protections is straightforward: it does not threaten workers at existing firms while benefiting only entrepreneurs and the workers they hire at their new firms. Of course, there is a danger that workers at current firms would nonetheless view such a reform as the proverbial "camel's nose under the tent," opening up the possibility that existing enterprises might form new enterprises or, more boldly, close down and reform themselves entirely simply to take advantage of the exemption. From a purely economic point of view, we would not be concerned about this possibility; to the contrary, it could be a desirable way of leading to much more rapid reform of European economies on a much larger scale. But practically, any reform that could be so easily expanded in this fashion could morph into the radical shock therapy whose political viability we questioned in the first place. For this reason, protections probably would have to be written into any laws creating regulatory exemption for new firms to prevent existing firms from moving part or all of their operations into new entities solely to take advantage of the exemption (although it may be possible politically to preserve the ability of existing companies to form new subsidiaries or affiliates that employed *additional workers* to take advantage of any labor exemption).

It may be useful and necessary to go even further to ease European workers' anxiety that changes at the margin will affect them. Denmark provides one role model. It permits firms to hire and fire without significant hurdles and also puts strict limits on its (high) unemployment compensation benefits, but at the same time the government shares in the cost of retraining and subsidizes the wages of workers who take new jobs. According to at least one media account, this system appears to account for the fact that Denmark's unemployment rate is about half that of its European neighbors, and the reported rates of anxiety about job security are far below those found in its European counterparts (Walker, 2006a). A related approach is the concept of wage insurance. Under this system, governments would compensate displaced workers for a limited period (perhaps two years) for some portion of any loss in income if they take a new job that pays less than the old one. Indeed, to its credit, Germany has adopted a limited version of wage insurance for older workers (as has the United States, but only for those who can prove they were displaced by foreign imports) and reduced the term of unemployment compensation payments instead.[10]

Promoting innovative entrepreneurship may be more difficult for Japan, where formal labor protections are not the main problem but where the difficulty stems from the system of lifetime employment. The government could begin to change this without directly challenging the employment system itself. Specifically, the government could give Japanese companies tax credits or other tax-related incentives for investments in enterprises founded by their employees. The reason for limiting the credits to employee-initiated ventures is that otherwise companies could "game" the tax system simply by creating new entities and thereby reap tax credits in the process. Indeed, to avoid this result, it may be necessary to limit the eligibility for any tax credits to companies where the employees who form the new enterprises own at least a minimum percentage of the equity of their companies.

Finally, some might think that European and Japanese universities could play a stronger role in facilitating the launching of entrepreneurial enterprises, as Cambridge University appears to be doing with some success in the United Kingdom. In particular, some of the suggestions we advance in this regard for the United States in the next chapter, in principle at least, would seem to be applicable to Europe and Japan (if not elsewhere). This may well be true, but we are reluctant at this point to bet too much on this possibility. As a gross overgeneralization that nonetheless we believe to be true, faculty at universities in Europe and Japan do not have a history of pursuing entrepreneurial ventures or of conducting research that could be readily commercialized.[11] More broadly, in some European countries (France, for example), university faculty collaboration with industry is frowned upon and thus not attempted. Instead, commercially relevant R&D is typically found only within large firms, which is one reason we have labeled these economies as leading exemplars of big-firm capitalism.

If, however, innovative entrepreneurship takes hold in either or both of these economies in the future, it is possible that university faculty gradually will take a different attitude. Should this occur, then the kinds of policies we advocate in the next chapter for facilitating the commercialization of university-based innovations in United States universities would indeed become relevant for Europe and Japan.

In any event, without more aggressive steps to promote the growth and formation of new enterprises, such ambitious Lisbon agenda goals as a substantial increase in the level of R&D spending throughout Europe, perhaps to 3 percent of GDP, have little chance of being realized, as one recent European "experts" report has recognized.[12] R&D spending is an input into the innovation process, not an output. Firms are the agents for translating R&D into commercially successful products and services. So far, already high R&D spending in some European countries has failed to generate large social gains precisely because the overall environment has not been conducive to new firm formation and growth (Henrekson and Rosenberg, 2001). This must be changed or else more resources thrown into research and development are likely to be wasted.

Concluding Comments

The economies discussed in this chapter are generally examples of big-firm capitalism. For this form of capitalism, growth has two basic requirements: elimination of obstacles to the entry of new firms created by innovative entrepreneurs, and creation of incentives for large firms to engage energetically in innovative activity. Little has been said here about measures that can help to achieve the second objective as this subject is addressed in some detail in chapter 8 with respect to the United States. The lessons outlined there, for the most part, apply with equal force to Europe and Japan.

In this chapter we have focused on the other and comparably critical task, the stimulation of innovative entrepreneurship in the countries of Europe and Japan whose regimes are examples of big-firm capitalism. We do not know, and indeed find it difficult to predict, whether and to what extent the incremental suggestions we have proposed for fostering innovative entrepreneurship in continental Europe and Japan actually would work, but we see little downside in trying. If the measures are not effective, they will at least set the stage for more aggressive policy steps. The pessimists may hold that this will not work because there is an anti-entrepreneurial culture in Europe that cannot be easily changed. For reasons that should be clear by now, we are not of this view, or at least not yet.

The central problem with our recommendations, if there is any problem, is that there is no immediate crisis in the economies of either Japan or continental Europe that would call for such measures. It is one thing, for example, for the leaders of continental European governments to declare their intention to reform their economies through such a process as the Lisbon agenda. It is quite another, as recent European elections attest, for substantial reforms to be welcomed by voters and then implemented. One possible ray of hope is that citizens in the medium- and lower-income EU countries, such as Spain and the Eastern European countries, feel a stronger need for their countries to catch up to the living standards of the continental core—France, Germany, and Italy—and because of this reform will proceed faster at the fringes. As it does, voters in the core countries, out of envy, may be shaken into supporting more aggressive reforms.

The Chinese approach to reform—do it at the margin without transparently threatening existing interests—should nonetheless provide reformers in Europe and Japan with the best and most immediate source of hope. Young voters in each economy are the obvious potential beneficiaries of reforms that lead to more entrepreneurial success and hence economic growth. Our advice to leaders in these countries is to sell the reforms to them, while assuring their parents that the reforms will not immediately threaten their own interests. Indeed, such steps are the best hope for providing for their children's welfare while also ensuring that health and retirement benefits promised to them by their governments can be paid for out of the resulting future growth.

8

THE CARE AND MAINTENANCE OF
ENTREPRENEURIAL CAPITALISM

Success breeds complacency. Complacency breeds failure. Only the
paranoid survive.

—attributed to Dr. Andrew S. Grove, cofounder of Intel Corporation

For roughly a century, the United States has been the leading
economic power in the world. Part of the reason for its success is that
the United States has been the quintessential exemplar of a mixture of
entrepreneurial and big-firm capitalism. But can Americans, and others
in the world who are now emulating the U.S. model, safely assume that
the American economy will continue to be as successful as it has been in
the past? Or is the United States—like other once-great civilizations (ancient Rome and Greece come to mind)—doomed in the foreseeable future to fall or at least stagnate? We make no claim to be prophets, but we
believe that while there is much to be optimistic about, there also are dangers ahead. In this chapter, we will celebrate the former and call attention
to the latter in the hope that current and future policy makers will take
steps to help us avoid the fate to which the dangers could condemn us.

Put in a nutshell, we will suggest in this chapter that one of the most immediate perils facing the U.S. economy is the possibility of transforming
into a much less entrepreneurial big-firm regime, one characterized by
ossification, limited incentives, and a paucity of breakthrough inventions.
There is no simple formula for preventing such an outcome, but the analysis of this book suggests the importance of two key principles: provide

incentives for productive entrepreneurship and discourage diversion of entrepreneurial talent into unproductive or destructive sources of wealth. In this closing chapter, we will provide a number of suggestions about how best to maintain the critical balance of big-firm and entrepreneurial capitalism, in part by simply bringing together the observations of the two preceding chapters.

One cannot simply dismiss the big-firm regime peril. For one thing, the U.S. economy has not always had such a nice blend of big-firm and entrepreneurial capitalism. In the 1950s and 1960s—the heyday of Big Auto, Big Steel, and Ma Bell (the old AT&T telephone system)—the economy was much closer to a regime of big-firm capitalism. Then came the oil price shock of 1973–74, the years of stagflation, and two decades of disappointing productivity growth. A resurgence of entrepreneurial innovation—largely in information technology and communications—coupled with more intense foreign competition (which forced the older big firms to become vastly more efficient and to improve the quality of their products) helped to turn the U.S. economy around. But, as the saying goes, nothing lasts forever. It is conceivable that the U.S. economy might revert to a more strictly big-firm regime, and it is wishful thinking to believe that this pattern could not reemerge.

Indeed, one farsighted economist, the late Mancur Olson, argued that something like this is likely to be the destiny of *all* economies, especially those in democratic societies (Olson, 1982). As economies age, Olson asserted, special-interest groups grow in number and power; as this happens, it becomes more likely that they will come into conflict. Like physical objects subject to Newtonian laws, calls for action by some special-interest groups meet with counterreactions from others, all aimed at thwarting each other's ambitions. Too often, the result can be paralysis or "rent-seeking" of the worst sort with regulations and policies that benefit particular groups without conferring benefits on, and even detracting from, the general welfare. The proliferation of trade associations and lobbyists—which was apparent when Olson wrote his book in the early 1980s and is even more so now—is powerful confirmation of his insight.[1] A reversion to big-firm capitalism would threaten analogous effects, leading to interest-group paralysis via a slowing of the rate of radical innovation.

In this chapter we will focus on the United States, in particular considering what it can do to maintain its unusual blend of big-firm and entre-preneurial capitalism in the future. We direct our attention to the United States for three reasons. First, it is the economy we know best. Second, we suspect that many of our readers are Americans. And third, even for read-ers outside the United States, we believe there is much to learn from the American experience.

We will follow the structure of earlier chapters, where we laid out four broad preconditions for the right of blend of entrepreneurial and big-firm capitalism and four types of economic-health-sustaining measures we con-sidered critical. Here, we will assess current trends relating to three of the most relevant of these requirements to the U.S. economy. In some cases, there is little cause for concern; in others cases, there is plenty cause for worry, and where that is true, we will offer some possible solutions. But lest readers think we are concluding this book by wringing our hands, we begin with the good news: evidence of what is right about the American economy.

The Productivity Miracle, So Far

Look through the business media and you'll find a plethora of sta-tistics—about stock prices, the inflation rate, the growth rate of the econ-omy over the past quarter or year, and the current unemployment rate. But in the long run, only one economic statistic really matters: the *growth of productivity,* which measures increases in output for given inputs. Be-cause the most important input, judged by its share of national income and thus cost for generating goods and services, is labor, many economists fo-cus much of their attention on *labor productivity.* We do the same here.

Labor productivity, by definition, measures output generated per unit of labor input, typically per hour. Again, by definition, the *level* of labor pro-ductivity at any one time reflects the *average* standard of living of the resi-dents of any economy, while the *growth* rate of labor productivity measures the rate at which that average living standard improves.[2] This is not to im-ply that if a worker's productivity rises by 7 percent, she deserves all the credit. Improved technology, the availability of more and better raw mate-rials, and other such developments make a critical contribution, and there is good reason to argue that in recent centuries innovation has been the primary source of productivity growth. Thus, while it is relatively easy to

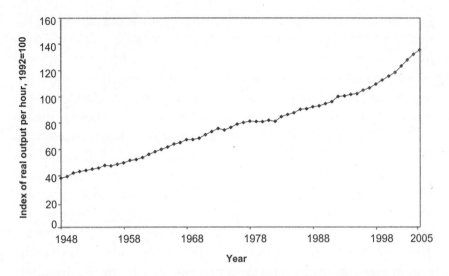

Figure 6. Index of U.S. Productivity (Nonfarm Business), Real Output per Hour, 1948–2005. *Source:* U.S. Bureau of Labor Statistics, Major Sector Productivity and Costs Index, 2006. Available at http://data.bls.gov/PDQ/servlet/SurveyOutput Servlet.

measure productivity and its growth, full determination of what was responsible for that growth is exceedingly difficult.[3]

We do know, however, that productivity in the United States and other wealthy economies, despite accelerations and slowdowns, has been growing virtually without interruption for the past two centuries (see figure 6). The rate of growth has been beset by ups and downs. In the United States, for the first quarter-century after the World War II—that is, between 1948 and 1973—productivity grew at an average rate of 2.8 percent per year, according to the U.S. Bureau of Labor Statistics. Between 1973 and 1995, it grew far more slowly: about 1.4 percent annually. But between 1995 and 2002, it recovered to 2.8 percent per year and through 2005 advanced at an even higher rate (a little more than 3 percent). The difference between a 1.4 percent and a 2.8 percent rise per year in our incomes may not seem like much, but the difference increases every year because it is compounded like interest in a bank account. At a steady growth rate of 1.4 percent per year, our descendants one hundred years from now will receive incomes on average four times as large as ours in purchasing power. But if, instead, the steady rise continues at 2.8 percent a year, our descendants' purchasing power will have risen to be sixteen times as large as ours. In the rate of growth of productivity, what appear to be minor differences soon matter very much indeed.

Many economists believe the resurgence in productivity in the 1990s was to a considerable degree attributable to what has been labeled IT (information technology), including computers, computer software, the Internet, and the like. There has been spectacular growth in productivity in the IT sector itself. For example, data collected by the U.S. Bureau of Labor Statistics show that labor productivity (output per hour) in the computer and electronic products manufacturing industry rose at an average annual rate of 15 percent between 1993 and 2003, compared to an average of 4 percent for manufacturing as a whole (U.S. Bureau of Labor Statistics, 2006; and Schweitzer and Zaman, 2006). This extraordinary productivity growth rate in computer manufacturing has been driven by advances in computer technology and the technology employed in the production processes of the computer industry. The rapid growth rate also illustrates "Moore's law," the prediction by Gordon Moore (cofounder of Intel, the world's largest computer chip manufacturer) that the number of transistors on a chip will double every eighteen months or so.

Productivity in the rest of the economy that uses IT has also benefited from the IT miracle. As was the case with the introduction of electric power for industrial and household use, it took decades before IT had much of an influence on productivity growth in other sectors of the economy. But once other industries learned to make use of it, the results were substantial, and there is reason to ascribe a significant part of the rise in growth of labor productivity in the 1990s to the expanded role and capacity of IT.[4]

The most recent data indicate that labor productivity in the United States has advanced at a more rapid rate since 2000: at an extraordinary 3.5 percent through 2005. Economists are deeply divided about whether this high rate can be sustained in the future, and if not, how much of a fallback is likely. The most likely outcome, in our view, is some falloff in productivity growth because, eventually, the diffusion of productivity-enhancing information technology will slow down, and, indeed, official government projections reflect that. The Congressional Budget Office and the Social Security Administration, for example, project long-run future productivity growth to be little more than 2 percent—above the disappointing 1.4 percent average of 1973–95 but well below the 3 percent growth rate of the past decade. History suggests that periods of extraordinarily rapid or especially slow productivity growth do not last very long. Indeed, after surging at close to a 4 percent annual clip since 2001, labor productivity grew at less than 3 percent in 2005.

There is much at stake here for future generations. The difference, in terms of the long-run earnings consequences, between an annual rate of productivity growth of, say, 2 percent and 3 percent is enormous, as indicated in table 17, below.

Which of these growth rates the future will bring is very likely to depend on the nature of the next big innovation breakthrough(s)—that is, whether or not it or they will be something as important as the Internet has been. Some breakthroughs may provide huge social benefits but not show up that way in the economic statistics; major advances in biotechnology or other health endeavors are likely examples. These will result in a longer lifespan for many of us, but the benefits of added longevity will not show up in higher GDP. On the contrary, as the population ages, the burden of current entitlement programs on current and future workers will grow, leading to higher taxes and/or higher interest rates that result from added government borrowing, both of which are likely to dampen growth. Other breakthroughs, such as nanotechnology or some combination of new products and production techniques that cannot be foreseen now will show up in measured GDP. If our argument in this book is correct, these radical breakthroughs are more likely to come from smaller and newer firms, although larger, established firms will be essential to mass production and increased reliability and capacity of whatever innovations the smaller firms come up with.

Continued economic growth is not just important to satisfy Americans'

Table 17 Long-Run Consequences of Different Growth Rates in Labor Productivity

If average annual growth of labor productivity is	In 50 years average earnings will rise	In 100 years average earnings will rise
2 percent	170 percent	620 percent
3 percent	340 percent	1820 percent

Source: Authors' calculations.

competitive desire to remain "number one." Growth is imperative if we want to continue to improve the quality of our lives along many dimensions. Growth is also critical in light of the rapid aging of our population, a trend that is even more apparent in Japan and Western Europe. An aging population will impose large and increasing obligations on our government to make good on the promises of the nation's entitlement programs—Social Security and, perhaps more important, Medicare—at a time when the country faces many other urgent priorities, including increased spending for national security at home and abroad, to defend against terrorism, as well as pressures to expand health insurance for the nearly 50 million Americans under the age of sixty-five who do not have it. Under these circumstances, anything that can be done to enhance the underlying rate of technological change, and hence economic growth, will be welcome.

For all these reasons, it will be critical for the United States to maintain and, ideally, improve upon the institutions that satisfy the four preconditions outlined in chapter 5 for ensuring the right blend of entrepreneurial and big-firm capitalism. Here, and in the rest of this chapter, it will be convenient to combine the four preconditions into three:

1. Adequate incentives for *productive* entrepreneurship, including appropriate rewards and adequate security of those rewards and of the earnings processes, must be maintained and ideally strengthened;
2. Disincentives for *unproductive* entrepreneurship must be restricted and ideally eliminated; and
3. Continued rivalry among and innovation by large firms must be ensured.

Incentives for Productive Entrepreneurship

The first of our three growth preconditions is the body of incentives for people to become entrepreneurs and to employ productive means of pursuing their personal goals, presumably some combination of wealth, power, and prestige. For this purpose, in simplest terms, society must offer some of its highest rewards to the most successful productive entrepreneurs. In particular, the rules and institutions must remove impediments to such activities, they must provide or at least not interfere with financial rewards for success, and they must provide security for these rewards, offering some degree of assurance that they cannot simply be taken away.

The last of these issues is, in general, no longer a matter of serious contention as it used to be in earlier periods of history in some noncapitalist societies, when kings or robber barons or warlords could simply expropriate the earnings from productive activity. Today, laws defining property rights and the penalties for fraud or theft provide reasonable security for the earnings of the productive entrepreneur, at least in economically advanced nations. Only one element in the set of institutions that ensures the requisite security of these asset accumulations—the patent system—requires more extensive discussion below, and it makes most sense to do so in the United States context. Although patents are necessary to provide incentives for productive entrepreneurship, the United States system in recent years appears to have become *too* protective, which can not only discourage new entrepreneurs from creating new markets but also insulate existing firms from the hot breath of competition.

On most other scores, the United States maintains a good record for encouraging productive entrepreneurship on all the requisite fronts. It has well-developed systems of property rights, and in recent years it has cut back marginal income tax rates as well as some regulations that hamper the task of the productive entrepreneur. Nonetheless, the income tax system will be under increasing pressure as the U.S. population ages and funds are needed to fund entitlement programs, such as pensions and health care. The corporate income tax, assuming it remains in place, can be restructured to strengthen the incentives for growth. Recent new regulations related to financial reporting and corporate governance—enacted after the financial reporting scandals earlier in this decade—now appear to be unduly burdensome for new enterprises. We will take up each of these subjects in the material that follows.

Removing Impediments to the Launch of Productive Enterprise

The most obvious step to make productive entrepreneurship attractive is to remove any handicaps to the creation of new firms. This is more difficult than it may seem. In many parts of the world, the bureaucratic impediments to firm-creation are substantial. In the United States, the technical, legal, and institutional costs associated with starting a business, fortunately, remain low, as the World Bank's *Doing Business* reports have consistently documented. The Internet is likely to further reduce these costs as more states and localities make it possible to obtain necessary licenses and approvals without having physically to appear at a government office. The same will be increasingly true in other countries as they embrace the Internet for the same purpose.

More broadly, the technological advances in the information technology (IT) and communications industries have substantially reduced the capital costs associated with entering some IT- and many Internet-related businesses. For retailers and middlemen, the costs may amount to as little as several thousand dollars, representing the cost of acquiring a computer, some related equipment (such as a printer, scanner, and fax machine), and some off-the-shelf Web site preparation software.[5] Indeed, with start-up costs now so low, many Internet businesses no longer need venture capital to finance their inauguration because they can attain positive cash flows in a relatively short period of time. This is clearly a beneficial development. The Internet is becoming a powerful engine that can wring out costs and increase productivity throughout the economy (Litan and Rivlin, 2000).

Yet here, as elsewhere, there are grounds for concern about the more distant future arising from the increasing tendency, at least in the United States, of many start-up companies to sell out to larger firms rather than to "go public," which was a common exit strategy for founders of and early-stage investors in high-tech companies in the 1990s. Indeed, a substantial number of larger firms—Microsoft, Cisco and Intel, among others—effectively have been outsourcing much of their R&D to the entrepreneurial marketplace, waiting for innovative companies to prove themselves and then snapping them up, or at least purchasing stock in them, much as the venture capitalists did for many high-tech companies in the 1990s. This has left some venture capitalists searching for other investment opportunities.

Our concern here is not for the welfare of the venture capitalists, but we do worry that small, young innovative companies built on or around radical and disruptive technologies will not be able to attain their true potential capacities—nor will their innovations—if they are regularly absorbed by larger, more bureaucratic firms, which may not have the same entrepreneurial spirit or culture. True, this has gone on in the recent past to a substantial degree, and so far the depleted ranks of innovative firms appear to have been replaced by entrants who grasp the opportunities provided by the departure of their successful predecessors. But this process remains a matter to be watched, and in the future policy adjustments may be required to keep the pipeline of innovative start-ups full.

One other worrisome public policy development that may affect the launch of future innovative companies is the unintended effect of the recent tightening of the bankruptcy law. Congress amended the U.S. bankruptcy laws in 2005 unaware that as many as 20 percent of all personal bankruptcies may, in fact, be business-related (Lawless and Warren, 2005). Since many entrepreneurs begin by bankrolling their activities with credit card charges, the modifications of the bankruptcy law, which force those who declare bankruptcy to repay more of their debts (seemingly a good thing), may unintentionally discourage the formation of new enterprises. Effective bankruptcy laws are important because the more difficult it is to exit from a business, the less likely it is that innovative entrepreneurs will take the risk of getting started in the first place. We must not forget that impediments to the exit of an unsuccessful firm can be, in effect, the equivalent of an increase in the cost of entry.

Taxation Policy

It is common in books that, like this volume, focus on forces the authors believe to be crucial for growth to recommend that governments provide some added incentives to strengthen those forces. The incentives perhaps most frequently proposed are tax deductions, tax credits, or lower tax rates for activities that contribute to economic expansion. In fact, federal policy makers in the United States in recent years have provided substantial tax incentives for all kinds of activity, which account for the complexity of the current tax code. In 2001 and 2003, President George W. Bush proposed and the United States Congress approved two tax bills, substantially lowering marginal income tax rates for individuals, especially for upper-income taxpayers, and (through 2007) establishing a 15 percent rate on payment of corporate dividends. In combination, the two tax bills lowered the federal income tax share of GDP to roughly 17 percent, from 20 percent in 2000. In November 2005, a special advisory panel on tax reform appointed by President Bush outlined broad recommendations to simplify the tax code by disallowing a number of personal deductions (notably, the one for state and local income taxes) and, as a trade-off, reducing the marginal income tax rates for individuals still further. The panel also offered recommendations related to the corporate income tax to enhance the incentives for investment (by proposing the immediate expensing of all new investment, thus shielding it from taxation, but denying any deduction for interest on borrowing). One study has argued that by reducing some of the distortions in the current tax system, the simplification elements in the panel's tax recommendations should benefit entrepreneurs (Bruce and Gurley-Calvez, 2006).

As important as simplicity is in structuring a tax system, the central objective of any tax system is *sufficiency*—that is, collection of enough revenues to support government expenditures. For this purpose, the Bush tax panel's mission was of no value because it was instructed only to examine proposals that would not affect total revenue collected. Yet this instruction ignored some clear budget mathematics. With the impending retirement of a generation of baby boomers, coupled with near-certain continuation of rapidly rising health care costs (albeit while research and technical progress improve its quality), federal spending on the government's three main entitlement programs—Social Security, Medicare, and Medicaid—is projected to rise rapidly. In particular, unless the benefit structures are changed, federal spending on these programs, which totaled a bit more than 8 percent of GDP in 2005, is projected to reach nearly 14 percent by 2025 and to hit 19 percent by 2050.[6] Because other federal spending, including interest, is likely to total at least 12 percent of GDP throughout this period (its level in 2005), it is clear that the tax share of GDP cannot remain at 17 percent without having an explosion of the deficit as a share of GDP. At some point, it is inevitable that a future Congress and president must agree on a budget package that cuts spending growth in the entitlement program and *also raises taxes*.

Of course, no one likes a tax increase, and selling one to a public accustomed to the lower marginal income tax rates implemented through the 2001 tax bill will be extremely difficult. From an economic perspective, it will be important that any tax increase do the least harm to long-term economic growth. What kind of tax increase best meets that test?

In principle, additional revenue raised through taxes on consumption rather than higher income tax rates should do the least economic harm because consumptions taxes should encourage private saving, which in turn should reduce interest rates and thereby increase investment (which could conceivably lead to *higher* growth in the long run though slower growth in the short run due to the depressing effect of consumption taxes on aggregate demand). In contrast, raising income tax rates entails some risk of discouraging work effort, although an across-the-board increase in income tax rates for everyone (employees and business owners alike) would not necessarily discourage entrepreneurial activity in particular.[7]

Consumption taxes have their drawbacks, however. For one thing, it is difficult to design a tax on consumption that is progressive in impact, namely, one under which taxpayers with low incomes pay lesser amounts relative to their incomes than those with higher incomes. In addition, and more pertinent to our subject at hand, certain kinds of consumption taxes—a value-added tax, for example—could actually hurt entrepreneurs by requiring them to pay taxes on inputs of production before they earn revenues on the sales of their products and services (and thus become eligible for rebates on those input taxes). Entrepreneurs may also suffer an adverse impact on their cash flow from a straight sales tax on certain inputs.

Accordingly, a more progressive way of raising revenue without discouraging work effort or entrepreneurship would be to "broaden the income tax base"—that is, to keep marginal income tax rates where they are but cut back on deductions and exemptions. This may be the ideal economic outcome, but a broaden-the-base approach may be the least politically palatable way of raising additional revenue since it would target specific, identifiable groups—those that now benefit from the deductions (the home-building industry, state and local government officials, and charitable organizations, to name just a few)—rather than impose burdens across the board.

Clearly, it is not to our comparative advantage to outline here the tax package that is least politically damaging and that least hurts growth and entrepreneurship. All we can do is highlight the trade-offs involved while underscoring that the alternative, doing nothing—that is, taking no action to raise revenue, given the certain continuation of Social Security, Medicare, and Medicaid in something resembling their current form—is worse than any of the revenue-enhancing options, for entrepreneurs and for all Americans, in the long run.

Financial Reporting Requirements and Sarbanes-Oxley

Legal requirements and the effort and costs needed to meet them can hinder entrepreneurial development. These costs may not be imposed when the firm is first created, but if they dim the prospects for profitable expansion later on (should the new firm should prove successful), they could constitute a disincentive to productive entrepreneurial activity.

A significant illustration is provided by the policies recently adopted in an effort to prevent the financial misconduct associated with Enron, WorldCom, and a number of other high-flying companies, whose failures led to the 2002 Sarbanes-Oxley Act (SOX) and related changes in listing requirements of the major stock exchanges. Among the reforms are requirements for: a majority of public company boards to be made up of independent directors (rather than in-house corporate managers); public companies to undergo extensive annual internal and external audits of their internal controls (the mechanisms to assure that corporate funds are not being misspent); and the remaining four large public accounting firms (as well as any smaller ones that audit public companies) to be subject to the oversight of a new regulatory body, the Public Company Accounting Oversight Board (PCAOB).

Of particular interest to us are the extensive auditing and independent director requirements. The open question is whether the costs of such measures deliver sufficient benefits—that is, a reduction in misconduct beyond what was likely with the previously existing criminal penalties for those involved in corporate financial scandals. At the very least, the additional costs of "going public"—that is, of a firm that formerly was privately held inviting the public to acquire part of its ownership via the purchase of company stock—may be contributing to the tendency of successful start-ups to avoid public offerings and to sell out to large established companies instead. In addition, there are anecdotal reports that whether or not SOX deters young companies from going public, it may be discouraging their founders from staying with the enterprises after they have done so. More public companies are also "going private," perhaps to avoid the regulatory burdens associated with SOX.

It is difficult to know how significant any or all of these effects are and will be in the future, but as the saying goes, "where there's smoke, there's fire." Although we are not ready to conclude that the costs of SOX have outweighed the benefits—it is conceivable that in the aggregate the reverse has been true—there seems to be sufficient "smoke" surrounding the impacts of SOX to warrant further examination of the law by academic researchers and policy makers to determine whether it or the regulations implementing the law might be modified to make it more cost-effective.

One good place to start would be to refine the Section 404 rules to make audits of internal controls more risk-based than they currently appear to be. Such a review should apply to the implementation of SOX-related rules for smaller and larger public firms alike. At this writing, the Securities and Exchange Commission (SEC) appears to be engaged in just such an activity and in December 2006 proposed clarifications to accomplish this.[8]

Another, more ambitious idea is for the SEC to specify different levels of "404 intensity" and then let shareholders choose which ones they want. Thus shareholders who are suspicious, wary of, or concerned about current management may vote to have the most intense (and costly) audit of internal controls performed; shareholders more trusting of management would be likely to opt for a less onerous version. Admittedly, it would take some work to flesh out the details of these options, but in principle at least, we suspect there would be a lot less second-guessing about the relative costs and benefits of 404 audits if investors had some say in the matter.

Legal Protection of Intellectual Property

The legal protection of ideas—in the form of patents, trademarks, copyrights, and trade secrets law—has long been part of the American legal fabric. Patents and copyrights, in particular, are mentioned in the Constitution. Patent rights have their origins in Italy, dating from the fifteenth century.

In principle, so-called intellectual property rights are supposed to encourage inventors and entrepreneurs to engage in activities that generate and propagate innovations. Reality is more complicated. When it comes to promoting entrepreneurship, the protection of intellectual property rights cuts both ways. On one hand, some legal protection surely is warranted to provide incentives for innovation, though the lion's share of the rewards for innovation accrues to society as a whole, not to the inventor or original entrepreneur.[9] On the other hand, too much legal protection—in particular, mistaken protection of products or methods of production or service delivery that are not truly novel—can retard innovation and entrepreneurship. Inappropriate or excessively broad legal protection raises barriers to entry by entrepreneurs, discouraging some from developing or promoting new processes or products altogether. Finding the right balance, or threading the needle between these two outcomes, is difficult and yet vitally important.

Institutions created for the protection of intellectual property give rise to a second conflict of purpose. Patents and copyrights, as the means of protecting society's interests in intellectual products, have two primary objectives. One goal is to ensure that the creators of the property have an opportunity to obtain some reward from their efforts, both as a matter of equity and as an incentive for the expenditure of further creative effort. But the second and apparently rather incompatible goal is ease of access and dissemination to others, to ensure that the benefits of the innovation to society as a whole are as substantial and as widely available as is reasonably feasible.

The conflict between these two goals is widely recognized. The lower the hurdles to accessing intellectual property, the less its creators can hope to charge for its use. If just anyone can make use of new, legally protected ideas, with no impediment whatsoever, the price of access is apt to be driven toward zero. There is a way, however, to reconcile these two goals, at least in principle. Contrary to what one might suppose, patents generally have not served primarily to impede dissemination, but in a wide range of circumstances they have facilitated and encouraged it. To appreciate this, it is useful to take a quick historical detour before returning to how patent law can promote both invention and its disclosure.

The historical oddity is that patents began not so much to reward the creation of new, commercially useful knowledge but rather to promote its transfer from one country to another. As North and Thomas (1973) have shown, so-called letters patent date from the 1300s in England and, as is true today, granted a monopoly to the recipients, for a specified period, over production and sale of the item named in the letter.[10] Initially these rights were granted not to the creator or inventor of the invention, but to a *foreign producer* who could steal the idea from his own country and export its use to England. In other words, patents were used to induce technology *transfer,* not necessarily technology *creation.* One of the first such letters was awarded to a Flemish weaver for this purpose. In the ensuing years, England encouraged the relocation of many other activities (aside from weaving) from the Continent across the English Channel: mining, metal working, silk manufacturing, ribbon making, and so on. Indeed, of the fifty-five grants of monopoly privilege made under Elizabeth I, twenty-one were issued to aliens or naturalized subjects for a variety of products.[11]

The modern practice of awarding patents primarily to the *inventors* within a country was adopted into English law in the Statute of Monopolies of 1623 in the wake of parliamentary anger over royal misuse of letters patent to reward royal favorites, and for other purposes having no connection with incentives for generating innovations. Since then, and particularly in recent decades, the voluntary dissemination of patented material has become a major economic activity. More to the point, patent laws around the world since have required holders of patent rights to disclose the technical details that justify the patent. Thus it is that patents, rather than impeding the process, have played a key role in making efficient and voluntary dissemination possible and attractive to the patent owner. Indeed, since at least the latter half of the nineteenth century, the sale or rental of access to intellectual property has become so attractive that it has resulted in the creation of markets dedicated to such transactions with the assistance of professionals who have specialized in the required activities.

In fact, today the sale, licensing, and trading of technology has become a large-scale activity. Arora, Fosfuri, and Gambardella list a sample of "leading deal makers in markets for technology" that includes numerous large companies.[12] They further report the results of a survey of 133 companies by a British consulting firm, indicating that 77 percent of the companies studied had licensed technology from others, while 62 percent had licensed technology to others. But they also note: "When compared to internal R&D, however, licensing is a fairly modest activity in terms of budgets involved. The survey estimated that expenditures for licensing technology from others amount to 12 percent, 5 percent and 10 percent of the total R&D budgets of North American, European and Japanese respondents, respectively" (Arora, Fosfuri, and Gambardella, 2001, 30–31).

For a number of firms, participation in markets in technology is of critical importance. For example, the sale of access to polypropylene technology has constituted a major activity of the Union Carbide Corporation. IBM has informed one of the present authors (Baumol) that it has a technology exchange contract with every major manufacturer of every significant computer part throughout the world. It is clear that voluntary dissemination is no isolated and unusual phenomenon.

Yet, there is much room for improvement in the operation of patent law, particularly in the United States, where mounting evidence suggests that the balance between too-strict and too-loose patent rules is not being struck as well it could, and thus patents are being awarded for inventions that are "obvious" rather than "novel." The most infamous example is the decision by the Patent and Trademark Office (PTO) to grant a "business process patent" to Amazon for the "one click" feature on its Web site ("click here to purchase"). But the marked increase in the raw numbers of patents granted strongly suggest that the PTO has become overwhelmed and thus more inclined to give patent applicants the benefit of any doubt. In 2004, for example, the PTO issued 181,000 patents, up from 99,000 in 1990. New applications are running at the rate of 400,000 per year. With the current PTO staff, it would take two years just to clear the backlog let alone process the continuing avalanche of new applications (Orey, 2006).

Professors Adam Jaffe and Josh Lerner argue that the PTO has become more liberal in part because the judges on the specialized appellate court that Congress created in 1982 to hear intellectual property cases have sided overwhelmingly with patent claimants (Jaffe and Lerner, 2004). These judges arguably are behaving much like government bureaucrats who seek to maximize the reach of their agencies' activities. Another contributing factor is that the PTO is short-staffed and its budget is tied to the fees it collects on the basis of patents granted. As a result, examiners have insufficient time to determine independently whether a patent application is truly novel, and the agency, in general, has a monetary incentive to grant more patents. Whatever the reason for the apparent shift in patent decisions, Jaffe and Lerner are not alone in their critique of the current system.

Two prestigious bodies—the National Research Council (Merrill et al., 2004) and the Federal Trade Commission (FTC, 2003)—have reached similar conclusions.

Of course, interests defending strong legal protection of intellectual property—especially the software and entertainment industries—hold a very different view. At a minimum, they favor strict enforcement of existing patent and copyright laws, especially against such new technology as Napster, which allows Internet users to easily copy music and videos. (The courts have been sympathetic to these efforts.) Some support stronger intellectual property laws. There is also a middle view, one that recognizes the potentially sclerotic effect of proliferating patents and copyrights, but which downplays this danger knowing that because few firms can monopolize all the intellectual property necessary to manufacture increasingly complicated products, most will have powerful incentives to cross-license their IP rights.[13]

Our view is that there are crevices in the system that can stand improvement. Jaffe and Lerner, the National Research Council, and the FTC have each have offered a number of technical suggestions with the objectives of improving "patent quality" (so that patents are granted only for truly new and nonobvious innovations), reducing uncertainty about the likelihood of gaining patent protection, and lowering the costs of obtaining a patent. These are unobjectionable proposals, at least in principle, and the specific suggestions they outline merit serious consideration.

For example, there are calls to permit third parties to contest a patent before it is granted and to give stronger teeth to any post-grant administrative review (for example, by changing the legal standard for overturning a patent from one requiring "clear and convincing evidence" to one based on the "preponderance of the evidence"). Another idea is to enhance the ability of judges or specially appointed masters (rather than juries) to decide the very technical issue of whether a particular invention is novel and nonobvious. There is a growing consensus, even among opponents to the foregoing reforms, that the PTO should be given additional resources to do its job, though any new funding should be decoupled from patent fees (so as not to encourage the PTO to engage in rubber-stamping of applications). Admittedly, to the nonspecialist these recommendations seem like technical fixes, but taken together, they move in the right direction: toward a better system that grants protection to worthy advances while reducing the likelihood that undeserving applications will be approved.[14]

United States policy makers might also do well to emulate several features of the Japanese patent system, which is designed to encourage dissemination of inventions. These include:

- Awarding of patents to those *first to file* rather than the party proving that it was the *first to invent* the item in question. Such a system that encourages early filing would make technical information available sooner than under the current U.S. system. (Such a system is used widely throughout the world, but not in the United States.)
- Allowing others to use a prospectively patentable invention during the period after a patent application has been filed and requiring them simply to pay royalties that are deemed "reasonable." During this disclosure period, the user is obligated to pay such royalties only if it can be shown that the applicant's invention has been used "knowingly." This system clearly adds to the risks applicants face in failing to reach early agreement with prospective users.
- Defining the coverage of a patent in a very narrow sense, so that only the unsanctioned production of items whose technology is extremely similar to the patented item is prohibited. At the same time, the requirement, found in any patent system, that the patented idea be novel, is interpreted relatively loosely in Japan. As a result, rivals who have learned the technology of an innovation during the disclosure period after the patent application, and have used the knowledge to design minor modifications of the original invention, are entitled to apply for patents of their own to cover these variations. This clearly weakens the power of a patent to exclude use by others. In addition, the original inventor may be boxed in by the derivative patents and prevented from using her own invention in her production process for fear of violating imitators' "improvement patents."[15]

Each of these patent provisions puts strong pressure on Japanese innovators to enter into cross-licensing arrangements with rivals. The mere presence of these rules constitutes a threat not only to the success of the initial patent application (via the prospect of direct opposition), but also to the right to use the patent should it be granted but then hemmed in by patented improvements. In Ordover's words, "The Japanese patent system subordinates the short-term interests of the innovator in the creation of exclusionary rights to the broader policy goals of diffusion of technology" (Ordover, 1991, 48). The Japanese model thus illustrates one way the "rules of the game" can be designed to provide the incentive for managements, particularly large firms with substantial stocks of proprietary innovations, to increase their contribution to the economy's productive capacity and to its growth.

There was a time, not so long ago, when the idea of reforming the patent system along these lines would have been viewed as politically inconceivable. The forces behind "strong IP" looked too strong to permit any changes that could be depicted as "weakening" IP protection. But one highly visible episode during 2005 and 2006 may have changed the political landscape and set the stage for constructive patent reform in the near to intermediate future. During that time, the inventor of one of the key technologies underlying the widely used Blackberry device (which permits wireless e-mailing), NTP, Inc., came close to obtaining a court injunction that would have shut down the service. The threat was perceived to be so serious that United States government attorneys urged the court to grant employees of the federal government and the congressional and judicial branches an exemption from such an order if it were issued. At the end of the day, the shutdown threat was removed when, at the last minute, the Blackberry manufacturer (Research in Motion, or RIM) settled out of court for more than $600 million. Because of the wide number of Blackberry users, this seemingly arcane lawsuit by a company that engaged in no manufacturing itself—but merely held a portfolio of patents—awakened policy makers and the public to the potentially enormous significance that patent principles and their application can have not only on innovation but on all those who use and depend on it.

Discouraging Unproductive Entrepreneurship

The second element in the three-pronged program we advocate is reducing or, ideally, eliminating incentives for individuals with entrepreneurial talent to turn their abilities in unproductive directions, which can actually damage a nation's productivity. Unproductive entrepreneurship can take many forms; for example, enterprising corruption, the formation of organized crime syndicates, or engaging in activities that are legal, such as lobbying legislatures to induce them to adopt laws that bring profits to the lobbyists or their clients. The courts and regulatory agencies provide many opportunities for a clever lawyer-entrepreneur. Relative to other countries, the United States has little problem with corruption, at least as measured by the rankings of Transparency International, a nongovernmental organization that ranked the United States seventeenth out of the 150 on its 2005 corruption perception index.[16] A larger problem, presaged by the late Mancur Olson (1982), is the mounting collection of interest groups and lobbies, which lead, at best, to inefficiency and, at worst, detract from growth. Examples are not hard to find: unsuccessful efforts to seriously reform large government-sponsored entities (GSEs), such as Fannie Mae and Freddie Mac; lobbying by U.S. farmers to obtain large subsidies (which makes it difficult for the United States to advance trade liberalization); lobbying by the high-tech and entertainment industry to extend intellectual property rights (which, as noted above, may well have gone too far); and rent-seeking litigation, in which firms compete to obtain monopoly licenses or sue their more successful competitors in hopes of obtaining protection from competitive activities. Each of these activities makes use of the innovative efforts of those who represent the parties involved. Resourceful lobbyists can think of new approaches for attaining their objectives, and ingenious litigants can be innovative in their courtroom activities, thereby obtaining large payoffs if their efforts succeed but in the process simply transferring resources from one pocket to another without contributing anything to total output.

It is not easy to solve these problems. It may seem that the lobbying problem can be curtailed by such measures as publicizing monetary contributions to the campaigns of elected officials. But the proliferation of advocacy organizations, which are not subject to disclosure requirements and, perhaps, cannot be under the United States Constitution, has shown how easy it is to get around such rules.

Governments can also adopt rules that limit rent-seeking litigation, although these can be controversial and could be inconsistent with preserving the ability of injured parties to seek redress for legitimate grievances. An example of constructive change is legislation enacted by the United

States Congress in 2005 designed to stop "forum shopping" by class-action plaintiffs, that is, the search for friendly state courts in which to press their cases. Under the new legislation, when plaintiffs reside in different states than defendants (which are typically large corporations in class-action cases), the suits must be brought in federal court. A further reform that seems promising is placement of cases involving highly technical subjects—such as medical malpractice cases—in specialized courts, much as patent cases are. This may not be a panacea, however, since these courts, too, can be subject to capture by vested interests (as appears to be the case for the patent intellectual property system [Jaffe and Lerner, 2004]). Nonetheless, some further measures to curtail unproductive entrepreneurship might be implemented, at some point.

Avoiding Misuse of Antitrust Laws

History is replete with examples of firms that lose out to competitors because of their inefficiency or the inferiority of their products and then seek protection from their rivals, claiming that the competitive actions of their rivals are "unfair," "predatory," or "destructive." There are, of course, cases where one firm does, indeed, adopt measures whose only conceivable purpose is to destroy rivals, as when firms use their deep pockets to adopt prices well below any pertinent costs of their products in the hope that their rivals will be driven into insolvency trying to match them. But there are also examples of what has been called "sham litigation"— lawsuits launched, for example, when a rival's low costs permit it to adopt very low prices that really are legitimate and serve the public interest. Knowing that the high cost, the energy entailed, and the uncertain outcome of such litigation can induce the defendant firm to surrender and even pay the plaintiff firm an amount sufficient to induce it to withdraw its complaint, firms that otherwise fear they will not succeed on their own merits have incentives to file such suits as a form of insurance against failure.

Indeed, one of the authors of this volume was involved in precisely such a case, in which a group of manufacturers of soft drinks had joined together to form a cooperative enterprise to produce their bottles at about half the cost they had been charged by the then-monopolist bottle manufacturer. That manufacturer communicated with his former customers, telling them that unless they agreed in the future to buy from him exclusively, at whatever price he chose to set, he would launch an antitrust lawsuit against them. The customer firms refused and the bottle manufacturer proceeded to sue. Fortunately, in this case, the judge was made aware of the plaintiff's undisguised threat, and the lawsuit was thrown out. But such cases do not always end so appropriately, particularly because litigation with exactly the same appearance can be entirely legitimate.

There are a number of steps that can be taken to discourage such enterprising litigation. Under prevailing rules in the United States, if the plaintiff in such a case is victorious, it can expect to be awarded court costs as well as treble damages (see below). But if the defendant wins, and even if the plaintiff's case is determined to have no merit, the plaintiff is generally not expected to cover the legal costs incurred by the defendant. Clearly, this system can encourage the launching of baseless legal complaints, perhaps even ensuring that the plaintiff has little to lose in the process. One way to correct this problem is to adopt the "English rule" on attorneys' fees—the loser pays—for some classes of cases, such as commercial litigation, that is, those with commercial interests on both sides. To do it more broadly, however, can make it difficult for legitimately harmed consumers to gain redress of their grievances.

Another idea is to revisit the longstanding provision in U.S. antitrust law that allows successful plaintiffs to collect treble damages if they win. This only adds to the attraction of sham antitrust litigation of the sort under discussion, which can end not only by protecting the plaintiff from the competition of a more efficient rival but also with a substantial financial reward. Treble damages were adopted for two reasons. First, a firm that violates the antitrust laws stands a considerable chance of getting away with it, and if it is in no danger of having to pay its rivals more than the damage its illegitimate activities has cost them, it will proceed with the violation. If so, treble damages may constitute an appropriate deterrent. But the second justification for trebling of damages is more suspect: to enlist "private attorneys general" to uncover and prosecute antitrust abuses. Although some legitimate cases still start this way, the hard work of investigating and prosecuting cases is generally carried out by government officials, with private plaintiffs coming in after the fact to pick up a large damage award. Because plaintiffs would have an incentive to bring their complaints to the government even without trebled damages, we favor the removal of the treble-damage provisions in U.S. antitrust law.

Reining in Other Unmeritorious Litigation

Lawsuits without merit not only impose needless transaction costs, they can discourage entrepreneurship and growth. This is especially so in unmeritorious class action lawsuits, typically brought on a contingency basis, which can involve damage claims running well into the hundreds of millions, if not billions, of dollars.

A contingency lawsuit, commonly undertaken by increasingly sophisticated well-networked members of the plaintiff's bar, is one arranged so that the plaintiff pays no attorney's fees in advance; lawyers are compensated by a substantial share of the award if they win the case. This invites the practice of some lawyers of making their living by seeking out prospective cases, which would otherwise never reach the courts, and inducing prospective clients to serve as plaintiffs, at no financial risk to themselves, representing a much wider class of parties (technically, there are ethics rules to prevent all this, but successful plaintiffs' attorneys seem to have ways to avoid them).

Class action lawsuits proceed in two stages. First, the court must determine that all class members are "similarly situated"—or damaged by the same cause—so that the case can be treated as a "class" action. In considering whether to make this finding, courts implicitly assume that the defendant is liable, and thus no evidence on that issue can be presented. Second, once a class is certified, the court proceeds to consider whether the defendant should actually be liable, and if so, by how much (as to the entire class).

For defendants, the more important of these two stages is the first because even a nonmeritorious plaintiff can be an enormous risk once a class action has been approved by the court. If the class is large, so will be total damages. Accordingly, even if they are innocent (or believe themselves to be innocent), defendants in class actions where a class has been certified may simply choose to surrender and settle, in effect paying a ransom to escape the perils now threatened by the lawsuit. This, too, is evidently an incentive for enterprising litigators to seek out such cases.

One possible way to reduce the incentives for enterprising class actions that, in effect, blackmail defendants with deep pockets (on their own or with the backstop of their liability insurers) would be to permit the defendant in such cases a limited opportunity to introduce some evidence of its innocence (if it has any) before the class designation is approved or rejected by the court. The stronger this evidence, the higher the hurdle for plaintiffs if they are to sustain their class action. We encourage the legal profession and economists interested in this problem to think of other ways to address it.[17]

Competition and Innovation: Keeping Winners on Their Toes

We come now to the third element of the program we have recommended for encouraging productive entrepreneurship. Unlike the first and second elements, which focused largely if not exclusively on individual entrepreneurs and their inventor partners, the third element deals with large firms and measures to stimulate them to continue innovating. This is appropriate and necessary in "entrepreneurial" economies because large firms play an important and complementary role in such economies, by providing the cumulative improvement of entrepreneurial inventions that enables and encourages the mass of consumers to want and use them. Furthermore, it is only vigorous competition among these large firms that forces them to strive without letup to introduce such improvements before competitors beat them to the punch, resulting in a steady stream of innovation and technical progress.

We will focus on several policy instruments to help assure that this outcome—ongoing innovation, primarily by large firms—continues, beginning with a discussion of the proper role of antitrust law and the importance of continued openness to foreign goods, services, ideas, and capital in applying competitive pressure that fuels the innovation race. One part of the corporate income tax code—that dealing with stock options—also could be improved to prod large firms, in particular, to continue innovating. Ideas developed by university faculties, which already are important sources of innovation but are likely to be even more important in the high technology arena in the future, can be commercialized more rapidly, contributing to entrepreneurial success. All of these suggestions should spur both innovation and commercialization by larger firms. Finally, there is a need to ensure that the United States has a sufficiently well-trained workforce, well suited for the increasingly technical demands of the twenty-first century, to staff innovative large and small firms alike.

Antimonopoly Rules and Cooperative Innovative Activity

In chapter 5, we discussed the role of antitrust laws, not just in preserving but also in encouraging competition. It goes without saying that these laws should continue to be enforced. At the same time, it is equally important that antitrust authorities give more weight in their enforcement efforts to the benefits of certain sorts of *cooperation* among firms that serve the public interest. Innovation is an arena in which this is particularly true. Innovation helps to speed elimination of the obsolete. It enables firms to share the heavy costs of the research and development process and makes it easier for the individual enterprise to bear its contribution. Innovation reduces the risks of investment in R&D and reduces duplicative efforts. It also facilitates compatibility of design by making it easier for one firm's technological advances to work smoothly with those of another while enabling firms to learn from one another in undertaking their own innovation activities.

In practice, antitrust authorities can recognize these benefits of cooperation by applying a "relaxed rule of reason" test when weighing the competitive (or possibly anticompetitive) effects of research joint ventures, research consortia, and even mergers in high-technology industries—all of which may be socially optimal responses to market failures that beset the production and dissemination of knowledge. Indeed, mergers of firms with substantial current market shares in high-technology industries (where fixed costs of research, development, and deployment of new technologies are high) can be presumed to be conducive to long-run efficiency, more so than in industries that are less technology-driven.

In fact, both of the U.S. antitrust enforcement agencies—the Department of Justice and the Federal Trade Commission—have recognized the virtues of cooperation through their intellectual property guidelines.[18] A more formal announcement of a relaxed rule of reason would also clear away some remaining legal uncertainties.[19]

Open Borders to Enhance Competitive Pressure

Openness to trade and foreign direct investment is an economic arrangement that arouses the suspicion, and sometimes the enmity, of the general public. It is widely feared that putting out the welcome mat for other countries' exports, particularly countries with low wages and living standards, will lead to the loss of domestic jobs, loss of business, and depression of wage levels toward the pitiful levels of developing countries. For many decades, popular opinion makers have railed against the unfair competitive threat posed by importing goods made by "cheap foreign labor." Now, a similar complaint has been lodged against "outsourcing" (or, more accurately, "off-shoring") of work to service providers in countries paying lower wages.

There are wrong and right responses in rich countries where work is being off-shored. Shutting the door on trade—even partly, via tariffs, quotas, or other impediments to imports—is one rather sure wrong response. The standard conclusion of economists that there are generally mutual gains from trade is fundamentally correct (although, as Baumol and Gomory [2005] have shown, foreign competition can reduce the *share* of those gains received by countries that off-shore jobs without offsetting advances in innovation). Trade gives importing countries products that manufacturers in other lands can produce more economically in exchange for items made by less costly producers in the exporting countries. Denying the benefits of this beneficial exchange to ourselves—a process that we welcome and openly encourage when all parties to the exchange are located inside the United States—can only add to whatever pains open trade and off-shoring already would inflict upon us.

The right response is for producers in countries where firms are engaged in off-shoring (such as the United States) to innovate more rapidly, developing ever-better and cheaper products. There is emerging evidence that companies that outsource or off-shore some or much of their routine work are exploiting their comparative advantage in bringing innovations to market more rapidly and more cost-effectively (Engardio, 2006). As innovation advances, nations can increase trade and at the same time experience the benefits of economic growth, the creation of more jobs, and the rising overall wages. This outcome is evident from recent United States history.

As a share of total output, imports have risen from just 11 percent in 1995 to nearly 17 percent in 2004. Yet during this period, median family income increased by 8 percent, GDP rose by more than 30 percent, and total employment by 12 percent.[20] Clearly, nations can increase trade and enjoy improvements in their standard of living at the same time.

Indeed, freer trade, coupled with direct investment by foreigners who build their own plants, keeps U.S. firms on their competitive toes and enables U.S. consumers to reap the benefits of a broader range of products and services, available at lower prices. For example, without the competition from more fuel-efficient and higher-quality Japanese automobiles, U.S. auto companies would be producing less fuel-efficient and less reliable autos than they are today. The same process has occurred in the steel and textile industries, among others.

This is not to deny the legitimate concerns about foreign progress in technological fields. There continue to be "first mover" advantages, which can make it difficult (but not impossible) to dislodge firms that are the first to achieve commercial success in new fields. Economies of large-scale production, the lessons learned by an experienced labor force, and the mutual support that related industries derive from one another all can give the early incumbent industries and the nations that host them a powerful defensive position against incursion of technology from other countries. Location still offers advantages even in the age of the Internet, which enables numerous products to be designed and assembled from all parts of the world. Once a locality or region obtains a firm place in some specialty, it seems to embark on a virtuous cycle: the pool of specialized labor and related support services attracts more firms, and this in turn attracts more such people and infrastructure and so forth. Examples are found not only in the United States (most prominently in Austin, Boston, Raleigh, Seattle, and the San Francisco Bay area), but also around the world: Bangalore, India (for software), northern Italy (for design), and Taiwan (for manufacture of consumer electronics). Richard Florida of Carnegie-Mellon University has pointed to this geographical agglomeration as evidence that the world is "spiky" rather than "flat," as argued by *New York Times* columnist Thomas Friedman (Florida, 2005; and Friedman, 2005).[21]

At the same time, it is important to put the concerns about the diffusion of economic progress throughout the world in some perspective. As

Americans, we should want the Indias and the Chinas of the world to grow because the richer they are, the larger the markets they provide for our exports. And, just because new ideas are developed elsewhere does not mean that Americans derive no benefits from them. We can gain, just as the rest of the world has been benefiting from our technological progress for decades, by importing capital goods that embody technical change and by accepting foreign direct investment that typically comes with cutting-edge process and/or managerial skills. In fact, the United States has benefited from precisely this sequence of events throughout its history—from British railroads in the nineteenth century to Japanese "just in time" manufacturing and quality circles more recently.

In the long run, all citizens of the world, including those in rich countries like the United States, can expect to be better off if there are more skilled people working to advance the technological frontier. As the popular author Malcolm Gladwell recently put it: "With the pace of development in China and India and other parts of the developing world, we're just adding to the available brainpower and unlocking these large populations of people and their ingenuity and giving them an education. *How much easier will it be to solve the problems of the world when we've got 10 times as many brains working on them*" (*Time*, October 24, 2005, p. 86; emphasis added).

All this is not to sound defeatist, but to caution against hysteria. Of course, U.S. leaders in both the private and public sectors should strive to maintain U.S. leadership in innovation and commercialization. We will be better off with this scenario since we will benefit both from the profits generated by innovation and from the virtuous circle of being an economic leader. But closing off our borders to foreign goods, services, ideas, and capital cannot help us in any respect. On the contrary, by depriving U.S. consumers and U.S. producers of what is best in the world, a protectionist retreat is the surest route to second-rate economic status.

The key challenge for policy makers in the United States (and other rich countries) is to maintain a commitment to freer trade in the face of mounting concern across the political spectrum and among both blue-collar and white-collar workers about the threat that foreign competition poses to their job security and earnings advancement. This challenge would be easier to meet if the United States trade deficit were not so enormous. But this deficit is not likely to come down appreciably without major reductions in the long-term federal budget deficit, which acts as a drain on national savings and thereby requires foreign capital to finance United States investment. The counterpart of capital inflows is the high and rising current account deficit. In the meantime, whatever action or inaction may take place on the budget front, federal policy makers could reduce workers' anxiety about global competition if the government did more to cushion the loss in earnings that workers suffer upon being displaced from a job. One way to do this is to provide limited wage insurance that compensates permanently displaced workers for some portion of any wage losses suffered upon accepting a new but lower-paying job. The United States Congress adopted a limited experiment along these lines in extending the president's trade negotiating authority in 2002, but only for workers over the age of fifty who could prove that trade was the dominant reason for their displacement. This program should be expanded for all workers, regardless of the reason for their displacement (which is most often the result of continued productivity improvements) and could be implemented at reasonable cost, perhaps less than $5 billion per year (easily financed by a modest increase in the federal unemployment insurance tax).[22] As we discussed in chapter 7, a similar program should be adopted in Europe as a way to effect a partial transition away from highly costly unemployment insurance programs.

Government Policies to Facilitate Transfer of Foreign Technology

The United States should remain open to foreign goods and ideas, and its government can and should take an active role in facilitating the use of foreign technology by U.S.-based firms. In fact, no country is an island in the global economy. No country has a monopoly on all innovation. Even the United States and Japan, by far the world's leaders in the number of patents awarded every year, each create no more than some 35 percent of the world's innovations, meaning that they must acquire (by purchase or by license) a substantial proportion of the remaining 65 or so percent in order to avoid falling hopelessly behind their competitors.[23] In fact, technology transfer is inherently an entrepreneurial activity. It entails recognition of foreign technological advances that are promising for importation, redesign of the innovations to adapt them to domestic needs, and then rearranging them for their introduction into the importing country's productive ventures.

Government can and should play a very helpful role in all of these activities. The main reason for this lies in the fact that new information can be very costly, difficult, and time-consuming to acquire, involving the hard work of many highly educated and skilled individuals. But once these initial expenses are paid, delivery of the information so acquired to others can be virtually costless and the same whether to ten, a thousand, or even more users. In other words, the cost of providing the information to an additional user is virtually zero. Because of this, a central gatherer of information—such as a governmental body—can simultaneously serve the needs of a multiplicity of users at costs far lower than those that would be incurred if each user were to seek to obtain the information for itself. For example, the work of monitoring foreign technical journals and of providing translations of pertinent technical articles can be carried out nearly as cheaply for a multiplicity of that economy's firms, or even for a considerable number of industries, as it can on behalf of any single business enterprise.

Countries appear to differ substantially in the quantity of resources they devote to this purpose, and the United States is clearly not a leader. Although the following survey is more than fifteen years old, we doubt that the main thrust of the results is any different today than when the survey was conducted. Edwin Mansfield reported in 1990 on the basis of a survey of one hundred American firms in thirteen industries, that these respondents believed only 29 percent of U.S. firms spend as much (as a percentage of sales) on the monitoring of foreign technology development as their Japanese rivals. Forty-seven percent of these American firms reported that they spent as much as their German counterparts, 51 percent as much as their French rivals, and 70 percent reported spending as much as their British rivals on the monitoring of foreign technology (Mansfield, 1990, 343). Such disparities, assuming they continue to persist today (and we suspect they do), may well constitute an opportunity for a growing economy to gain a differential advantage in its monitoring and adoption of foreign technology.

One way to narrow the technology gap would be for the federal government to establish an office of technology monitoring, with a staff of specialists qualified to monitor, translate, and disseminate pertinent materials from foreign publications. Such an office could be lodged in an existing agency, such as the Commerce Department, or even be an arm of the Patent and Trademark Office (provided the new office was given additional funds and existing overworked PTO personnel were not diverted from their current tasks). The office also need not be large. Much of its work could perhaps be outsourced to U.S. universities. In addition, the federal office could be aided by a small army of technical personnel lodged in U.S. embassies around the world, whose main job would be to monitor technological developments—in technical journals, patent applications, and company newsletters and reports—and to report back regularly to Washington. The results could be compiled in a database, translated into English, and made widely accessible through the Internet. The embassy specialists could also help facilitate technology transfer agreements between U.S. and foreign firms and native enterprises.

Universities represent another potentially important transmission link for transferring foreign technology to the United States. For much of the post–World War II period, foreign students traveled to the United States to study at our best universities, often at their government's expense, gaining cutting-edge technical and managerial skills and knowledge to be put to use in their home countries. Indeed, the balance between native and foreign-born individuals gaining science and engineering Ph.D. degrees from U.S. universities has shifted markedly over time: in 1966, 77 percent of such degrees were awarded to native-born Americans, but by 2000, this figure had fallen to 61 percent (Freeman et al., 2004). Since the terrorist attacks of September 11, 2001, U.S. immigration authorities have made it far more difficult for students from abroad to continue their science and engineering studies here. We believe that this is a mistake and that U.S. immigration policy should be more accommodative to foreign students, granting long-term work visas, or even immediate citizenship, to foreign students who earn degrees in math- and science-related fields (Becker, 2005; and Schramm and Litan, 2005). In 2006, U.S. policy makers agreed with this line of argument. Congress lifted the annual cap on "H1-B" guest worker visas for immigrants in science and engineering from 65,000 to 115,000, and during the summer of 2006, it was debating whether to let more foreign students become permanent residents (we would prefer automatic citizenship) after obtaining advanced degrees in math, engineering, technology, and the physical sciences in the United States.

At the same time, we also urge the U.S. government to learn a lesson from other governments by providing more scholarship aid for *American* students to study engineering and science in foreign universities. Such a program would extend the existing Fulbright postgraduate fellowships and reach down into the undergraduate and graduate schools, and it would provide subsidies for U.S. students to learn the languages of the countries where they intend to study. In the increasingly global economy of the twenty-first century, it is only appropriate that formal government policy enable U.S. students to be better prepared for working and starting businesses that compete globally. Recognizing that we have much to learn from the rest of the world is a good way to start.

Finally, technology transfer could be accelerated not only by sending Americans abroad, but also by welcoming highly trained foreigners here. Such a policy may be stoutly resisted by their high-skilled United States counterparts, whose earnings growth could be diminished by the added supply of well-trained workers—just as lesser-skilled workers typically object to labor-intensive imported goods or the immigration of low-skill workers themselves. But in a world where knowledge increasingly has no limits, it would be a collective mistake not to take advantage of the training and skills of workers from abroad.

Encouraging Innovation through the Corporate Income Tax System

Like the individual income tax, corporate income taxes can be used to encourage entrepreneurial firms. We have in mind one modification to corporate income taxes—whether or not those taxes are increased, reduced (as many economists have long argued), or left roughly where they are now in terms of raising revenue—that should help catalyze innovation both by large companies and among newer, more entrepreneurial firms.

Our specific subject is stock options, which since the early 1990s have become an increasingly popular means of compensating individuals, especially at high-growth, high-technology companies. Stock options afford their recipients the opportunity to buy a company's stock at a given price (the "strike price") and thus provide a potentially significant upside opportunity if stock prices increase but no downside risk (since the holders of options have no incentive to exercise them if stock prices do not increase). In principle, stock options help address what has come to be known as the principal-agent problem, with the stockholders being the principals and corporate managers their agents. The "problem" in this arrangement arises from the possibility that the agents will look after their own interests in the company and attend only secondarily, if at all, to the interests of the company's owners. By giving corporate managers an ownership stake, or at least a potential ownership position (once options are exercised), stock options theoretically better align the interests of corporate managers and shareholders.

But there is an important drawback to stock options, as they currently exist. If the value of the options is tied only to a company's stock price, and the stock price in turn can be temporarily boosted by higher-than-expected earnings, managers may be tempted to "cook the books"—that is, falsify their accounting records by understating expenses or overstating revenues, in an effort to beat earnings expectations (particularly the expectations of the stock analysts who follow the fortunes of public companies) in the hope of cashing in their options after the stock price has risen. The corporate scandals of the late 1990s and early 2000s can be explained by just such a sequence of events (Bogle, 2005; Bromwich et al., 2002).

Some of the abuses of stock options are likely to be corrected by the 2005 decision of the Financial Accounting Standards Board (FASB) to require public companies in the United States to begin recording stock options as a compensation expense, using any one of several approved techniques. The FASB took this step after a more than a decade of debate over the issue and after earlier congressional pressure against such a measure, largely at the behest of high-technology companies (which feared that "expensing" of options would inhibit them from attracting talented employees and executives). There is insufficient evidence to know whether this fear is or ever was justified, but even if it were, it could be addressed by exempting new public companies from the expensing requirement for a limited time after their listing on a public exchange.

The issue we want to address here, however, is how stock options are or should be treated for *tax purposes*. Unlike the FASB provisions, which essentially require companies to estimate expenses associated with stock option grants, current corporate income tax provisions allow deductions only when employees actually *exercise* the options. The value of stock options for tax purposes differs from their value for financial reporting purposes most likely because it is easier to verify stock-option expenses based on the difference between the exercise and strike price (the tax definition) than some estimate of the value of the options when they are granted (the reporting definition). More important for our purposes is that U.S. tax law permits companies to deduct expenses associated with stock options *regardless of how the firm itself has performed relative to other firms in the same industry or with respect to all other publicly traded firms.* Stock options structured in this manner (as virtually all options are) do not reward managers and employees for extraordinary performance; on the contrary, option holders can benefit from a sub-par performance by their companies since they can realize gains from the options as long as the price of their company's stock rises.

Furthermore, although companies generally restrict managers and employees from exercising their options for a period of time after they are granted, this limitation is often as short as six months. As a result, option holders have an incentive to maximize the short-run performance of their company's stock (including "cooking the books") regardless of the effect their activities may have on company performance in the long run.

We believe that the corporate tax law would better encourage extraordinary, long-term company performance—and thus innovation—if stock option expenses were deductible only if they meet the following conditions: (1) stock options cannot exercised for some substantial period, say five years, so that anyone who receives them will think beyond the short-term effects on stock prices; and (2) stock options must be performance based, with their amounts contingent on the firm's exceeding the performance of comparable firms or its own past record.[24] Separately, the Securities and Exchange Commission, which governs reporting by public companies, should require the prompt disclosure of stock sales by top management so that the investing public knows when "insiders" are selling their shares.

The proposed tax reform coupled with the proposed disclosure requirement should discourage managers from taking steps that may artificially boost a company's stock price and then taking their chips off the table by selling their shares. Viewed more positively, the proposed reforms should make clear to corporate managers that the only way they can enhance their own compensation is to improve their companies' pace of innovation, which is good for shareholders and for the economy as a whole.

Encouraging the Commercialization of University-Based Research

Entrepreneurs clearly must have incentives to bring innovations to the marketplace. So must large companies, although, as we have argued, their innovations are more likely to be incremental in nature and forthcoming only so long as these firms face competitive pressure to continue the innovations arms race.

Increasingly, at least in the United States, universities also have become sources of new technological knowledge and new products and processes.[25] As technology becomes more complex, universities may play an even more important role in advancing innovation by generating ideas that fuel the innovations arms race among large and small companies alike. Until 1980, there was some uncertainty about the extent to which universities and their faculties had rights to their innovations, which many believed discouraged their commercialization. This uncertainty was cleared up with the passage of the Bayh-Dole Act, which explicitly allowed universities and their faculties to commercialize, and thus to profit from, federally financed research. The aim of the legislation was to move university-based science "out the door" and into the commercial marketplace as rapidly as possible, whether through the formation of new ventures or the sale or licensing of the technology to large firms, many of which look to universities to fill their own innovation pipelines.

By a number of indicators, the Bayh-Dole Act appears on the surface to have been a success, gauged by a fourfold jump in the share of all domestic patents accounted for by universities from 1980 to the mid-1990s (Mowrey, 2005),[26] and the visibility of some of the high-technology companies that have spun out of universities: Google (Internet search), Genentech (biotechnology), Chiron (vaccines), Cirrus Logic (information technology), and Netscape (which developed the first widely used Internet browser, only to be eclipsed by Microsoft, in part through conduct that the United States courts later deemed to be in violation of the U.S. antitrust laws). Large companies and venture capital firms also eagerly line up outside university doors, not waiting to acquire the spun-out companies, but rather seeking to license the universities' best technologies from the outset. In recent years, other countries (which heretofore have discouraged the commercialization of university-developed innovations on the grounds that this would distract them from their core functions of teaching and basic research) have been seeking to implement or have already adopted their own versions of the Bayh-Dole Act.

For all this seeming success, it is our view that university research is not flowing as fast as it should to entrepreneurs and to larger companies that are trying to become more entrepreneurial by embracing and exploiting newly developed technologies. The lure of the rewards from commercialization seems to motivate only a handful of researchers at a relatively small number of universities. For example, only four universities generate more than 100 patents every year, and only ten report more than 270 disclosures, which represent the pre-patent stage of a new discovery. A summary of where the commercialization action really is taking place, showing how limited it is, is shown in table 18.

We believe that universities—even those where innovation and commercialization activity is already concentrated—could do a much better job of moving their discoveries to market if they were less bureaucratic, and more entrepreneurial, in doing so. One of the unintentional by-products of the Bayh-Dole Act is that universities somehow have come to believe that they can only, or at least best, implement the act by centralizing their commercialization activities in their in-house technology transfer offices. Universities had good reason for believing this. In principle, such offices should be able to help enterprising faculty members determine whether their innovations are patentable or protected by some form of intellectual property right and then pay for the necessary legal work to file the patent applications and negotiate licenses or uses in commercial start-ups. Accordingly, university technology trade offices, in theory, should be able to accelerate the commercialization of university-based innovation.

But research work documented by staff at the Ewing Marion Kauffman Foundation has revealed that in practice (with few exceptions) many university technology trade offices have become bottlenecks to commercialization. Given their situation within university bureaucracies, technology trade offices have difficulty paying for and thus attracting the sophisticated

Table 18 Cumulative University Licensing Revenues

	5-year total	FY 2004	FY 2003	FY 2002	FY 2001	FY 2000
University of California System	$575,096,000	$79,265,000	$67,019,000	$88,148,000	$72,899,000	$267,765,000
Columbia University	$460,377,115	n.a.	n.a.	$168,097,058	$143,342,000	$148,938,057
New York University	$291,979,740	$109,157,450	$85,946,382	$62,700,209	$25,691,655	$8,484,044
Stanford University	$225,707,852	$49,501,622	$45,383,189	$52,712,041	$41,167,000	$36,944,00
Florida State	$219,931,655	$14,316,563	$24,023,189	$52,077,120	$62,077,749	$67,437,034
MIT	$194,083,674	$30,031,032	$26,824,897	$28,706,848	$77,040,976	$31,479,921
Univ. of Wisconsin/WARF	$164,248,265	47,976,489	$36,765,393	$32,340,266	$24,230,361	$22,935,756
University of Florida	$159,298,772	$37,446,673	$35,278,127	$31,615,691	$28,683,282	$26,274,999
University of Minnesota	$150,611,500	$46,198,818	$38,083,275	$26,458,840	$16,727,250	$23,143,317
Michigan State University	$146,661,298	$36,578,455	$23,931,337	$30,032,740	$30,397,759	25,721,007
University of Rochester	$145,562,700	$33,736,882	$26,741,537	$42,095,533	$29,589,000	$13,399,748
University of Washington	$136,058,292	$25,202,792	$29,282,203	$24,823,037	$26,446,297	$30,303,963
All AUTM reporting institutions (universities, hospitals, research institutes in U.S. and Canada)	$6,348,048,669	$1,361,613,710	$1,250,818,557	$1,255,665,014	$1,153,534,736	$1,326,416,652
Total (top ten)	$2,587,995,871					
Total (top twelve)	$2,869,616,863					

Source: AUTM U.S. Licensing Survey, FY 2004 Survey Summary, ed. Ashley J. Stevens, Frances Toneguzzo, and Dana Bostrom (Northbrook, Ill.: Association of University Technology Managers, 2005).

negotiating, licensing, and legal talent that otherwise moves to the private sector. In addition, the typical university technology trade office is under-staffed, which inevitably slows the commercialization process. As a result, although they are technically bound to clear their commercialization activ-ity through the technology transfer office, many university faculty mem-bers commercialize through the "back door," circumventing that office al-together (Shane, 2004; Audretsch et al., 2006). Furthermore, it is rare for a technology transfer office to generate sufficient income to cover its ex-penses, again with certain exceptions for the universities with substantial licensing income.

In our view, the commercialization process could be much improved if universities experimented with a number of different arrangements. To re-duce the delays and transactions costs associated with licensing negotia-tions, universities could jointly develop or follow the lead of others to de-velop standardized licensing agreements. An obvious analogue is the typical publishing contract that contains a standard royalty rate applied to sales through different media. The royalty rate, and possibly other terms, might vary depending on whether the license is exclusive or nonexclusive. Admittedly, it may not be possible to standardize start-up arrangements, which most likely will continue to require custom agreements. But this process, too, could be accelerated if the technology transfer office were subjected to some competition.

One of the reasons technology transfer offices fail to generate a profit for their universities, which would seem to be a principal rationale for their ex-istence, is that they can neither reach a size sufficient to realize economies of scale nor attract licensing and other personnel with expertise compara-ble to that available in the private sector. These problems might be ad-dressed if universities in a region (at the very least public universities) com-bined their resources to share a single technology transfer office, rather than each continue to maintain its own office. To be sure, there would be up-front and perhaps continuing problems of "turf" in a sharing arrange-ment, but assuming these could be mostly resolved in advance (via agree-ments about which institutions get "credit" for which inventions), the economies of scale in such joint arrangements should clearly offset any op-erational difficulties.

Another notion is for the universities to change the objectives of their technology transfer offices—from maximizing profits (or at least minimizing losses) to maximizing the volume or numbers of "deals" that are arranged. Knowing that they will be graded by how many innovations their offices "get out the door" might loosen the bottleneck and reduce the delays that are now created when the transfer offices concentrate so much of their scarce time and money on negotiating the "perfect" licensing arrangement for one or a few technologies while ignoring the innovations that pile up, waiting for attention.

A fourth, more radical idea would be for universities to experiment with ending what amounts to the technology transfer office monopoly, which stems from the requirement that all faculty members use that office for any licensing or other commercialization of their innovations. Instead, universities could let faculty members choose between their own intellectual property agents or the university's technology trade office. Allowing competition should spur the transfer office to improve its performance, reducing delays and transactions costs.[27]

Perhaps the most radical suggestion of all is that universities, in some fields, simply abandon their quest for up-front profits and make certain intellectual property freely available, along the lines of the open-source model developed so successfully by Linux for computer operating system software. Such a policy would accelerate the introduction of new ideas into the marketplace. To the extent universities harbor any desire for future profits from the successful commercialization of ideas generated by their faculty, they could hope to realize them in a different form later, perhaps through generous gifts by individuals or companies who profit from them. The idea is not far-fetched. As it is now, universities rely heavily on grateful alumni for significant sources of endowment or operating expenses. Universities can realistically expect similar contributions from grateful faculty who have full rights to commercialize their innovations.

Though seemingly disparate, these suggestions have a common objective: to speed up the introduction of university-generated ideas into the marketplace. This can benefit the universities financially, but it is also an important social good, especially when, increasingly, companies headquartered around the world are deciding where to locate their R&D facilities, based in part on their ease of access to university-based research personnel and output (Thursby and Thursby, 2006).

Why, then, have university presidents not already adopted one or all of these measures? We suspect the answer, in part, is that most presidents are not themselves familiar with the commercialization process and treat it much like information-technology decisions, delegating them to some subset of individuals presumed to be knowledgeable in the area. In the case of IT, this may be a sensible strategy. But when it comes to the commercialization of technology, the danger of delegation to an independent office is that the manager and employees of the delegated office, namely, the technology trade office, may acquire vested interests of their own, seeking to preserve their own jobs and possibly expand their operations. Given the many responsibilities of university presidents, it is not unexpected that they would largely ignore what the technology trade office is doing and treat any commercialization as a success—as a "free good," one might say—without realizing what could be realized if the commercialization process were organized differently.

Here is where the federal government could play a constructive role. At a minimum, the key agencies that award significant research funds to universities (the National Institutes of Health, the National Science Foundation, the Department of Energy, and the Department of Defense) could collectively agree (perhaps with the guidance of the White House science advisor and/or the director of the National Economic Council) to convene university presidents to inform and persuade them of alternative models of commercialization. A more aggressive approach would be for the same agencies to condition their research monies on universities experimenting with one or more approaches to accelerating commercialization. However it is accomplished, when more universities become skilled at transferring technology, and when they become more efficient and inventive as organizations, entrepreneurs and large firms, the United States, and the rest of the world will benefit.

Maintaining a Well-Trained Workforce

The living standards enjoyed by residents of any economy depend on the productivity of its workforce. Workers are more productive if they work with more and better capital equipment. They are also more productive if they have the benefit of education and training.

Education and training also play a key role in the innovation arms race that is essential to sustain economic growth in any economy. Firms that have succeeded in "round one" cannot be expected to continue their success in subsequent "rounds" of competition unless their managers and workers have the skills necessary to generate innovations or, at the very least, to recognize and purchase the rights to innovations developed by others.

With the coming of the twenty-first century, Americans have grown worried about the quality of their elementary and secondary educational systems and their ability to continue to provide new generations of Americans with the requisite skills. A number of commissions, chaired by highly qualified and influential individuals, have pointed to a series of disappointing statistics about student achievement in mathematics and science, in particular. According to various international tests, American students rank well behind those in other parts of the world in these subjects, although there continues to be some debate about how poorly American students do on average, and whether their comparative performance declines in upper grades or essentially remains relatively flat as they age.

Meanwhile, at the university level, there seems to be declining interest in mathematics and science among our native-born youth, and the numbers of foreigners who in recent years have made up a substantial share of our mathematics and science graduates are now down as a result of immigration restrictions in the aftermath of the terrorist attacks of September 11, 2001. The United States was once first in terms of the percentage of its population of twenty-five to thirty year olds that attained tertiary education, but by 1991 it had fallen to third place among OECD countries, and by 2003 it had dropped to eighth position (Bowen, 2005).[28] All in all, one can paint a disturbing picture of the status of American education at all levels, with other nations catching up to us in educational attainment, paying much lower wages, while our system for training our future workforce seems plagued with problems. This situation seems especially dire given the increasing tendency for U.S.-educated foreign scientists to return to their home countries, where state-of-the-art research facilities often await them (Lemonick, 2006).

But the source and consequence of the challenges the United States faces must be properly understood. The K-12 statistics, as alarming as they are, are *average* rankings, mixing our best and brightest in excellent suburban public and private schools with many urban schools that are performing poorly. The real worry about the apparently poor math/science pre-college performance of U.S. students may be more about what it portends for future income inequality than what it means for continued technical change.

Meanwhile, the concern about the apparent inadequacy of engineers in the United States misses several important facts. For one thing, although the United States trails China and India in the *absolute* number of engineers produced at the college and graduate school levels, on a *per capita* basis, the United States still ranks well above both countries.[29] This should continue to be true for some time, if not the indefinite future. Second, the comparisons of absolute numbers do not take account of the difference in the *quality* of engineers produced in the United States and other countries. Although China, India and other countries have first-rank universities producing their engineers, the United States has many more such places of higher learning, turning out very well-trained engineers and scientists. And even if the rest of the world is producing and using more scientific talent, in the long run, this will benefit both other countries and the United States, for reasons we gave earlier. Finally, the marketplace in the United States is not signaling a shortage of engineers, for otherwise firms in need of their services would increase their salaries more rapidly than they have in the past, thereby inducing more people to enter the field. Policy makers would do well to heed what happened the last time alarm bells seemingly went off about the shortage of engineers: in 1987, when the National Science Foundation predicted a shortage of engineers, it prompted Congress to increase scholarship funding and to expand foreign visa allowances, resulting in a glut of American-trained engineers several years later, many of whom had difficulty finding jobs (Friel, 2006, 40).

Still it is likely that, as a group, engineers and scientists generate social benefits that exceed the private benefits that accrue to them; in this respect, engineers and scientists are like teachers. This is one reason why it makes sense, in our view, for government to continue to subsidize their education, as well as to provide research funds through universities, which indirectly increases the demand for their services and thus their job prospects and their earnings. As it is, federal support for basic R&D has fallen steadily over the years, from 2 percent of GDP in 1965 to less than half that in 2005. Further, the composition of federally supported R&D

has shifted over time toward health sciences and away from the physical sciences, engineering, math, and computer science,[30] a trend that the Bush administration's proposed federal budget for fiscal year 2007 would begin to reverse over the subsequent ten years. Industry R&D spending has fared better than federally supported R&D, but this is for applied research rather than the basic R&D that is more likely to spawn radical breakthroughs (Friel, 2006).

Whether the United States has too few, too many, or the just right number of scientists and engineers, there is little question that U.S. firms will demand better math and science skills of their *other* workers over time. Those without this training will find themselves at a competitive disadvantage in the workplace and thus cannot look forward to enjoying the living standards of those who have these skills. As long as skills are highly unevenly distributed across the population, so will be incomes. The standard prescription for rectifying these educational imbalances, of course, is to spend more money. Several prominent reports, as well as President George W. Bush himself, have offered various proposals for increasing funding—for more math and science teachers, equipment, remedial training, and so forth.[31] We are sympathetic with this approach only to the extent that any additional educational funds are channeled to teachers under the kind of performance-based pay systems that are prevalent in the private sector. Otherwise, additional funds have little prospect of improving educational performance among any set of students.

More fundamentally, as much if not more attention needs to be paid to *how education money is spent* than to the total sums involved. As contentious as educational policy is, it is generally agreed that America is not getting the largest "bang" out of its hundreds of billions of education "bucks" as it could. It is appalling, for example, that there is so little research on what educational practices actually work to improve the performance of underprivileged students. Our educational practices are much like health care was before the nineteenth century, when doctors proceeded without evidence and resorted to little more than bloodletting and cupping as the universal remedies for most illnesses. Whatever else is done, this lack of research on educational best practices must be remedied. Furthermore, improving educational performance for all students, but especially those from disadvantaged backgrounds, requires the promotion of more competition at the local level. Charter schools are a form of competition, but we would prefer to see at least some form of the voucher system recommended long ago by economist Milton Friedman. If vouchers for private schools prove to be constitutionally unacceptable, then, at a minimum, parents should have choices within the public schools about where to send their children.[32] And if sufficient choices are not available, then, again at the very least, public school authorities should treat public charter schools on equal footing with other public schools, by providing them with the equivalent amount of per pupil funding as is now directed to conventional public schools.

The Political Economy of Growth

One problem with many books like this one is that the policy suggestions they provide risk looking impractical or politically infeasible, at least in the short run. It is a sad but unfortunate fact that in any democracy, political leaders rarely anticipate problems but instead react to crises, real or manufactured. The critical question is: what policy levers are pulled when those crises occur? The answer, more often than not, is that policy prescriptions or ideas that have been percolating in the academy or in the think tank community are taken off the shelf and dusted, as it were, and written into law in some form. Examples of crises-led policy change abound throughout American history: the securities registration and disclosure laws of 1933 and 1934 and the Glass-Steagall Act of 1933 that walled off commercial banking from investment banking were adopted only after the Great Depression was already underway; the banking reform laws in the 1980s and 1990s were enacted after the wave of failures of depository institutions in the 1980s; and the Sarbanes-Oxley Act was adopted only after various corporate scandals in the early 2000s. Such steps typically close the barn door after the horses have escaped and in some cases turn out to be counterproductive yet difficult to repeal or modify (the best-known example being the Glass-Steagall Act, which Senator Carter Glass, one of its sponsors, urged be repealed only two years after enactment, advice that was not taken for more than sixty years).

Policy also changes when political leaders successfully "manufacture" crises over long-festering problems in order to create the urgency needed to mobilize policy action, especially when congressional action is required. Examples here include the War on Poverty in the 1960s; the tax code simplification of 1986; and welfare reform in the 1990s, which represented a partial undoing of the 1960s-era War on Poverty. Not all manufactured crises have resulted in public policy action, however. Examples in this category include President George W. Bush's attempt to reform Social Security during his second term, and President Bill Clinton's bold effort to reform health care during his first. Both foundered because the public failed to appreciate the urgency of the need for reform and/or because there was strong disagreement about how any reform should be structured.

Sustaining the appropriate mix of entrepreneurial and big-firm capitalism—in order to continue and accelerate long-run growth—is perhaps even more difficult than mobilizing the public and its elected representatives to address the problems that this book has emphasized. This is because the public tends to view economic growth more as a cyclical issue than a structural one, that is, something to attend to only during recessions. The public (or even economists) cannot be expected to distinguish between a cyclical shortfall in total output and a downward shift in economic growth. More difficult, neither the public nor political leaders can readily imagine that growth *could* be higher over the long run than it now is if certain policies were adopted to enhance innovation and the economy's expansion.

In short, in the absence of a crisis that impels them to act, policy makers cannot be expected to take apparently radical actions to raise long-term growth by creating the right mix of "capitalisms." In the absence of a recession, political leaders may conceivably be able to use the public's current anxiety about increased economic competition from India and China to manufacture such a crisis. But if the motive for taking action is solely to thwart a perceived foreign threat, then there is a great danger that policy makers will do the wrong things (such as turning inward by raising barriers to goods, capital, and ideas), rather than taking what we believe to be more constructive steps to strengthen our economy at home.

The more likely source of policy action is another recession that will be all too real to the millions of workers whose jobs are threatened. Of course, macroeconomic policy will be used to rescue the economy when that happens, although large federal budget deficits will inhibit the use of fiscal policy (either further tax cuts or spending increases) in the event of a future recession. But perhaps because only monetary policy will be left to help lift the economy out of a downturn, policy makers will be required to look to other measures to stimulate the long-term growth rate of the economy. If and when that occurs, the framework we have outlined here—one that focuses on enhancement of innovations, large and small—should be appealing to political leaders.

Many years ago, the British economist John Maynard Keynes wrote, "practical men, who believe themselves to be quite exempt from any intellectual influence, are usually the slaves of some defunct economist" (Keynes, 1965). Fortunately, none of us is yet defunct. But we hope the ideas we have presented here will be among those that influence the practical men and women of the future to do what it takes to sustain and indeed improve on the remarkable record of economic growth that the U.S. economy has so far achieved.

Concluding Thoughts: Why Accept Our Analysis?

After all this discussion and argument, it is understandable if readers retain more than a degree of skepticism. After all, a profusion of other books by eminent and qualified authors have recently made their appearance, each the strong proponent of his or her recipes for growth—how it can be preserved in advanced economies and how it can be accelerated by those that lag or are mired in poverty. In addition, various international organizations with substantial resources at their disposal have their own lists of actions deemed necessary and perhaps even sufficient to achieve these goals. Yet the economic growth miracles that have resulted—in Asia, Israel, India, and Ireland—were self-generated without the apparent help of much outside expert advice. If this is the case, then why pay much attention to any pronouncements about the ingredients for growth, by others or our own?

Because we believe that the successes of countries that have made it on their own provide an important body of experience that other countries can and should draw on, our book is largely a distillation of what we believe these experiences can teach. To be sure, there are and always will be major differences between countries in their histories and cultures, and so there can be no "one size fits all" recipe. We have tried to resist succumbing to that temptation and instead have offered a menu of potential ingredients we believe are important for economic growth, but how and in what manner the leaders of each country apply these ingredients must be shaped to that country's particular circumstances.

Nonetheless, our reading of the historical evidence and the experiences of prosperous, innovative, and rapidly growing economies suggests the central importance of two conclusions for all who want their economies to be as successful as they can be in delivering rising living standards to their peoples. First, incentives really matter. Countries where activities that promote growth are rewarded will grow faster than countries where this is not the case. Second, the contribution of the entrepreneur in the growth process is substantial.

In this book we have focused largely on the second of these propositions. But on what basis can we be confident that an abundance of productive entrepreneurs can make a substantial difference? Absolute certainty is, of course, impossible. History, in effect, offers us examples and anecdotes on which to base our conclusions, yet the inferences they suggest can be powerful and almost unequivocal.

Perhaps the most striking example is provided by the steam engine, which more than any single invention defined the Industrial Revolution. Yet it is useful to recall its history, as recapitulated by President Abraham Lincoln:

> The advantageous use of *steam-power* is, unquestionably, a modern discovery. And yet, as much as two thousand years ago the power of steam was not only observed, but an ingenious toy was actually made and put in motion by it, at Alexandria in Egypt.
>
> What appears strange is, that neither the inventor of the toy, nor anyone else, for so long a time afterwards, should perceive that steam would move *useful* machinery, as well as a toy. (Lincoln, 1858)

The answer—the explanation of Lincoln's riddle—is that in Rome truly remunerative entrepreneurship was primarily military conquest and its payoff. A similar story can be told for medieval China, the home to a remarkable series of inventions, which likewise did not find their way into commercial application, at least until centuries later. Contrast these experiences with that of James Watt, who after improving the steam engine joined forces with an outstanding productive entrepreneur, Matthew Boulton. Boulton proceeded to energetically market the device for its then-prevalent use, pumping water out of mines. After recognizing that this market was approaching saturation, he demanded that Watt devote himself at once to finding ways to adapt the engine to the profusion of other uses that soon revealed themselves. The Industrial Revolution that resulted reshaped the United States and Europe. The lesson we draw from this history is that without entrepreneurs, and without the right incentives for them to devote themselves enthusiastically and tirelessly to commercial use of their innovations, economic progress cannot be counted on and indeed is unlikely to occur.

These then—entrepreneurship and appropriate incentives—seem to us, from striking historical evidence, to be indispensable ingredients of any growing economy. That, in sum, is the central lesson of this book, a lesson we believe cannot and will not easily be refuted.

APPENDIX: DATA COLLECTION
AND MEASUREMENT ISSUES

Economists like to do two things: theorize and measure. The first is a job increasingly left to the most mathematically inclined or gifted and tends to be the most highly rewarded in the profession. Rare is the Nobel Prize winner who has demonstrated or explained what may seem like an elementary proposition without using some elegant mathematical tools. Although sometime derided by economists who don't have these skills and who believe that it is more important to focus on institutions, culture, and history of economies, the application of mathematics to economics is also useful because it can reveal some surprising and important insights.

Most economists who do not theorize do "empirical work"—testing theories through the use of (increasingly sophisticated) statistical techniques. We have already discussed the limits of such analysis when it comes to assessing the causal factors driving economic growth. Nonetheless, we concede that propositions about economic growth will not be widely accepted within the profession until there is at least some degree of statistical validation (although those outside the profession generally do not apply such exacting standards). For example, one would like to be able test various theories related to our four categories of capitalism. We would like to answer questions such as: Is it really true that oligarchic economies grow less rapidly than other economies? And at what point do state-guided and bureaucratic systems, which can generate growth for substantial periods of time, run out of gas? Is it inevitable that these economies reach that point and, if not, why not? And, as we asked earlier, what mix of entrepreneurial firms and large firms—perhaps measured by the relative output of each type—is likely to maximize growth? Does the answer depend on a country's stage of economic development (measured by its per capita income)?

These are among the questions one would like to examine if only one could measure and/or classify the extent to which capitalist economies fall into one or more of the four categories we have outlined. Alas, that job is difficult, conceivably impossible, but in any event, it is one that we do not undertake here. We trust that if our arguments resonate with at least some in the profession, others more expert than we will expend the effort and resources to collect and analyze the relevant data. But if we are correct that most economies exhibit *some combination* of several or even all of the categories of capitalism, then it may be a fool's errand to put entire economies into one box or the other. Instead, it would be more revealing to be able to track the *mix* of the different types of capitalism present in any economy, perhaps by value added generated by sector or by firms classified into one of the four categories.

Even this may be difficult, if not impossible, to do within any reasonable length of time. As we mentioned in chapter 5, the World Bank has just in the past two years assembled a set of indicators to measure the strength of legal systems and regulatory burdens, more than a decade after Peruvian economist Hernando De Soto popularized the notion that such factors are central to encouraging or handicapping growth in developing countries. But since the World Bank is unable collect such data for earlier periods, it will be many years before it has a series of data spanning a period of sufficient length to be useful for statistical analysis. The same would be true of any effort to collect data on the shares of different economies characterized by the various forms of capitalism we have outlined.

Until then, policy makers and economists who agree with us that our typology is useful will have to be satisfied with impressionistic views of different economies, supplemented by various nuggets of hard statistical data. Such data may be hard to come by for state-guided economies since, as we have noted, state guidance comes in many forms and is often too subtle for outside observers to detect, let alone measure. Data measuring or indicating oligarchic capitalism are a bit easier to assemble. Again, as we noted earlier, such economies tend to be characterized by high income inequality, the presence of a substantial underground (that is, informal) sector, and an abundance of corruption. Income inequality can readily be measured; corruption and the size of the informal sector can be approximated.

Testing Big-Firm Theories

It is tempting to conclude that measurement of big-firm capitalism is easier. For example, why not look to the share of value added or employment by the largest firms in the economy, say the top 100 or 500? The drawback to this deceptively simple approach is that country size matters greatly. In small economies, relatively few firms may account for a significant share of value added or employment, but the firms may be small by international standards. In other words, the firms in such economies may be competing in oligopolistic settings but still may be small in comparison to the large enterprises in bigger and richer countries. On the other hand, in such countries as the United States, India, and China, the largest firms might account for a relatively small share of total value added or employment but still would be characterized, on the basis of their size alone, as bureaucratic. Depending on the industry in which they do business, they may or may not be competing in oligopolistic markets. For these reasons, cross-country comparisons of the shares of value added by a fixed number of companies are likely not to be very revealing and, worse, could even be misleading. Instead, what may be more instructive is the *turnover* or *churn* among the top companies in an economy. In a dynamic big-firm economy, one would expect to see a reasonable amount of shifting of rankings among the largest companies over time, as some firms grow rapidly while others recede. In less dynamic settings, there would be little churn.

Table 19 illustrates the kind of data we have in mind, covering just the top twenty U.S. companies, by revenue, since 1955, with snapshots every ten years. Interestingly, although General Motors and Exxon Mobil topped the list for most of that period, by 2005 both had been eclipsed by Wal-Mart, a company that ranked fourth in 1995 and didn't even make the top twenty in 1975. The table shows an especially large movement of rankings among companies below the top five throughout the period. Expanding the focus to a larger group of companies reinforces the message in the table. According to one calculation, only about half of the one hundred largest manufacturing and industrial firms in the United States in the 1970s survived until the year 2000. The rest disappeared via takeovers or bankruptcies (Micklethwait and Woolridge, 2003, 130–31).

We do not know what a similar chart or data on the status of the largest companies over several decades would look like for Europe or Japan, or for other economies. Our educated guess, however, is that churning of the rankings of large companies in rapidly growing economies generally would be more evident than in more slowly growing ones. In any event, our impressionistic view of the U.S. data indicates that within the big-firm sector, the U.S. economy has been reasonably, and perhaps even remarkably, dynamic over the past five decades (if not more). The U.S. economy looks even more dynamic once account is taken of its entrepreneurial sector.

Entrepreneurship Data and Theory

And so we come to the polar opposite form of capitalism, calling for measures or indicators of entrepreneurial activity. Again, for reasons explained throughout the book, it would be a mistake to measure the vitality or the degree of entrepreneurial capitalism simply by counting the number of entrepreneurs, or small businesses, or those who identify themselves as self-employed. Such a measure is much too broad for our purposes since it would probably include a far greater number of replicative entrepreneurs than innovative entrepreneurs, the number of primary interest here. In principle, surveys can be designed to collect data on the number of innovative entrepreneurs and the growth in that number, and we describe one such effort at the end of this appendix. Given the extensive data collection on firms available in Scandinavian countries and in France, we suspect that such information already exists or could be generated for those countries without overwhelming difficulty. We doubt, however, that such data exist for the rest of the world.

Entrepreneurship Data

The entrepreneurship data that do exist are spotty and, unfortunately, of limited value for purposes of testing the hypotheses advanced in this book.[1] Nonetheless, there is a wealth of information available related to entrepreneurship that serves other

Table 19 Top Twenty U.S. Companies by Revenue, 1955–2005

Rank	1955	1965	1975	1985	1995	2005
1	General Motors	General Motors	Exxon Mobil	Exxon Mobil	General Motors	Wal-Mart Stores
2	Exxon Mobil	Exxon Mobil	General Motors	General Motors	Ford Motor	Exxon Mobil
3	U.S. Steel	Ford Motor	Ford Motor	Mobil	Exxon Mobil	General Motors
4	General Electric	General Electric	Texaco	Ford Motor	Wal-Mart Stores	Ford Motor
5	Esmark	Mobil	Mobil	Texaco	AT&T	General Electric
6	Chrysler	Chrysler	ChevronTexaco	Intl. Business Machines	General Electric	ChevronTexaco
7	Armour	U.S. Steel	Gulf Oil	DuPont	Intl. Business Machines	ConocoPhillips
8	Gulf Oil	Texaco	General Electric	AT&T	Mobil	CitiGroup
9	Mobil	Intl. Business Machines	Intl. Business Machines	General Electric	Sears Roebuck	American Intl. Group
10	DuPont	Gulf Oil	ITT Industries	Amoco	Altria Group	Intl. Business Machines
11	Amoco	AT&T Technologies	Chrysler	ChevronTexaco	Chrysler	Hewlett-Packard
12	Bethlehem Steel	DuPont	U.S. Steel	Atlantic Richfield	State Farm Insurance Cos.	Berkshire Hathaway

13	CBS	Esmark	Amoco	Shell Oil	Prudential Ins. Co. of America	Home Depot
14	Texaco	Shell Oil	Shell Oil	Chrysler	DuPont	Verizon Communications
15	AT&T Technologies	Amoco	AT&T Technologies	Marathon Oil	Kmart Holding	McKesson
16	Shell Oil	ChevronTexaco	Conoco	United Technologies	Texaco	Cardinal Health
17	Kraft	CBS	DuPont	ConocoPhillips	Citicorp	Altria Goup
18	ChevronTexaco	Bethlehem Steel	Atlantic Richfield	Occidental Petroleum	ChevronTexaco	Bank of America Corp.
19	Goodyear Tire & Rubber	Navistar International	CBS	Tenneco Automotive	Proctor & Gamble	State Farm Insurance Cos.
20	Boeing	Rockwell Automation	Occidental Petroleum	Sunoco	PepsiCo	J.P. Morgan Chase & Co.

Source: Fortune 500, 1995–2000, available at http://www.fortune.com/fortune/fortune500.

useful purposes. We are able, for example, to distinguish between the numbers of employed versus self-employed individuals, which may be relevant for understanding social behavior and learning about responses to regulatory or other incentives or disincentives. Similarly, we can use data on new firm formation to understand the effects of the regulatory and institutional climate in a given country for a particular type of entrepreneurial activity.

SELF-EMPLOYMENT DATA   In the United States, the Current Population Survey (CPS) and Census of Population provide estimates of the number of self-employed business owners annually and every decade, respectively. Data from these household surveys allow us to estimate the number of self-employed individuals at a particular point in time and to track changes in the number of self-employed individuals over time. The new Kauffman Index of Entrepreneurial Activity, compiled by Professor Robert Fairlie (of the University of California at Santa Cruz) takes these analyses one step further, using the matched basic monthly files from the CPS to learn about trends in the rate of business creation at a national level.

It is inherently very difficult, however, to find comparable self-employment data sources for cross-country comparisons. In addition to cultural differences that influence survey responses, definitions of self-employment may vary from country to country. There is variation among nations in reporting unpaid family workers as self-employed (likely a function of the particular tax regime and welfare system), and not all countries consider owners of larger businesses to be self-employed.

The Organization for Economic Cooperation and Development (OECD), an organization of largely rich countries (and thirty in all) has made considerable efforts to create comparable cross-country self-employment data. The OECD Labour Force Statistics, generally based on household labor force surveys, provide self-employment data for all OECD member countries. As the majority of these countries (with the exception of Iceland, Mexico, and Turkey) use the International Labor Organization Guidelines definition of self-employment for measuring employment, most of these statistics are comparable across countries. The population statistics that serve as the denominator when calculating these self-employment rates are from a mixture of labor force surveys, administrative records, and population censuses.

Unfortunately, neither the U.S. datasets nor the OECD data can be used to test the theories presented in this book. It is impossible to distinguish the portion of the self-employed population that started businesses for lack of better options for work from those who are taking advantage of an entrepreneurial opportunity. We cannot differentiate between individuals who seek business growth versus those who only have an interest in maintaining their market share. And there is certainly no way to identify those self-employed individuals who are creating truly innovative new entities.

NEW FIRM FORMATION   The United States also maintains data on new firm formation and on the number of small businesses in the country. Using business tax returns and administrative records, the U.S. Census Bureau maintains various programs that both extract relevant data from these files and use them as sampling frames for surveys of businesses.

These data are, however, of limited use for the study of entrepreneurship and certainly do not provide additional information for investigations of innovation and growth. Entrepreneurial activity may be overstated in those datasets that include all firms with receipts of $1,000 or more, which may include side or casual businesses. And efforts to use small businesses as a proxy for entrepreneurs may also overstate the number of new businesses. The Small Business Administration's definition of small businesses as those with fewer than five hundred employees means that this classification includes firms that may be much larger than what we think of as entrepreneurial companies and that may have been in existence for decades.

INTERNATIONAL DATA, GLOBAL ENTREPRENEURSHIP MONITOR The Global Entrepreneurship Monitor (GEM) is, in fact, designed to provide international data that would answer some of the important questions raised in the text. This survey of approximately forty countries is intended to provide comparative entrepreneurship data that include measures of innovation and distinguish between opportunity entrepreneurs and necessity entrepreneurs. GEM presents a Total Entrepreneurial Activity (TEA) index that measures both nascent and early-stage entrepreneurship, capturing individuals between the ages of eighteen and sixty-four who are involved in either the start-up phase or manage a business that is less than forty-two months old. In addition, GEM seeks to measure innovation by asking respondents if their product or service is completely new, and the dataset includes both a TEA-Opportunity and a TEA-Necessity measure, based on questions regarding the reasons for entrepreneurs' decision to start businesses. With this information, the principal investigators have concluded that there is a positive relation between entrepreneurial activity and economic growth.

Although GEM begins to identify the questions that must be part of future data collection efforts, methodological problems with the GEM data and inconsistent results over time suggest that this dataset is not appropriate for investigating the questions raised in the text in a rigorous and meaningful way. It is not clear that GEM's definition of entrepreneurial activity is sufficiently nuanced for scientific inquiry, and it is possible that interpretations of this definition may vary significantly across countries. Furthermore, while the response rate for these surveys is within the operational range for commercial marketing surveys, it is not necessarily high enough for academic analysis.

Inconsistencies in GEM survey results also cast doubt on the credibility of these data for academic research. The significant changes in the entrepreneurship rate for a single country from year to year, and conflicts between the GEM findings for the United States and U.S. Census Bureau data for the same time periods suggest that the measure is problematic for this type of research.

Improving Data Collection on Entrepreneurial Activity

The Kauffman Foundation is making significant efforts to improve the state of data collection related to entrepreneurial activity in the United States and in the world. Since we see the distinction between replicative and innovative entrepreneurship as fundamental to relating entrepreneurship and growth, several of the foundation's data collection initiatives are explicitly intended to bring greater clarity to this contrast.

First, the foundation is supporting a National Academies study of U.S. federal business statistics. The Committee on National Statistics (CNSTAT) has established a panel of experts to review existing data sources in light of researchers' need for better measurement of younger and smaller businesses, their evolution over time, their economic performance, and their role in the larger economy. The panel's final report, to be completed in 2007, will present recommendations for improving the sources and accessibility of data on high-growth firms. In addition, it will suggest new data collection efforts that will give researchers better information for measuring and analyzing the early life cycle dynamics of businesses and for evaluating theories of business formation, selection, and growth.

Similar efforts will need to take place at the international level in order for meaningful comparison to take place. The foundation is sponsoring a study through OECD that will begin to identify needs and make recommendations for international data collection. This assessment of existing data sources and identification of those entrepreneurship-related questions for which there are no international data available will call attention to the significant gaps in data sources for comparative analysis of high-growth companies and will provide a roadmap for future work.

As both of these studies are now in their early stages, the foundation has also taken steps to start collecting the type of data that will allow for greater insight into the difference between replicative and innovative entrepreneurship in the United States. The foundation is funding the Kauffman Firm Survey, a multiyear longitudinal study of new businesses started in the United States in 2004. An oversample of high-technology businesses is expected to yield a greater number of innovative firms than most business surveys, and a focus on the financial development of the firm will offer researchers new insight into new business financing and growth.

While the foundation can begin to identify the gaps in existing data sources and fund data collection efforts that further efforts to answer the important questions raised in the text, the comprehensive data collection efforts that are truly needed will require the support of multinational organizations like the United Nations or the World Bank. These organizations alone have the broad resources and the network of relationships that are required for this vitally important and incredibly difficult task.

Financial Data on Entrepreneurship

Some analysts find it useful to measure entrepreneurship by the financing—specifically third-party equity financing, venture, or angel capital—that supports it. Information about venture capital is available for the United States and Europe and, to a more limited degree, for other countries. Little or nothing is known about the magnitudes of angel investing among countries, though some effort is being expended on collection of such data in the United States.[2]

There are two caveats that must be mentioned regarding the venture figures, however. One is that since the bursting of the dot-com bubble in 2000, venture funds in the United States seem to be going predominantly to existing companies rather than to support firms that are in their "early stages." So even venture money raised or invested

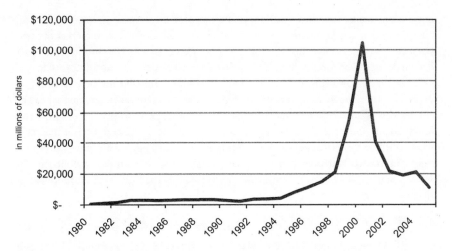

Figure 7. U.S. Venture Capital Investment by Year. *Source:* PricewaterhouseCoopers/ Thomson Venture Economics/ National Venture Capital Association MoneyTreeTM Survey.

may no longer be a good indicator of the risk-taking associated with start-up compa-nies. For the United States, angel money invested now is likely to be a better indicator of entrepreneurial activity (but so far comprehensive data for this measure are not yet available). A second caveat is that although venture money can be important—Paul Gompers and Josh Lerner of Harvard Business School have argued that it is critical for many "innovative" companies—many innovative firms get their start without it (Gom-pers and Lerner, 1999).

One financial indicator of entrepreneurial activity that does not have these difficul-ties is the number of companies raising money through initial public offerings (IPOs), whether on local or foreign stock exchanges. But even IPO data have their limits be-cause they do not include many privately held, but rapidly growing, companies in the United States and elsewhere around the world.

Furthermore, money going into venture (angel) funds and activity in the IPO mar-ket reflects only the willingness of particular types of investors to take on higher risks. There certainly is much more variation in these measures than in underlying entrepre-neurial activity. Figure 7 displays the gross flows into venture funds in the United States since 1980. The graph shows the peak in 2000 at roughly $100 billion, with flows drop-ping dramatically thereafter and recovering modestly in 2003–4. It is difficult to be-lieve that innovative entrepreneurial activity—or the kind that is most attractive to ven-ture (and angel) capital—has varied, and fallen, as much during this period.

Meanwhile, large companies in the United States do not appear to be abandoning the financing of early-stage companies via venture funds and IPOs.[3] It is true that this sort of financing may be less supportive of entrepreneurial activity in the long run since the less structured environment that leads to successful start-ups may often clash with the more bureaucratic structures and, more important, the incentive systems of the large companies that acquire them. Nevertheless, the existence of an active market in early-stage companies tempers the view that just because venture or IPO funding may have declined, entrepreneurial activity by implication must have dropped along with it.

All of this is not to dismiss the relevance of venture and IPO funding to entrepreneurial economies. As we discussed in chapter 5, as economies mature, the depth and complexity of an economy's formal financial system appears to play an essential role in enhancing entrepreneurship. Thus, the fact that the early-stage capital market—whether in the form of angel groups, venture funds, initial public offerings, or the outright purchase of early-stage firms by larger enterprises—is more developed in the United States than in other countries suggests strongly that it is more entrepreneurial than the others.

Indicators to Avoid

Finally, it is important to know what measures *not* to use as indicators of the degree of entrepreneurial activity in an economy. Here we have in mind various technological indicators, such as number of patents issued by the government or numbers of scientists and engineers.[4] Both of these measures may shed light on how innovative an economy may be, but not necessarily on how *entrepreneurial* it is. Patents can be obtained—and in the United States this seems increasingly easy to do, as we discussed in chapter 8—but a patent may sit on the shelf for years until some entrepreneur, in a current company or forming a new one, actually licenses or purchases it and puts it to use. Similarly, economies such those as India and China are turning out ever greater numbers of engineers, but many (perhaps most) of these highly trained individuals are going to work in existing bureaucratic enterprises, to tinker with incremental refinements, rather than to develop and take to the marketplace the truly radical innovations that characterize entrepreneurial economies. Japan is the world leader in the number of patents granted, but even the Japanese would concede that their economy is not a model of entrepreneurial capitalism. Rather, Japanese entrepreneurship essentially is synonymous with small retail stores, which are ways for former managers in large Japanese companies to finish their working careers and to supplement their retirement income.

Summary

In sum, existing data do not permit the kind of econometric testing of the various hypotheses we have advanced in this book. But we believe that the broad outline of our argument—and, specifically, our distinctions among the different types of capitalism—will strike a chord among many readers. It is sometimes true that informal evidence available to the trained eye is just as revealing as a mountain of numbers.

NOTES

Chapter 1. Entrepreneurship and Growth

1. One of the present authors has given considerable thought to why this is the case. Interested readers can consult Baumol, 2002.

Chapter 2. Why Economic Growth Matters

1. At that time, economists focused on increasing the demand for goods and services and not necessarily on the rate of growth in their supply, a distinction about which we will say more in chapter 3.

2. Based on data in the IMF's World Economic Database.

3. By comparison, per capita world output advanced by 248 percent in the nineteenth century, but by meager double-digit amounts in the eleventh through eighteenth centuries. See DeLong, 2000.

4. The enthusiasm about hydrogen replacing oil and gas may be misplaced. It takes energy to produce hydrogen. Though hydrogen may be "clean," the process of generating it—through electricity power plants—may not be. For a controversial but compelling case that the world faces no imminent shortage of energy, see Huber and Mills, 2005.

5. For one of the more thoroughly thought-out approaches along these lines, see McKibbin and Wilcoxen, 2002.

6. The pollution reductions so far have been brought about through command-and-control mandates rather than more market-oriented approaches, such as cap and trade. One reason for moving in the market direction, however, is that it is cheaper—that is, one can gain the same pollution reduction at lower cost by using techniques that simulate the market.

7. For a compelling discussion of how ethnic elites within many countries have benefited disproportionately from globalization, see Chua, 2003.

8. For a superb discussion of all of the arguments surrounding the controversial issue of "globalization" one couldn't do better than to read Wolf, 2004.

9. For more recent summaries of the economics of "happiness," see Kahneman and Krueger, 2006, and Di Tella and MacCulloch, 2006.

10. As Martin Wolf has noted, life expectancy in the developing world has risen from two-thirds of the level in rich countries in 1950 to 82 percent of that level in 2000 (Wolf, 2004, 164).

11. As has recently been shown, however, the gains from trade may not be as great when other countries are growing as rapidly as (or more rapidly than) one's own country (Baumol and Gomory, 2005; Samuelson, 2004). Still, trade can generate gains.

12. Of course, nationalism and ethnic and/or religious allegiances may triumph over economic growth and democracy and result in military action. All we are claiming is that growth, which should lead to democracy, should also reduce the probability that a nation will choose military over diplomatic means of resolving disputes with neighboring countries.

13. For one outline of possible measures to fix the long-term budget problem, see Rivlin and Sawhill, 2005.

14. For example, in one of the pioneering studies of economic growth in the United States, the late Edward Denison calculated that a more experienced workforce raised the annual growth rate of labor productivity by 0.13 percent between 1909 and 1957. See Denison, 1962, 148.

Chapter 3. What Drives Economic Growth?

1. Solow built on earlier growth models developed by Roy Harrod and Evsey Domar, and by Nicholas Kaldor, that emphasized the difficulty economies had in staying on their long-run potential growth path. The Harrod-Domar model, in particular, implied that economies constantly were poised on a knife edge between growth and collapse, which Solow and others have since rejected as unrealistic. For a useful survey of the growth models of the 1950s and beyond, see Solow, 1994.

2. A model that has this characteristic is called a Cobb-Douglas production function, named after economists Charles W. Cobb and Paul H. Douglas (the latter was a United States senator from Illinois after having had a distinguished academic career as an economist).

3. See, e.g., North, 1981, 1990, and 2005; North and Thomas, 1973; and Baumol, 1952.

4. There are ethical and other technical issues associated with conducting such experiments. For one early guide to this subject, see Rivlin, 1971.

5. The Summers and Heston data project stems from an effort by them and the late Irving Kravis (also of the University of Pennsylvania) that started in the 1970s, expanded in the 1980s, and has since come to be known as the Penn World Tables (see Heston, Summers, and Aten, 2002).

6. These studies are summarized in Barro and Sala-i-Martin, 2004, 14.

7. Romer advanced his theory of endogenous growth in his Ph.D. dissertation and has since refined it in a number of ways. He reviews much of this work, as well as the work of others who have followed in a similar vein, in Romer, 1994.

8. For a more formal analysis of this "intertemporal price discrimination," see Baumol, 2006.

9. For a thorough review of the studies on each side of the debate, see Dam, 2006.

10. The most prominent study to reach this conclusion is Barro and Sala-i-Martin, 2004. See also Bosworth and Collins, 2003.

11. This saying is usually attributed to the British statesman Benjamin Disraeli and was popularized in the United States by Mark Twain.

Chapter 4. Capitalism

1. We are not the only authors who have recognized that capitalist systems are of different varieties. For the presentation, discussion, and analysis of a different classification scheme (one that distinguishes between "coordinated market economies" and "liberal market economies"), see Hall and Soskice, 2001.

2. The Gini coefficient is calculated as the area between two curves. The first of these curves, called the Lorenz curve, depicts the actual income distribution of the population in question. It does so by dividing the population by income into, say, the lowest-income 10 percent, the second-lowest 10 percent, and so on. Then for each such group it indicates the share of the total income of the population that accrues to that group (e.g., the lowest 10 percent of the population receives only 4 percent of the population's total income). The second curve shows the same thing for the hypothetical case in which there is perfect equality of distribution so that each 10 percent of the population receives 10 percent of total income. The greater the space between the two curves, the greater actual inequality must be. The Gini coefficient is simply a measure of the size of that space.

3. Of course, with some exceptions, Latin American countries suffered some hard times between 1980 and 2000 and thus were not able to grow rapidly even if they had tried to do so. A number (Argentina, Brazil, and Mexico) borrowed too much foreign currency, some incurred excessive domestic debt, and were unable to pay it back because of sluggish growth at home coupled with flat or declining prices of their export commodities on world markets.

4. Arvelund (2005) also notes that small-size and medium-size businesses account for only about 15 percent of Russia's GDP, in contrast to the near 50 percent figure in the United States.

5. The finding of a negative statistical relationship between growth and corruption is not universal, however. In his survey of the subject, Jakob Svensson finds no linkage in cross-country statistical tests but also cautions that corruption may not be well measured in these regressions (Svensson, 2006).

6. Wei (2000) also finds that corruption tilts capital inflows toward foreign bank loans and away from foreign direct investment. To the extent that this is true, it in-

creases the risks of currency crisis, since banks can "run" from borrowing countries by not rolling over the loans, whereas foreign direct investment tends to be "sticky" (controlling interests in companies being much more difficult to unwind).

7. The statistical studies by Wei and others who have done work in this area use measures of corruption derived from surveys, and they thus are subject to the limitations affecting much statistical work on growth that we highlighted in the last chapter. Nonetheless, the negative relationship between these corruption measures and foreign investment is consistent with common sense, and thus believable, at least to us.

8. For a thorough analysis of the economic conditions in Saudi Arabia, see "Long Walk," 2006.

9. In 2006, one of Dubai's most important firms, Dubai Ports, sought to acquire a British port company, Peninsular & Oriental Stream Navigation Company, which operates a number of U.S. ports. The proposal sparked a firestorm of criticism from congressmen and senators from both political parties, and according to polling data, was deeply unpopular with the American public. Dubai Ports ultimately called off the deal and later agreed to divest itself of certain other ports that it held in the United States. The affair wounded the relationship between the United States and Dubai, up to then an important United States ally, and tarnished United States relations with other countries in the Arab world, although how lasting this effect will be is uncertain.

10. For a stimulating summary of Galbraith's many writings and professional career, and why his view of the ideal economy now seems somewhat outdated and at odds with current realities, see DeLong, 2005.

11. This problem was recognized in the 1930s by Adolphe Berle and Gardiner Means as inherent when ownership is separate from control (see Berle and Means, 1932). Economists in recent decades have relabeled it the "principal-agent problem."

12. See Cheesebrough, 2003.

13. Henry Ford did invent a self-powered vehicle, but so did others before him (Carl Benz, Charles Edgar, J. Frank Duryea, Elwood Haynes, Hiram Percy Maxim, Charles Brady King, George Selden, among many others); Ford's genius was in applying assembly line manufacturing to the mass production of affordable automobiles.

14. For two recent, comprehensive analyses of the linkage between entrepreneurship and economic growth in the United States and elsewhere, see Acs and Armington, 2006, and Audretsch, Keilbach, and Lehmann, 2006. These studies are complementary in many respects to the views we express here.

15. See Baumol, 2006.

16. For further evidence of churning among U.S. firms, see the appendix.

Chapter 5. Growth at the Cutting Edge

1. The commission's final report is United Nations, 2004. Among other things, it recommended that developing countries improve their systems of business and property registration.

2. For example, it is somewhat surprising, at least to us, that the costs of property registration are zero in Saudi Arabia and very low in Belarus, Mongolia, Azerbijan, and

Estonia; that among the countries with the lowest cost of hiring new workers are a number of Arab countries, Russia, and Kazakhstan (which we claim are essentially oligarchies); and that Saudi Arabia also is among those countries where it is easier to fire employees.

3. The United States recently adopted amendments to its bankruptcy code that impose greater repayment obligations on individual debtors. Although generally this is a constructive move, since it imposes more responsibility on individuals, the law unintentionally may discourage entrepreneurs whose businesses fail but who declare personal bankruptcy, having incurred debts on their credit cards. We discuss this issue in chapter 8.

4. The risks of entrepreneurship are somewhat overstated by the raw figures about failure rates of new enterprises. Many entrepreneurs fail simply because they don't know what they are doing.

5. One exception is Gentry and Hubbard (2004). These two analysts address features of the income tax system that are least likely to penalize entrepreneurship. In brief, they conclude that the flatter the tax schedule, the less likely entrepreneurship is to be discouraged.

6. We also discuss in chapter 8 how the income tax system can be modified to provide greater incentives for growth than is now the case.

7. See generally the work of Clifford Winston documenting the benefits of "economic" deregulation (Winston, 1993).

8. This is true even in the case of Thomas Edison, widely regarded as the greatest American inventor (or inventor, period) ever: As Hargadon (2005, 120) explains: "The stock ticker—[Edison's] first profitable product—combined a telegraph system with a crude early typewriter. The incandescent light was really invented forty years earlier. Edison's brilliance lay in combining advances in lighting with advances in generators, wiring from the telegraph industry, and business models from the gas industry to create the first viable system of electric light for the home and office."

9. Indeed, one author has persuasively argued that the central problem posed by Microsoft's monopoly in operating systems for personal computers was not the abuse of the power by the company, which was the heart of the U.S. government's antitrust case against it, but instead the extensive, multilayered systems of intellectual property protection that surrounded the operating system (Abramson, 2005).

10. Data from www.ppic.org/content/pubs/R_502ASR.pdf, p. 12.

11. The case for redistribution through the tax system rests largely on the notion that as individuals' incomes grow, their "utility" or satisfaction from an extra dollar or unit of income declines. If the objective of the tax system is to assess taxes in a way that equalizes the "pain" of losing a dollar or unit of income at the margin, then a declining "marginal utility of income" implies that tax rates should be progressively higher with income. Otherwise, a flat income tax would impose greater loss of satisfaction or pain, at the margin, on those with lower incomes than those with higher incomes.

12. Readers interested in the antitrust laws and their enforcement can consult a wide variety of economic or legal textbooks on the subject.

13. One of us (Litan) has reluctantly come to this conclusion from direct experience, after serving in the Antitrust Division at the Justice Department in the 1990s. Another author (Baumol) has reached this conclusion after extensive experience as an expert witness in antitrust and regulatory matters.

14. One recent book argues that antitrust, or more precisely a set of policies that encourage competition from both domestic and foreign sources, is not as important, and may even be detrimental, in less developed economies as in economies closer to the technological frontier (Aghion and Griffith, 2005). This is because in a global marketplace, firms in developing economies are not likely to be able to compete effectively with those from richer countries. For rich economies, however, it would be a mistake, in the authors' view, to shield firms from competition as it will dull their incentives for innovation. We refer to this analysis again in chapter 7 when discussing the economic difficulties confronting the continental European economies.

15. Based on conversations and unpublished material Phelps has provided to us.

16. Furthermore, if workers have multiple skills, the easier it should be for them to find other jobs if they lose their current ones, through no fault of their own, when demand for their firms' products declines and managers have no choice except to shrink the workforce.

17. Gary Becker from the University of Chicago won his Nobel Prize, in part, based on this work documenting the economic returns to education. Another Chicago economist, Theodore Schultz, also carried out similar work. See Becker, 1976, and Schultz, 1961.

18. For one discussion of this issue, see Krueger, 2005.

19. One study supports a related finding that democracy enhances growth by decreasing the probability of military coups, which can destabilize rules upon which both domestic and foreign business rely in making investment decisions (Persson and Tabellini, 2006).

20. Halperin et al., 2005, 72–74. The authors report that there was a 2.5 percent probability that a democracy will backtrack in any given year. This probability rises to 4.3 percent if average per capita income growth over the preceding three years is less than 1 percent.

Chapter 6. Unleashing Entrepreneurship in Less Developed Economies

1. Yale development expert T. N. Srinivasan has highlighted a series of other "accidental events" that also contributed to India's IT success (Srinivasan, 2005). For example, the decision by the Indian government in the mid-1980s to adopt the Unix computer operating system standard ultimately enabled India's software industry to become expert in Unix technology, which turned out to be highly useful later when Unix software became dominant in Internet servers. India also profited from the Y2K crisis, the widespread fear in the late 1990s that computers would suddenly quit working when clocks turned to January 1, 2000. To "fix" this problem, many companies from around the world turned to low-cost Indian programmers to carry out the mun-

dane task of changing the o's and 1's in assembly language. But what could not have been predicted at the time is that the companies found the programmers so efficient that it awakened them to the possibility of off-shoring more routine and advanced computer programming in subsequent years.

2. See "Planning the New Socialist Countryside," *Economist,* March 11, 2006, pp. 37–38; "A Survey of China," *Economist,* March 25, 2006; and Dollar, 2005.

3. See http://english.people.com.cn/200311/30eng20031130_129338.html.

4. This projection is contained in one of the organization's "Trade Facts of the Week" published in 2006 and available on the organization's Web site, www.dlcppi.org.

5. Quadir's remarkable efforts are more fully described in "Power to the People," *Economist,* March 11, 2006, pp. 37–38.

6. Professor Kenneth Dam of the University of Chicago has provided, in our view, the most comprehensive overview of this somewhat inconclusive legal and economic literature. See Dam, 2006.

7. For the Indian banking data, see Caprio et al., 2004, and "Thinking Big: A Survey of International Banking," *Economist,* May 20, 2006, pp. 18–19.

8. For example, China has capped foreign ownership of its state owned banks, when privatized, at 25 percent, because of fears that excessive foreign ownership, especially in private hands, would lead the banks to take on additional risk. See "A Survey of China," *Economist,* March 25, 2006, p. 13.

9. Several of the essays in Caprio et al., 2004, document the benefits of foreign financial institutions operating in developing country markets.

10. For a recent, thoughtful guide to this important topic, see Barth et al., 2006.

11. Bruns, Mingat, and Rakotomalala, 2003.

12. "Survey of China," p. 12.

13. For a thorough discussion of why elections are not enough to produce true democratic government see Haass, 2005.

14. In the fall of 2006, the Kauffman Foundation initiated such a program for students from the United Kingdom and Italy. We are suggesting here a much larger, government sponsored initiative (though the details could be outsourced to a provider or providers), and aimed at developing countries, which most likely would not have the resources to pay for it.

15. For a thorough review and critique of Sachs' book, see Easterly, 2006a.

16. Statement of Alan Patricoff at the Brookings Blum Roundtable—The Private Sector in the Fight against Global Poverty, August 4, 2005.

17. Again, William Easterly outlines in detail how recipient governments have inhibited foreign aid from being effective (Easterly, 2006b).

18. For a thorough guide to the economics of microfinance, see Aghion and Morduch, 2005. See also "The Hidden Wealth of the Poor: A Survey of Microfinance," *Economist,* November 5, 2005, on which we draw heavily in our discussion here.

19. For a thorough review of the most recent progress of micro-lending, especially among established financial institutions, see Barr, Kumar, and Litan (2007). This book

includes a chapter on the growing trend toward profitability from micro-lending. See also Barr, 2005.

Chapter 7. The Big-Firm Wealthy Economies

1. Thus, one OECD study has found that although new firm entrants in the United States tend to be smaller than in Europe, after the initial start-up phase, successful U.S. firms grow more rapidly than their European counterparts, which tend to remain small (Scarpetta et al., 2002).

2. Table 12 illustrates that the populations of both Ireland and Great Britain also will age rapidly in the years ahead, but the fiscal burdens of this trend will be much less pronounced than in the other countries because retirement benefits are not as generous in Ireland and Great Britain as they are elsewhere. Of course, this may leave elderly citizens, on average, to face more difficult economic circumstances in these countries than in those with more ample government retirement programs.

3. Hoshi and Kashyap attribute much of the increased importance of banks in financing Japanese businesses to their role in reorganizing many of the firms that were deeply in debt as a result of the war.

4. In particular, fiscal stimulus has been limited to no more than 3 percent of GDP, the upper ceiling for central government deficits under the European Union's "Stability Pact" that European countries adopting the Euro have had to sign; and monetary growth has been limited by the new European Central bank, which has adopted the strong anti-inflation tradition of the Bundesbank, the German central bank.

5. This is not to dismiss the role of high marginal tax rates for low- and middle-income workers, which probably do diminish incentives for these workers to participate in the labor force. See Baily and Kirkegaard, 2005, 14, 19 (who at the same time also do not find evidence that high marginal tax rates for upper-income workers are a significant barrier to output or employment growth).

6. For an overview of the Lisbon agenda and related information, see www.europa.eu.int/comm/lisbon_strategy/index_en.html.

7. The *Economist* of January 7, 2006, reported, for example, that as of early 2006, several large Japanese banks were looking to lend to small- and medium-sized enterprises (SMEs) because, as in America, larger companies increasingly are raising funds in the capital markets.

8. In particular, by 2007, the foundation will have funded two rounds of competitively determined awards to multiple universities to further this goal.

9. These data are preliminary figures provided by the European Venture Capital Association and can be found at http://www.evca.com/images/attachments/tmpl_8_art_190_att_935.pdf.

10. This idea was promoted through work done at the Brookings Institution. See Burtless and Schaefer, 2002.

11. For a thorough analysis of some of the problems besetting universities in Europe and other countries, see Weber and Duderstadt, eds., 2006.

12. See Independent Expert Group on R&D, 2006.

Chapter 8. The Care and Maintenance of Entrepreneurial Capitalism

1. See also Jonathan Rauch, 1994.

2. There are a number of adjustments that have to be made to convert productivity statistics into fully defensible indicators of average standards of living. First, one must disentangle the effects of inflation—a worker who produced goods worth $10 in an hour in 1950 and produced goods selling for $20 in an hour in 2005 will not have doubled his productivity because inflation reduced the purchasing power of a 2005 dollar well below that of a 1950 dollar. Then there is the fact that workers differ in the sizes of their families. If two workers earn the same amount, the one with the larger family will not be able to achieve as high a living standard as the smaller-family worker. Finally, there is the fact that some part of the U.S. worker's output is exported rather than being consumed at home, while he consumes some items that were produced abroad. Statisticians adjust their data to take all of these and other complications into account.

3. To reflect the fact that capital equipment (and buildings) are also necessary for the production of goods and services, some economists look to a broader measure of productivity—so-called multifactor productivity—to measure the performance of economies in the long run. This measure is defined by dividing total output by a weighted average of the two main inputs, labor and capital. The weights typically represent the share of national income each input, or "factor of production," generates (assuming a particular form of the "production function" that relates output to these two inputs). Although these fractions vary somewhat from country to country, as a rough generalization, labor typically takes home about two-thirds of national product, while the suppliers of capital earn the other one-third.

4. Much of the credit for sorting out the role of the IT-generating and IT-using sectors in contributing to the increase in U.S. productivity goes to several economists within the Federal Reserve system, Stephen Oliner, Kevin Stiroh, and Daniel Sichel, and to Harvard economist Dale Jorgenson. See Jorgenson et al., 2002, and Oliner and Sichel, 2002.

5. For some new software, the major investment is human capital—and ingenuity—or, so-called sweat equity. A dramatic illustration is the success of Skype, the long-distance Internet telephone service invented by two Finns, which parlayed their ingenious service into $2.6 billion, after selling it to eBay in 2005.

6. Data are from the Web site of the Congressional Budget Office, www.cbo.gov (intermediate spending scenario).

7. Gentry and Hubbard (2004), for example, show that the schedule of tax rates has a more important impact on entrepreneurship than the level of tax rates. Specifically, they show that the more progressive the tax rate schedule is—that is, the more steeply the marginal tax rate rises with income—the less inclined individuals are to become entrepreneurs. Assuming these findings hold, then an across-the-board increase in marginal income tax rates should raise revenues without adversely affecting entrepreneurship to a significant degree.

8. In April 2006, an advisory commission on small business to the SEC recom-

mended that smaller public companies be exempted from, or subject to a less onerous version of, 404 rules than larger companies. The commission rejected this proposal, which would have introduced an artificial distinction between smaller and larger companies that unintentionally might have discouraged smaller firms from growing larger. A less risky course along these lines is one that the commission had already taken, by delaying the effective date of compliance with all of the provisions of SOX for smaller public companies until the end of 2007.

9. Yale University economist William Nordhaus has carried out very careful computations indicating that inventors, on average, capture only about 3 percent of the total value of their innovations (Nordhaus, 2004). This figure, which at first sight may seem implausible, becomes easier to accept when we consider what a small share the income of Bill Gates and other highly successful entrepreneurs constitutes in the total rise in incomes since the Industrial Revolution in all of the world's wealthier countries; most of this increase arguably is attributable to invention and discovery.

10. The term "letters patent" refers to letters issued by the monarch meant to be visible (patent) to all (as distinguished from confidential "letters close").

11. Examples include soap, machines for dredging and draining land, ovens and furnaces, oils, leather, grinding machines, salt, glass, drinking glasses, force pumps for raising water, writing paper, and machines for introducing processes for tempering iron, milling corn, extracting oil from rapeseed, and dressing, drying, and calendaring cloth (North and Thomas, 1973, pp. 153–54).

12. These include Microsoft, IBM, AT&T, Monsanto, Motorola, Bell South, Daimler-Benz, Eli Lilly, Eastman Kodak, Sprint, Philips Electronics, Siemens, General Motors, Honeywell, Boeing, Fiat, Ford, General Electric, Hitachi, Toshiba, Dow Chemical, Johnson & Johnson, and many others (Arora, Fosfuri, and Gambardella, 2001, pp. 34–37).

13. This is the view expressed in a thorough review of the controversies in the field by the *Economist* magazine ("Market for Ideas," 2005).

14. To its credit, the PTO itself has been working with a number of technology companies to try to make the patenting process more efficient and more reliable. Thus, as of early 2006, it was exploring the creation of a central repository of all open-source code and related documentation; an indexing system to rank the viability of patent applications; and a way to tap into the knowledge about current state of the art held by experts in the private and public sector (in much the same way that *Wikipedia*, an Internet-based encyclopedia, has done for several years).

15. The content of these paragraphs is a summary of materials in an extremely illuminating paper by Janusz Ordover (1991), which describes the pertinent Japanese arrangements and analyzes their consequences.

16. This information can be found at http://www.transparency.org.

17. We are less enamored, however, of what seems to be a favorite proposal for tort reform in the United States: statutory caps on noneconomic damages (those for "pain and suffering"). Although there is evidence that caps have the intended effect of deterring lawsuits (Danzon et al., 2004), they are also inherently unfair to individuals who have suffered severe pain and suffering as a consequence of negligence by defendants.

18. U.S. Department of Justice and the Federal Trade Commission, *Antitrust Guidelines for the Licensing of Intellectual Property,* Washington, D.C., April 6, 1995.

19. For a recent attempt to shed further light on the issues involved, see Swanson and Baumol, 2005.

20. Figures from *The Economic Report of the President, 2006* (Washington, D.C.: Government Printing Office).

21. But Professor Florida is much less worried about the Indian and Chinese patent challenge than many others (both of these countries continue to lag well behind patents generated in the United States), and he provides data to support this judgment.

22. For details of this proposal, see Kletzer and Litan, 2001, and Brainard, Litan, and Warren, 2005. For a set of broader "safety net" proposals to address worker anxiety, see Sperling, 2005.

23. The Organization for Economic Cooperation and Development (2005b) provides the following information about patents: A "patent family" is a set of patents taken in various countries for protecting a single invention. "Triadic patent families" are those filed at the European Patent Office, the Japanese Patent Office, and the U.S. Patent and Trademark Office. Such triadic patent families eliminate the "home advantage" bias and generally represent patents of high value. In 2002, there were approximately 51,500 triadic patent families, with country shares as follows: United States, 35.6 percent; Japan, 25.6 percent; European Union, 31.5 percent; and other countries, 7.3 percent.

24. Since the FASB required expensing of stock options for financial reporting purposes, some firms (Microsoft being a prominent example) have replaced option awards with grants of stock, which often have holding period restrictions. As an incentive, stock awards are in one respect superior to options, because managers lose when stock prices decline, unlike options, whose prices cannot fall below zero. Nonetheless, the incentive value of stock awards could be enhanced if the tax law allowed them to be expensed only under the same conditions we have just suggested for options.

25. For a list of some of the major commercial innovations that have come out of U.S. universities, including the Google search engine and the PSA test for prostate cancer, see the Web site of the Association of University Technology Managers Better World Project, www.autm.net/betterworldproject.cfm.

26. Mowrey himself is skeptical, however, over the extent to which Bayh-Dole can claim responsibility for this pickup in patenting and licensing activity.

27. To our knowledge, among major universities that have technology trade offices or their equivalent, only the University of Wisconsin currently allows competition of this sort.

28. The raw data were obtained from the OECD, the organization composed mostly of the world's wealthiest countries.

29. For example, while China is turning out 500,000 engineering college graduates annually, India 200,000, and the United States less than 100,000, on a per capita basis, the United States in the same year graduates engineers at roughly twice the rate of China and five times the rate of India (see Friel, 2006, based on data supplied by the National Academy of Sciences).

30. In particular, while federal support of physical sciences, engineering, math, and science combined has remained relatively stable at $5–6 billion (in 2004 dollars) since the mid-1980s, federal support for life sciences has increased by roughly a factor of three, from $5 billion in 1984 to roughly $15 billion in 2004 (see the National Summit on Competitiveness, 2005).

31. For example, the National Academy of Sciences, National Academy of Engineering, and the Institute of Medicine recommend, among other things, the annual recruitment of 10,000 science and math teachers through the award of four-year college scholarships (in amounts of up to $20,000 per student per year) in return for a commitment of five years of public service in a K-12 school (along with a $10,000 bonus for teachers in underserved communities). At an average of $10,000 per year, a steady-state class of 10,000 graduating students per year would cost $100 million, a seemingly small price to pay. The report, however, contains numerous other recommendations that would considerably add to the overall cost (see National Academy of Sciences, 2005).

32. In January 2006, the Florida Supreme Court struck down private school vouchers, which were granted to parents of students in poorly performing schools. Earlier, the Ohio Supreme Court had handed down a similar ruling.

Appendix

We are grateful for the extraordinarily able assistance of Alyse Freilich in preparing this appendix.

1. For similar complaints about the adequacy or usefulness of existing data on entrepreneurship, see Audretsch, Keilbach, and Lehman, 2006, 7–9.

2. That effort has begun with the formation of the Angel Capital Association, an organization that, as of June 2006, had approximately 130 angel investing groups as members. The Ewing Marion Kauffman Foundation provided the initial funds for the organization.

3. For an extensive study of large company acquisitions of newer, smaller enterprises, see Christiansen and Raynor, 2003.

4. Gross patent counts have several shortcomings even as measures of innovation. Patents do not include innovations that are not formally patented but nonetheless entail important breakthroughs in know-how, especially in production or specific products. These innovations may be protected by "trade secret" law, but government agencies (or even their private equivalents) do not, and cannot, count trade secrets. Another limitation is that mere counts of patents do not reflect their importance. One patent may generate billions of dollars in revenue, while another may lie in a drawer and never be used. There is no good way to distinguish between the two in official government statistics that count the number of patents issued.

BIBLIOGRAPHY

Abraham, Katherine G., and Christopher Mackie, eds. 2005. *Beyond the Market: Designing Nonmarket Accounts for the United States* (Washington, D.C.: National Academies Press).

Abramson, Bruce. 2005. *Digital Phoenix* (Cambridge: MIT Press).

Acemoglu, Daron, Simon Johnson, and James A. Robinson. 2001. "The Colonial Origins of Comparative Development: An Empirical Investigation," *American Economic Review* 91 (5): 1369–1401.

———. 2002. "Reversal of Fortune: Geography and Institutions in the Making of the Modern World Income Distribution," *Quarterly Journal of Economics* 117 (4): 1231–94.

Acs, Zoltan, and Catherine Armington. 2004. "Employment Growth and Entrepreneurial Activity in Cities," *Regional Studies* 38: 911–27.

———. 2006. *Entrepreneurship, Geography, and American Economic Growth* (Cambride: Cambridge University Press).

Acs, Zoltan, and David B. Audretsch. 1990. *Innovation and Small Firms* (Cambridge: MIT Press).

Acs, Zoltan, and Lawrence A. Plummer. 2005. "Penetrating the 'Knowledge Filter' in Regional Economies," *Annals of Regional Science* 39: 439–56.

Aghion, Beatriz Armendáriz de, and Jonathan Morduch. 2005. *The Economics of Microfinance* (Cambridge: MIT Press).

Aghion, Phillippe, and Rachel Griffith. 2005. *Competition and Growth: Reconciling Theory and Evidence* (Cambridge: MIT Press).

Alesina, Alberto, Edward Glaeser, and Bruce Sacerdote. 2005. "Work and Leisure in the United States and Europe," NBER Working Paper 11278 (Cambridge, Mass.: National Bureau of Economic Research).

Amarante, Massimiliano, and Edward Phelps. 2005. Unpub. report prepared for the Ewing Marion Kauffman Foundation.

Arora, Ashish, Andrea Fosfuri, and Alfonso Gambardella. 2001. *Markets for Technology: The Economics of Innovation and Corporate Strategy* (Cambridge: MIT Press).

Arrow, Kenneth J. 1962. "The Economic Implications of Learning by Doing," *Review of Economic Studies* 29 (June): 155–73.

Arvelund, Erin E. 2005. "In Russia's Boom, Riches and Rags," *International Herald Tribune,* April 15, p. 3.

Askari, Hossein, and Roshanak Takhavi. 2006. "Economic Failure in the Middle East," *Banca Nazionale Del Lavoro Quarterly Review* (March).

Audretsch, David A., Taylor Aldridge, and Alexander Oettl. 2006. *Scientist Entrepreneurship: The Sleeping Giant of University Commercialization.* Unpub. report prepared for the Ewing Marion Kauffman Foundation.

Audretsch, David A., Max C. Keilbach, and Erik E. Lehmann. 2006. *Entrepreneurship and Economic Growth* (New York: Oxford University Press).

Baily, Martin, and Diana Farrell. 2006a. "Waking up Europe," *Milken Institute Review* (first quarter): 8–15.

———. 2006b. "Breaking Down Barriers to Growth," *Finance and Development* (March).

Baily, Martin Neil, and Jacob Funk Kirkegaard. 2005. *Transforming the European Economy* (Washington, D.C.: Institute for International Economics), September.

Baker, Raymond. 2005. *Capitalism's Achilles Heel: Dirty Money and How to Renew the Free-Market System* (Hoboken, N.J.: Wiley).

Barone, Michael. 2005. *Hard America, Soft America* (New York: Three Rivers Press).

Barr, Michael S. 2005. "Microfinance and Financial Development," *Michigan Journal of International Law* 26: 271–96.

Barr, Michael S., Anjali Kumar, and Robert E. Litan, eds. 2007. *Access to Finance: Building Inclusive Financial Systems: A Framework for Access to Finance* (Washington, D.C.: World Bank and the Brookings Institution Press), forthcoming.

Barro, Robert J., and Xavier Sala-i-Martin. 2004. *Economic Growth,* 2nd ed. (Cambridge: MIT Press).

Barth, James A., Gerard Caprio, Jr., and Ross Levine. 2006. *Rethinking Bank Regulation: Till Angels Govern* (New York: Cambridge University Press).

Baumol, William J. 1952. *Welfare Economics and the Theory of the State* (London: Longmans Press).

———. 1986. "Productivity Growth, Convergence, and Welfare: What the Long-Run Data Show," *American Economic Review* 76, no. 5 (December): 1072–85.

———. 2002. *The Free Market Innovation Machine* (Princeton: Princeton University Press).

———. 2005. "Entrepreneurship and Innovation: Toward Their Microeconomic Value Theory," AEI-Brookings Joint Center for Regulatory Studies, Related Publication 05–38.

———. 2006. "Return of the Invisible Man: The Microeconomic Value Theory of Investors and Entrepreneurs." Paper presented at the 2006 annual meeting of the American Economic Association (also available at www.aei-brookings.org).

Baumol, William J. (with Klaus Knorr). 1961. *What Price Economic Growth?* (Englewood Cliffs, N.J.: Prentice-Hall).

Baumol, William J., and Ralph Gomory. 2005. "Foreign Productivity Growth, Outsourcing, and the Benefit or Damage to the Domestic Economy."

Becker, Gary S. 1976. *Approach to Human Behavior* (Chicago: University of Chicago Press).

———. 2005. "Give Us Your Skilled Masses," *Wall Street Journal,* November 30, A18.

Berle, Adolph, and Gardiner C. Means. 1932. *The Modern Corporation and Private Property* (New York: Commerce Clearing House).

Bhagwati, Jagdish. 2004. *In Defense of Globalization* (Oxford: Oxford University Press).

Bhalla, Surjit S. 2002. *Imagine There's No Country: Poverty, Inequality, and Growth in the Era of Globalization* (Washington, D.C.: Institute for International Economics).

Bhide, Amar. 2006. "How Novelty Aversion Affects Financing Options," *Capitalism and Society* 1, no. 1 (Berkeley Electronic Press).

Blustein, Paul. 2001. *The Chastening* (New York: Public Affairs).

———. 2004. *And the Money Kept Rolling In (and Out): Wall Street, the IMF, and the Bankrupting of Argentina* (New York: Public Affairs).

Bogle, John C. 2005. *The Battle for the Soul of Capitalism* (New Haven: Yale University Press).

Bok, Derek. 2003. *Universities in the Marketplace* (Princeton: Princeton University Press).

Bosworth, Barry P., and Susan M. Collins. 2003. "The Empirics of Growth: An Update," *Brookings Papers on Economic Activity* 12: 113–78.

Bowen, William G. 2005. "Extending Opportunity in Higher Education." Speech delivered at New York University, December 8.

Brainard, Lael, Robert E. Litan, and Nicholas Warren. 2005. "Insuring America's Workers in a New Era of Offshoring," *Brookings Policy Brief,* no.143.

Branscomb, Lewis. 2004. "Where Do High Tech Commercial Innovations Come From?" *Duke Law and Technology Review,* no. 0005.

Breznitz, Dan. 2006. *Innovation and the State* (New Haven: Yale University Press).

Bromwich, Michael, et al. 2002. *Following The Money: Corporate Financial Disclosure after Enron* (Washington, D.C.: AEI-Brookings Joint Center for Regulatory Studies).

Bruce, Donald, and Tami Gurley-Calvez. 2006. "Federal Tax Policy and Small Business." Paper presented at a Hudson Institute Seminar, March.

Bruns, Barbara, Alain Mingat, and Ramahatra Rakotomalala. 2003. *Achieving Universal Primary Education by 2015: A Chance for Every Child* (Washington, D.C.: World Bank).

Bueno de Mesquita, Bruce, and George W. Downs. 2005. "Development and Democracy," *Foreign Affairs* 84 (5): 77–86.

Burtless, Gary, and Holger Schaefer. 2002. "Earnings Insurance for Germany," *Brookings Policy Brief,* no. 104, July.

Bush, Jason. 2006. "Shoppers Gone Wild," *Business Week,* February 20, pp. 46–47.

"The Business of Giving: A Survey on Wealth and Philanthropy." 2006. *Economist,* February 25.

Cantillion, Richard. 1931. *Essai Sur la nature de Commerce en General* (New York: Sentry Press).

Caprio, Gerard, et al., eds. 2004. *The Future of State-Owned Financial Institutions* (Washington, D.C.: Brookings Institution Press).

Cheesebrough, Henry. 2003. *Open Innovation: The New Imperative for Creating and Profiting from Technology* (Cambridge: Harvard Business School Press).

CHI Research, Inc. 2003. *Small Serial Innovators: The Small Firm Contribution to Technical Change.* Prepared for the Small Business Administration's Office of Advocacy, February 27.

Christiansen, Clayton. 1997. *The Innovator's Dilemma: When New Technologies Cause Great Firms to Fail* (New York: Harper Collins).

Christensen, Clayton M., and Michael E. Raynor. 2003. *The Innovator's Solution: Creating and Sustaining Successful Growth* (Boston: Harvard Business School Press).

Chua, Amy. 2003. *World on Fire: How Exporting Free Market Democracy Breeds Ethnic Hatred and Global Instability* (New York: Doubleday).

Coase, Ronald H. 1988. *The Firm, the Market, and the Law* (Chicago: University of Chicago Press).

Commission of the European Communities. 2003. *Green Paper: Entrepreneurship in Europe* (Brussels: European Commission).

Congressional Budget Office. 2003. *Long-Term Budget Outlook.* Available at http://www.cbo.gov/ftpdocs/49xx/doc4916/LongTermBudgetoutlook.

Council on Competitiveness. 2004. *Innovate America* (Washington, D.C.: Council on Competitiveness).

Cox, W. Michael, and Jahyeong Koo. 2006. "Miracle to Malaise: What's Next for Japan?" *Economic Letter: Insights from the Federal Reserve Bank of Dallas* 1, no. 1 (January).

Dam, Kenneth. 2006. *The Law-Growth Nexus: The Rule of Law and Economic Development* (Washington, D.C.: Brookings Institution Press).

Danzon, Patricia, Andrew J. Epstein, and Scott J. Johnson. 2004. "The 'Crisis' in Medical Malpractice Insurance," *Brookings-Wharton Papers in Financial Services,* pp. 55–96.

DeLamarter, Richard Thomas. 1986. *Big Blue: IBM's Use and Abuse of Power* (New York: Dodd, Mead).

DeLong, J. Bradford. 2000. "Cornucopia: The Pace of Economic Growth in the Twentieth Century," NBER Working Paper 7602 (Cambridge, Mass.: National Bureau of Economic Research).

———. 2005. "Sisyphus as Social Democrat," *Foreign Affairs* (May/June): 126–30.

Denison, Edward F. 1962. *Sources of Economic Growth in the United States and the Alternatives Before Us* (New York: Committee for Economic Development).

———. 1967. *Why Growth Rates Differ* (Washington, D.C.: Brookings Institution Press).

————. 1974. *Accounting for Economic Growth* (Washington, D.C.: Brookings Institution Press).

De Soto, Hernando. 1989. *The Other Path: The Invisible Revolution in the Third World* (New York: Harper & Row).

————. 2000. *The Mystery of Capital* (New York: Basic Books).

Dew-Becker, Ian, and Robert Gordon. 2005. "Where Did the Productivity Growth Go? Inflation Dynamics and the Distribution of Income," NBER Working Paper 11842 (Cambridge, Mass.: National Bureau of Economic Research).

Di Tella, Rafael, and Robert MacCulloch. 2006. "Some Uses of Happiness Data in Economics," *Journal of Economic Perspectives* 20, no. 1 (winter): 25–46.

Dixit, Avinash. 2004. *Lawlessness and Economics: Alternative Modes of Governance* (Princeton: Princeton University Press).

Djankov, Simeon, et al. 2005. "Who Are Russia's Entrepreneurs?" *Journal of the European Economic Association* 3 (April-May): 587–97.

Dollar, David. 2005. "China's Economic Problems (and Ours)," *Milken Institute Review* (third quarter): 48–58.

Dollar, David, and Art Kraay. 2002. "Growth Is Good for the Poor," *Journal of Economic Growth* 1 (3): 195–225.

————. 2003. "Institutions, Trade, and Growth," *Journal of Monetary Economics* 50 (1): 133–62.

Drucker, Peter F. 1985. *Innovation and Entrepreneurship: Practice and Principles* (New York: Harper & Row).

Easterbrook, Gregg. 2003. *The Progress Paradox* (New York: Random House).

Easterly, William. 2001. *The Elusive Quest for Growth: Economists' Adventures and Misadventures in the Tropics* (Cambridge: MIT Press).

————. 2006a. "The Big Push Déjà vu: A Review of Jeffrey Sachs's *The End of Poverty*," *Journal of Economic Literature* 44 (1): 96–105.

————. 2006b. *The White Man's Burden: Why the West's Efforts to Aid the Rest Have Done So Much Ill and So Little Good* (New York: Penguin Press).

Easterly, William, and Ross Levine. 2001. "It's Not Factor Accumulation: Stylized Facts and Growth Models," *World Bank Economic Review* 15 (2).

————. 2003. "Tropics, Germs and Crops: How Endowments Influence Economic Development," *Journal of Monetary Economics* 50 (1): 3–39.

Elliott, Kimberly A., Gary C. Hufbauer, and Jeffrey J. Schott. 1990. *Economic Sanctions Reconsidered* (Washington, D.C.: Institute for International Economics).

Engardio, Pete. 2006. "The Future of Outsourcing," *Business Week* (January 30): 50–58.

European Commission. 2003. *Green Paper: Entrepreneurship in Europe* (Brussels: Commission of the European Communities), January 21.

European Council. 2002. "Increasing Labor Force Participation and Promoting Active Aging." Council document, August 3.

Federal Trade Commission. 2003. *To Promote Innovation: The Proper Balance of Competition and Patent Law and Policy.* Available at www.ftc.gov/opa/2003/10/cpreport. htm.

Fischer, Stanley. 2003. "Globalization and Its Challenges," *American Economic Review* 93, no. 2 (May): 1–30.

Fisher, Franklin M., John J. McGowan, and Joen E. Greenwood. 1983. *Folded, Spindled and Multilated: Economic Analysis and U.S. v. IBM* (Cambridge: MIT Press).

Florida, Richard. 2005. "The World Is Spiky," *Atlantic Monthly* (October).

Frank, Robert H. 2004. "How Not to Buy Happiness," *Daedalus* 133, no. 2 (spring): 69–79.

Frankel, Jeffrey. 1997. *Regional Trading Blocs in the World Economic System* (Washington, D.C.: Institute for International Economics).

———. 2003. "Comments on Bosworth and Collins," *Brookings Papers on Economic Activity* 2: 189–99.

Freeman, Richard B., Emily Jin, and Chia-Yu Shen. 2004. "Where Do New U.S.-Trained Science-Engineering PhDs Come From?" NBER Working Paper 10554 (Cambridge, Mass.: National Bureau of Economic Research).

Friedman, Benjamin M. 2005. *The Moral Consequences of Economic Growth* (New York: Knopf).

Friedman, Thomas. 2005. *The World Is Flat* (New York: Farrar, Strauss & Giroux).

———. 2006. "The First Law of Petropolitics," *Foreign Policy* (May/June): 28–35.

Friel, Brian. 2006. "The Science Scare," *National Journal* (January 14): 36–41.

Fukao, Mitsuhiro. 2004. "Japan's Lost Decade and Its Financial System," in Gary R. Saxenhouse and Robert M. Stern, eds., *Japan's Lost Decade: Origins, Consequences and Prospects for Recovery* (Malden, Mass.: Blackwell Publishing), 99–118.

Fukuyama, Francis. 1996. *Trust: The Social Virtues and the Creation of Prosperity* (New York: Free Press).

Galbraith, John Kenneth. 1967. *The New Industrial State* (Boston: Houghton Mifflin).

Gentry, William M., and R. Glenn Hubbard. 2004. "Success Taxes, Entrepreneurial Activity and Innovation," NBER Working Paper 10551 (Cambridge, Mass.: National Bureau of Economic Research).

Glaeser, Edward L., Rafael La Porta, Florencio Lopez-de-Silane, and Andrei Shleifer. 2004. "Do Institutions Cause Growth?" NBER Working Paper 10568 (Cambridge, Mass.: National Bureau of Economic Research).

Goldstein, Morris. 2000. *IMF Structural Conditionality: How Much Is Too Much?* (Washington, D.C: Institute for International Economics).

Gompers, Paul, and Josh Lerner. 1999. *The Venture Capital Cycle* (Cambridge: MIT Press).

———. 2001. *The Money of Invention: How Venture Capital Creates New Wealth* (Boston: Harvard Business School Press).

Graham, Carol, and Stefano Pettinato. 2002. *Happiness and Hardship: Opportunity and Insecurity in New Market Economies* (Washington, D.C.: Brookings Institution Press).

Haass, Richard. 2005. *The Opportunity* (New York: Public Affairs).

Hall, Peter A., and David Soskice, eds. 2001. *Varieties of Capitalism: The Institutional Foundations of Comparative Advantage* (Oxford: Oxford University Press).

Hall, Robert E., and Charles I. Jones. 1999. "Why Do Some Countries Produce So Much More Output Per Worker Than Others?" *Quarterly Journal of Economics* 114 (1): 83–116.

Halperin, Morton, Joseph T. Siegle, and Michael Weinstein. 2005. *The Democracy Advantage: How Democracies Promote Prosperity and Peace* (New York: Routledge).

Hanson, James A. 2004. "The Transformation of State-Owned Banks," in *The Future of State-Owned Banks,* ed. Gerard Caprio et al. (Washington, D.C.: Brookings Institution Press).

Hargadon, Andrew. 2003. *How Breakthroughs Happen: The Surprising Truth About How Companies Innovate* (Cambridge: Harvard University Press).

———. 2005. "Understanding the Innovation Process: The Power of Social Networks," *Kauffman Foundation Thoughtbook,* 117–122.

Helpman, Elhanan. 2004. *The Mystery of Economic Growth* (Cambridge: Harvard University Press).

Henrekson, M., and N. Rosenberg. 2001. "Designing Efficient Institutions for Science-Based Entrepreneurship: Lessons from the United States and Sweden," *Journal of Technology Transfer* 26 (3).

Heston, Alan, Robert Summers, and Bettina Aten. 2002. *Penn World Table Version 6.1.* Center for International Comparisons at the University of Pennsylvania (CICUP), October.

Hicks, J. R. 1969. *A Theory of Economic History* (Oxford: Clarendon Press).

Hoshi, Takeo, and Anil K. Kashyap. 2001. *Corporate Financing and Governance in Japan: The Road to the Future* (Cambridge: MIT Press).

———. 2004. "Japan's Financial Crisis and Economic Stagnation," *Journal of Economic Perspectives* 18 (1): 3–26.

Huber, Peter W., and Mark Mills. 2005. *The Bottomless Well: The Twilight of Fuel, The Virtue of Waste, and Why We Will Never Run Out of Energy* (New York: Basic Books).

Hufbauer, Gary, ed. 1990. *Europe 1992* (Washington, D.C.: Brookings Institution Press).

Hurst, E., and A. Lusardi. 2004. "Liquidity Constraints, Household Wealth, and Entrepreneurship," *Journal of Political Economy* 112: 319–47.

Independent Expert Group on R&D and Innovation. 2006. "Creating an Innovative Europe." Report. January. Available at http://europa.eu.int/invest-in-research.

International Monetary Fund. 2004. *World Economic Outlook: The Demographic Transition* (Washington, D.C.: International Monetary Fund).

Jaffe, Adam B., and Josh Lerner. 2004. *Innovation and Its Discontents: How Our Broken Patent System Is Endangering Innovation and Progress, and What to Do About It* (Princeton: Princeton University Press).

Johnson, Chalmers. 1982. *MITI and the Japanese Miracle: The Growth of Industrial Policy, 1925–1975* (Stanford: Stanford University Press).

Jorgenson, Dale W., Mun S. Ho, and Kevin J. Stiroh. 2002. "Projecting Productivity Growth: Lessons from the U.S. Growth Resurgence." Resources for the Future Discussion Paper 02–42 (July).

Kahneman, Daniel, and Alan B. Krueger. 2006. "Developments in the Measurement of Subjective Well-Being," *Journal of Economic Perspectives* 20, no. 1 (winter): 3–24.

Kamara, Ehud, Pinar Karaca-Mandic, and Eric Talley. 2005. "Going-Private Decisions and the Sarbanes-Oxley Act of 2002," Kauffman-Rand Center for the Study of Small Business Regulation, September.

Kauffman, Daniel, and Shang-Jin Wei. 1999. "Does 'Grease Money' Speed Up the Wheels of Commerce?" NBER Working Paper 7093 (Cambridge, Mass.: National Bureau of Economic Research).

Keynes, John Maynard. 1965. *The General Theory of Employment, Interest, and Money* (New York: Harcourt Press).

Khalil, Elias L. 1967. "The Red Queen Paradox: A Proper Name for a Popular Game," *Journal of Institutional and Theoretical Economics* 153, no. 2 (June): 411–15.

Klapper, Leora, Luc Laevan, and Raghuram Rajan. 2004. "Business Environment and Firm Entry: Evidence from International Data. Unpub. manuscript (June).

Klemens, Ben. 2006. *Math You Can't Use: Patents, Copyright and Software* (Washington, D.C.: Brookings Institution Press).

Kletzer, Lori, and Robert E. Litan. 2001. "A Prescription for Worker Anxiety," *Brookings Policy Brief*, no.73, March.

Kneese, Alan, and Charles L. Schultze. 1975. *Pollution, Prices and Public Policy* (Washington, D.C.: Brookings Institution Press).

Krueger, Anne. 2005. "Comment on Srinivasan," *Brookings Trade Forum*, 232–36.

Kuczynski, Pedro-Pablo, and John Williamson. 2003. *After the Washington Consensus: Restarting Growth and Reform in Latin America* (Washington, D.C.: Institute for International Economics).

Landes, David. 1999. *The Wealth and Poverty of Nations: Why Some Are So Rich And Some So Poor* (New York: W.W. Norton).

Lawless, Robert M., and Elizabeth Warren. 2005. "The Myth of the Disappearing Business Bankruptcy," *California Law Review* 93: 743–47.

Lazear, Edward. 2006. "The State of the U.S. Economy and Labor Market." Remarks before the Hudson Institute, May 2. Unpub., on file with the authors.

Lemonick, Michael D. 2006. "Are We Losing Our Edge?" *Time*, February 5.

Levine, Ross. 2004. "Finance and Growth: Theory and Evidence," NBER Working Paper 10766 (Cambridge, Mass.: National Bureau of Economic Research).

Levine, Ross, and David Renelt. 1992. "A Sensitivity Analysis of Cross-Country Growth Regressions," *American Economic Review* 82 (4): 942–63.

Lincoln, Abraham. 1858. "Lecture on Discoveries and Inventions," in *Collected Works of Abraham Lincoln,* ed. Roy P. Basler. Available at http://showcase.netins.net/web/creative/lincoln/speeches/discoveries.htm.

Lincoln, Edward J. 2001. *Arthritic Japan: The Slow Pace of Economic Reform* (Washington, D.C.: Brookings Institution Press).

Litan, Robert E., and Alice M. Rivlin. 2000. *Beyond the Dot.coms* (Washington, D.C.: Brookings Institution Press).

"A Long Walk: A Survey of Saudi Arabia." 2006. *Economist,* January 7.

Maddison, Angus. 1982. *Phases of Capitalist Development* (New York: Oxford University Press).

Mandel, Michael J. 2004. *Rational Exuberance: Silencing the Enemies of Growth* (New York: Harper Collins).

Mansfield, Edwin. 1990. "Comment on Zvi Grilliches and Jacques Mairesse," in *Productivity Growth in Japan and the United States: Studies in Income and Wealth*, vol. 53, ed. Charles R. Hulten (Chicago: University of Chicago Press), 341–46.

Mansfield, Edwin, Mark Schwartz, and Samuel Wagner. 1981. "Imitation Costs and Patents: An Empirical Study," *Economic Journal* (December): 907–19.

"A Market for Ideas: A Survey of Patents and Technology." 2005. *Economist*, October 22. Available at http://www.economist.com.

Matthews, R. C. O., C. H. Feinstein, and J. C. Odling-Smee. 1982. *Slower Growth in the Western World* (London: Heinemann).

McKibbin, Warwick J., and Peter Wilcoxen. 2002. *Climate Change Policy after Kyoto: Blueprint for a Realistic Approach* (Washington, D.C.: Brookings Institution Press).

Merrill, Stephen A., Richard C. Levin, and Mark M. Meyers, eds. 2004. *A Patent System for the 21st Century* (Washington, D.C.: National Academies Press).

Micklethwait, John, and Adrian Wooldridge. 2003. *The Company: A Short History of a Revolutionary Idea* (New York: Modern Library).

Mohuiddin, Shamarukh, and Julie Hutto. 2006. "Connecting the Poor," *Progressive Policy Institute Policy Brief*, March.

Moore, Gordon, and Kevin Davis. 2004. "Learning the Silicon Valley Way," in *Building High-Tech Clusters: Silicon Valley and Beyond*, ed. Timothy Bresnahan and Alfonso Gambardella (Cambridge: Cambridge University Press).

Mowrey, David C. 2005. "The Bayh-Dole Act and High-Technology Entrepreneurship in U.S. Universities: Chicken, Egg, or Something Else?" in *University Entrepreneurship and Technology Transfers*, ed. Gary Libecap (Amsterdam: Elsevier), 38–68.

Naim, Moises. 2005a. "Arabs in Foreign Lands," *Foreign Policy* (May/June): 94–95.

———. 2005b. *Illicit: How Smugglers, Traffickers, and Copycats are Hijacking the Global Economy* (New York: Doubleday).

National Academy of Sciences. 2005. *Rising Above the Gathering Storm: Energizing and Employing America for a Brighter Economic Future* (Washington, D.C.: National Academy of Sciences).

National Research Council. 2001. *The Advanced Technology Program, Assessing Outcomes* (Washington, D.C.: National Academy Press).

National Science Board. Various years. *Science and Engineering Indicators* (Washington, D.C.: U.S. Government Printing Office).

National Summit on Competitiveness. 2005. *Investing in U.S. Innovation* (Washington, D.C.: National Summit on Competitiveness), December 6.

"The New Organization." 2006. *Economist*, January 21.

Nordhaus, William. 2004. "Schumpeterian Profits in the American Economy: Theory and Measurement," NBER Working Paper 10433 (Cambridge, Mass.: National Bureau of Economic Research).

Nordhaus, William D., and James Tobin. 1972. "Is Growth Obsolete?" in National Bureau of Economic Research, *Economic Growth,* General Series #96E (New York: Columbia University Press).

North, Douglass C. 1981. *Structure and Change in Economic History* (New York: W. W. Norton).

———. 1990. *Institutions, Institutional Change, and Economic Performance* (Cambridge: Cambridge University Press).

———. 2005. *Understanding the Process of Economic Change* (Princeton: Princeton University Press).

North, Douglass C., and Robert Paul Thomas. 1973. *The Rise of the Western World* (Cambridge: Cambridge University Press).

Okun, Arthur M. 1976. *Equity and Efficiency: The Big Tradeoff* (Washington, D.C.: Brookings Institution Press).

Oliner, Stephen D., and Daniel E. Sichel. 2002. "Information Technology and Productivity: Where Are We Now and Where Are We Going?" *Federal Reserve Bank of Atlanta Economic Review,* pp. 15–44.

Olson, Mancur. 1982. *The Rise and Fall of Nations* (New Haven: Yale University Press).

Ordover, Januscz. 1991. "A Patent System for Both Diffusion and Exclusion," *Journal of Economic Perspectives* 5, no. 1 (winter): 43–60.

Orey, Michael. 2006. "The Patent Epidemic," *Business Week,* January 9, pp. 60–62.

Organization for Economic Cooperation and Development (OECD). 2003. *The Sources of Economic Growth in the OECD Countries* (Paris: OECD).

———. 2006. *Going for Growth* (Paris: OECD).

Patel, Urjit R. 2004. "Role of State-Owned Financial Institutions in India: Should the Government 'Do' or 'Lead,'" in *The Future of State-Owned Financial Institutions,* ed. Gerald Caprio et al. (Washington, D.C.: Brookings Institution Press).

Perez, Carlota. 2002. *Technological Revolutions and Financial Capital: The Dynamics of Bubbles and Golden Ages* (Cheltenham, U.K.: Edward Elgar).

Persson, Torsten, and Guido Tabellini. 2006. "Democratic Capital: The Nexus of Political and Economic Change," NBER Working Paper 12175 (Cambridge, Mass.: National Bureau of Economic Research).

Phelps, Edmund S. 2006. "The Economic Performance of Nations: Prosperity Depends on Dynamism, Dynamism on Institutions," in *Entrepreneurship, Innovation, and the Growth Mechanism of the Free-Enterprise Economies,* ed. William Baumol, Eytan Sheshinski, and Robert J. Strom (Princeton: Princeton University Press).

Prahalad, C. K. 2005. *The Fortune at the Bottom of the Pyramid: Eradicating Poverty through Profits* (Philadelphia: Wharton School Publishing).

Prestowitz, Clyde V., Jr. 1988. *Trading Places: How We Allowed Japan to Take the Lead* (New York: Basic Books).

Rajan, Raghuram G. and Arvind Subramanian. 2005. "Aid and Growth: What Does the Cross-Country Evidence Really Show?" IMF Working Paper WP/05/127.

————. 2006. "What Undermines Aid's Impact on Growth?" NBER Working Paper 11657 (Cambridge, Mass.: National Bureau of Economic Research).

Rauch, James E. 2005. "Getting the Properties Right to Secure Property Rights: Dixit's *Lawlessness and Economics,*" *Journal of Economic Literature* 63, no. 2 (June): 480–87.

Rauch, Jonathan. 1994. *Demosclerosis: The Silent Killer of American Government* (New York: Crown).

Ricardo, David. 1821. *On the Principles of the Political Economy and Taxation* (London: John Murray).

Rivlin, Alice M. 1971. *Systematic Thinking for Social Action* (Washington, D.C.: Brookings Institution Press).

Rivlin, Alice M., and Isabel Sawhill. 2005. *Restoring Fiscal Sanity* (Washington, D.C.: Brookings Institution Press).

Rodrik, Dani. 2003. *Growth Strategies* (Cambridge: Harvard University Press).

Roe, Mark J. 2002. "Corporate Law's Limits," *Journal of Legal Studies* 31 (June): 233–71.

Romer, Paul M. 1986. "Increasing Returns and Long Run Growth," *Journal of Political Economy* 94, no. 5 (October): 1002–37.

————. 1994. "The Origins of Endogenous Growth," *Journal of Economic Perspectives* 8, no. 1 (winter): 3–22.

Sachs, Jeffrey D. 2005. *The End of Poverty: How We Can Make It Happen In Our Lifetime* (New York: Penguin Press).

Samuelson, Paul A. 2004. "Where Mill and Ricardo Rebut and Confirm Arguments of Mainstream Economists Supporting Globalization," *Journal of Economic Perspectives* 18 (3): 135–46.

Saxenian, AnnaLee. 1999. *Silicon Valley's New Immigrant Entrepreneurs* (San Francisco: Calif.: Public Policy Institute of California).

————. 2006. *The New Argonauts: Regional Advantage in a Global Economy* (Cambridge: Harvard University Press).

Say, Jean-Baptiste. 1834. *A Treatise on Political Economy* (Philadelphia: Grigg & Elliot).

Scarpetta, Stefano, Philip Hemmings, Tressel Thierry, and Jaujoon Woo. 2002. "The Role of Policy and Institutions for Productivity and Firm Dynamics: Evidence from the Micro and Industry Data," OECD Economics Department Working Paper, no. 329.

Schaffer, Jonathan. 2003. "Millennium Challenge Account: A New Compact for Global Development." An electronic journal of the U.S. Department of State.

Schramm, Carl. 2004. "Building Entrepreneurial Economies," *Foreign Affairs* (July/August): 104.

Schramm, Carl, and Robert Litan. 2005. "Why Democracy Is America's Second Most Valuable Export," *Inc. Magazine* (October).

Schultz, Theodore. 1961. "Investment in Human Capital," *American Economic Review* 51 (March): 1–17.

Schultze, Charles L. 1977. *Public Use of the Private Interest* (Washington, D.C.: Brookings Institution Press).

Schumpeter, Joseph A. 1911. *Theory of Economic Development* (Cambridge: Harvard University Press).

———. 1942. *Capitalism, Socialism, and Democracy* (New York: Harper).

Schweitzer, Mark, and Saeed Zaman. 2006. "Are We Engineering Ourselves Out of Manufacturing Jobs?" Federal Reserve Bank of Cleveland, Research Department, January 1.

Segal, Adam. 2005. *Digital Dragon: High-Technology Enterprises in China* (Ithaca: Cornell University Press).

Servan-Schreiber, Jean Jacques. 1968. *The American Challenge* (London: H. Hamilton).

Shane, Scott. 2004. *Academic Entrepreneurship* (Cheltenham, U.K.: Edward Elgar).

Sheshinski, Eytan. 1967. "Optimal Accumulation with Learning by Doing," in *Essays on the Theory of Optimal Economic Growth,* ed. Karl Shell (Cambridge: MIT Press), 31–52.

Slater, Martin. 1980. Foreword to Edith T. Penrose, *The Theory of the Growth of The Firm,* 2nd ed. (White Plains, N.Y.: M. E. Sharpe).

Smith, Adam. 1976. *An Inquiry into the Nature and Causes of the Wealth of Nations* (Oxford: Clarendon Press).

Solow, Robert. 1956. "A Contribution to the Theory of Economic Growth," *Quarterly Journal of Economics* 70: 65–94.

———. 1957. "Technical Change and the Aggregate Production Function," *Review of Economics and Statistics* 39: 312–20.

———. 1994. "Perspectives on Growth Theory," *Journal of Economic Perspectives* 8, no. 1 (winter): 45–54.

Sperling, Gene. 2005. *The Pro-Growth Progressive: An Economic Strategy for Shared Prosperity* (New York: Simon & Schuster).

Spindle, Bill, and Yasmine El-Rashidi. 2006. "In Quest to Build a Financial Center, Hurdles for Dubai," *Wall Street Journal,* March 2, p. A1.

Srinivasan, T. N. 2005. "Information-Technology-Enabled Services and India's Growth Prospects," *Brookings Trade Forum,* 203–31.

Stiroh, Kevin J. 2002. "Information Technology and the U.S. Productivity Revival: What Do the Industry Data Say," *American Economic Review* 92, no. 5 (December): 1559–76.

Summers, Robert, and Alan Heston. 1991. "The Penn World Table (Mark 5): An Expanded Set of International Comparisons, 1950–88," *Quarterly Journal of Economics* 106 (May): 327–68.

Surowiecki, James. 2005. "All Together Now," *New Yorker,* April 11, p. 26.

Svensson, Jakob. 2006. "Eight Questions about Corruption," *Journal of Economic Perspectives* 19, no. 3 (summer): 19–42.

Swan, Trevor W. 1956. "Economic Growth and Capital Accumulation," *Economic Record* 32 (November): 334–61.

Swanson, Daniel G., and William Baumol. 2005. "Reasonable and Nondiscriminatory

(RAND) Royalties, Standards Selection, and Control of Market Power," *Antitrust Law Journal* 73 (1): 1–58.

Tanzi, Vito. 2000. "Taxation in Latin America in the Last Decade," Center for Research on Economic Development and Policy Reform, Working Paper no. 76.

Thurow, Lester C. 1980. *The Zero Sum Society: Distribution and the Possibilities for Economic Change* (New York: Basic Books).

———. 1992. *Head to Head: The Coming Battle among Japan, Europe, and America* (New York: Morrow).

Thursby, Jerry, and Marie Thursby. 2006. "Here or There? A Survey on the Factors in Multinational R&D Location." Unpub. report prepared for the Ewing Marion Kauffman Foundation. Available at www.kauffman.org.

United Nations. 2004. *Follow-Up to the Second World Assembly on Aging: Report of the Secretary-General* (New York: United Nations).

United Nations Development Programme. 2003. *Human Development Report* (New York: United Nations).

United Nations Educational Scientific and Cultural Organization (UNESCO). 2005. *Education for All, Global Monitoring Report 2005—The Quality Imperative* (New York: United Nations).

———. 2006. *Education for All, Global Monitoring Report 2006—Literacy for Life* (New York: United Nations).

U.S. Bureau of Labor Statistics. 2006. Industry Productivity and Costs. Available at http://www.bls.gov.

Vogel, Ezra. 1979. *Japan as Number One: Lessons for America* (Cambridge: Harvard University Press).

Walker, Marcus. 2006a. "For the Danish, a Job Loss Can Be Learning Experience," *Wall Street Journal,* March 21, p. A1.

———. 2006b. "Germany's Merkel Gains Favor by Backing Away fom Pledges," *Wall Street Journal,* May 2, p. A1.

Warsh, David. 2006. *Knowledge and the Wealth of Nations: A Story of Economic Discovery* (New York: W. W. Norton).

Weber, Luc E., and James J. Duderstadt, eds. 2006. *Universities and Business: Partnering for the Knowledge Society* (London: Economica).

Wei, Shang Jin. 2000. "Local Corruption and Global Capital Flows," *Brookings Papers on Economic Activity* 2: 303–46.

———. 2001. "Corruption and Globalization," *Brookings Policy Brief,* no. 79, April. Available at http://www.brookings.edu/comm/policybriefs/pb79.pdf.

Williamson, John, ed. 1994. *The Political Economy of Policy Reform* (Washington, D.C.: Institute for International Economics).

———. 2004. *The Washington Consensus as Policy Prescription for Development.* Lecture given at the World Bank, January 13. Available through the Institute for International Economics.

Winston, Clifford D. 1993. "Economic Deregulation: Days of Reckoning for Microeconomists," *Journal of Economic Literature* 31: 1263–89.

Wolf, Martin. 2004. *Why Globalization Works* (New Haven: Yale University Press).

World Bank. 1993. *The East Asian Miracle: Economic Growth and Public Policy* (New York: Oxford University Press).

———. 2005. *Doing Business in 2005: Removing Obstacles to Growth* (Washington, D.C.: International Bank for Reconstruction and Development/World Bank Group).

———. 2006. *Doing Business in 2006: Creating Jobs* (Washington, D.C.: International Bank for Reconstruction and Development/World Bank Group).

INDEX

ACCION International, 183
Advanced Technology Program, 220
Africa, 175, 179; education in, 163
aging populations: benefits paid to, 28–
32, 294n2; economic implications of,
189–92, 233
agriculture, technological advances in, 17
Airbus, 198
Amarante, Massimiliano, 101
Angel Capital Association, 298n2
antimonopoly regulation, 106, 117, 118–
19
antitrust laws, 117, 118–19, 195–96,
292n13; and cooperative innovation,
253; misuse of, 249–51
Apple, 84
Arab Americans, economic success of,
123
Arafat, Yassir, 171
Argentina, 56
Arora, Ashish, 243–44
Arrow, Kenneth, 48, 50
Asian Tiger economies, 141, 142–43, 151,
179
AT&T, antitrust litigation against, 118–
19
Aten, Bettina, 47–48
Audretsch, David, 86
auto industry: American, 119–20; Japa-

nese, 120; mass production in, 83,
290n13

Bahrain, 78
Baily, Martin, 211, 212
banking: and access to capital, 101–2,
196–97; in China, 68, 293n8; in
Japan, 64, 68, 102, 185–86, 196, 204,
294n3, 294n7; privatization of, 156–
59, 168; in South Korea, 64, 67–68;
under state-guided capitalism, 63–64,
156–59. *See also* micro-credit
bankruptcy laws, 100–101, 291n3; impact
of on entrepreneurs, 237
Barro, Robert, 48
Baumol, William J., 46–47, 87, 244,
254
Bayh-Dole Act, 111, 263, 264
Becker, Gary, 292n17
Bell Laboratories, 88, 89
Berle, Adolphe, 290n11
Bhide, Amar, 85
Blackberry, patent issue involving, 247
Blair, Tony, 216
Boeing, 88
Bosworth, Barry, 48
Boulton, Matthew, 276
Breznitz, Daniel, 148–49, 166
brute force, growth by, 5, 36